THE CONSTITUTIONAL POLITY

Essa
Foun f
Amer

Edited by

Sidne r.

UNIVERSITY
PRESS OF
AMERICA

Copyright © 1983 by

University Press of America, Inc.

P.O. Box 19101, Washington, D.C. 20036

Library of Congress Cataloging in Publication Data

Main entry under title:

The Constitutional polity.

    1. Political science—United States—Addresses,
essays, lectures. I. Pearson, Sidney A.
JA84.U5C66   1982   320'.01'0973   82-15953
ISBN 0-8191-2744-2
ISBN 0-8191-2745-0 (pbk.)

For M.A.

iv

Acknowledgements

In addition to the contributors to this volume, a number of other people gave valuable assistance to its preparation at various stages. Among them are Joseph E. Goldberg of Hampton-Sydney College, Virginia; Robert E. Wood of the U.S. Navy War College, Newport, Rhode Island; and Anthony T. Sullivan of the Earhart Foundation, Ann Arbor, Michigan.

Financial assistance was provided by a generous grant from the Earhart Foundation through its President, Richard A. Ware.

Special thanks is also extended to the faithful typists, Evelyn Benson and Carolyn Kirk, who helped prepare the final manuscript.

Table of Contents

Preface

viii

Preface

This collection of essays is devoted to understanding the founding principles of the American constitutional system as those principles were expounded
by the Founders and how they have been viewed in the
works of both critics and defenders of those principles who came later. It is inevitable that in any
collection of this sort certain arbitrary limitations
must be imposed on the selection of authors, works, and
topics to be covered. Comprehensiveness is virtually
impossible so we have opted instead for the outlines
of an analysis that must of its very nature remain
incomplete. We believe that the scope of what is
included will partially compensate for those omissions.

The specific selection of authors and works included has been subjected to several considerations.
First, because the emphasis is on the founding principles as the common demoninator of American political
philosophy, an introductory discussion of certain of
the Founders was deemed essential. Our interest in
the Founders was born in large measure by the brilliant
and extraordinarily influential work of Martin Diamond.
He is one of the preeminent teachers of the founding
principles and most of the contributors to this volume
have been affected in one way or another by various
aspects of Diamond's work. Not all contributors are
in equal sympathy with his interpretation, but it can
fairly be said that all recognize the importance and
seriousness of his work and appreciate its challenge
to much of the modern reading of the Founders' intentions. In a very real sense we are all students of
Martin Diamond in that he has taught us to reread the
Founders with a fresh eye to viewpoints we had not
always considered before. This is perhaps the most
lasting and important achievement of any scholar; to
know what questions to ask and point the way to those
who come after. It is not unlike the achievements of
the Founders themselves.

Criteria for the selection of the remaining
authors and certain of their works followed more or
less logically from the first set of conditions. We
have sought to review the work of those authors that
seemed to be most in need of revision in the light of
Diamond's work or who have highlighted in some way the
concerns about American political philosophy Diamond
expressed. This has meant the inclusion of a few

authors who we feel have remained too long in relative obscurity. It seemed, for example, that President William Howard Taft's Our Chief Magistrate and His Powers is a much neglected minor classic that ought to be recalled to the attention of a new generation of readers. The same point could be made for the inclusion of a number of other authors. In each case, however, the overriding concern has been to try to establish a dialogue between opposing points of view on how the founding principles ought to be interpreted and what they mean today. Both well known as well as lesser known works have been selected for this purpose.

The focus on specific authors also represents an essential ingredient of our philosophical perspective. We have dealt with individual authors and specific works because we are ever mindful that the substance of political philosophy is the thought of individual persons. The frequent tendency of many similar essays on American political philosophy is to focus on the ebb and flow of Liberal and Conservative tides in American history. This gives to political philosophy a certain disembodied character and an abstractness that is partially overcome by attention to the thought of specific authors and their writings. In addition, we have tried to keep in mind that while the substance of political philosophy is thought, the object of political philosophy is politics as distinct from thought alone--in this case, the politics of the American polity. We have tried to balance these considerations in what we hope will be a deeper understanding of how the founding principles continue to operate and guide politics in contemporary America.

Contributors:

1. Edmund D. Carlson is Assistant Professor of Political Science, Virginia Wesleyan College.

2. Robert M. Gill is Associate Professor of Political Science, Radford University, Virginia.

3. Margaret Hrezo

4. William E. Hrezo is Assistant Professor of Political Science, Radford University, Virginia.

5. Gary J. Jacobsohn is Assistant Professor of Political Science, Williams College, Massachusetts.

6. Sanford Kessler is Associate Professor of Political Science, North Carolina State University.

7. Rev. Edward Krause, C.S.C., is at Gannon University, Erie, Pennsylvania.

8. Richard E. Krouse is Associate Professor of Political Science, Williams College, Massachusetts.

9. Gordon Lloyd is Associate Professor of Political Science, Redlands University, California.

10. David Marion is Associate Professor of Government and Foreign Affairs, Hampden-Sydney College, Virginia.

11. Sidney A. Pearson, Jr., is Associate Professor of Political Science, Radford University, Virginia.

12. James F. Pontuso is Assistant Professor of Political Science, Hampton Institute, Virginia.

13. Peter Schultz is Assistant Professor of Political Science, Catholic University of America, Washington, D. C.

14. Peter Shotten is Assistant Professor of Political Science, Augustana College, South Dakota.

15. Robert Webking is Assistant Professor of Political Science, University of Texas, El Paso, Texas.

Introduction

The beginning point for the study of American political philosophy is the study of the American founding. And for Americans political philosophy is an unusually practical enterprise because it is indissolubly linked to expounding a constitution. Sooner or later almost every issue in American politics becomes a constitutional question and constitutional questions have a way of becoming questions about the founding principles of the American polity. Any serious probing of American politics must then eventually return to the political science of the Founders. Because the Founders have determined the shape of current politics through the construction of our constitutional system, they can be said to occupy a living position in the perennial dialectic between the past, the present, and the future of the American polity.

In the American political tradition there is no symbolism more powerful than the founding. Successive generations have revered the Constitution as the unifying basis for the nation and the Founders have become the larger-than-life models of the ideal American statesman -- practical, yet also possessed with a profound wisdom and nobility of character that sometimes reaches biblical proportions. Nevertheless, there is a subtle irony in the genuine popular reverence for the Founders' historical accomplishments. For many Americans, the historical magnitude of the Founders has largely obscured their role as the pre-eminent teachers of democratic constitutionalism. The symbolic power of the Founders then, has often been more potent than their political arguments. There are some signs of change; and the renewed interest in their philosophy will lead to an awareness and its importance for any adequate understanding of current American politics.

This renewal of interest in the Founders' political philosophy corresponds to a widely perceived crisis in the contemporary American political order. The political turmoil in the United States during the 1960's and early 1970's compelled Americans to re-examine and to think anew about the nature of their political system; and, of course, the problem of the founding could not be avoided. Central to the questions raised during this turmoil was that of the intentions of the Founders. What was the true nature of the American polity? Was it flawed from the outset, or had something gone radically wrong since the founding itself? Was America a beacon of hope in a world engulfed by tyrannical regimes, or was America itself an anachronism in a world becoming progressively enlightened and freed from the yoke of a peculiarly American form of tyranny? While the answer to these questions might have seemed obvious to an earlier generation, to a younger generation of Americans they were not. Further, the answers frequently given were negative, since the Founders were increasingly depicted as the source of our problems rather than the root of our enlightenment. The crisis has not in the least abated, but thanks to such scholars as Martin Diamond, we now have a more rational and perceptive view of the Founders' political science and its continued applicability to the continuing crisis.

The reawakened interest in the teaching of the Founders is to be distinguished from historical curiosity chiefly in that its object is to learn from them rather than about them. This renaissance is based on the conviction that the most prominent Founders have left us with an enduring and pertinent legacy of practical statesmanship and an enlightened political philosophy. They remain, after almost two hundred years, the most important spokesmen for liberal constitutional government; and we cannot understand either freedom or modern tyranny without their perspective. As Americans, we habitually turn to the Founders in times of crisis because we find in their writing a delicate and elusive wedding between the theory and practice of good government. Put another way we perennially confront the problem stated by Hamilton of "whether or not societies of men are really capable of establishing good government from reflection and choice, or whether they are forever destined to depend for their political constitutions on accident and force." The Founders' answer was the Constitution: good government based on reflection and choice.

Even if the modern world should reject their solution, the Founders' answer remains the starting point for contemporary American political philosophy. Political philosophy always begins with questioning the nature of our present condition, and for Americans a substantial part of that condition is citizenship

xiv

under a Constitution that is almost two hundred years
old. We begin by asking, "does that Constitution still
serve our needs"? Is the Constitution competent to
its modern tasks? Is the founding political philosophy
adequate today? In approaching American politics from
this perspective there can be no final, sovereign
word; but, likewise, there can be no shirking from
the inquiry itself. The following essays are an
attempt to understand our present political condition
in the light of the founding of the American polity.

A full discussion of the principles of American
politics must necessarily take us through the
approximately two hundred years of American history.
This is not because philosophical answers are
historically conditioned, but rather because the full
implications of the founding principles were not all
readily apparent to the Founders themselves. Problems
and peculiar crises arose about which the Founders
could have no prescience. It was left to others to
think about these problems and try to relate them to
the constitutional order, always in time of crisis
rethinking the founding principles either implicitly
or explicitly. These essays are organized accordingly,
as we attempt to understand the Founders and their
impact throughout the history of the American Republic.

In an attempt to clarify the major issues of
American political philosophy, the essays are divided
into four sections. They are intended to be suggestive
rather than exhaustive in scope. Part I, "The Founding
Principles," is a discussion of the Founders and some
of the sources of their ideas. Part II, "Democracy
Defined and Redefined," is an effort to understand the
changing definitions of democracy in America that have
helped to shape the modern critique of the Founders.
Part III, "The Principles Critiqued," deals with the
major criticisms of the Founders from a variety of
perspectives. Part IV, "The Principles Defended," is
a discussion of some of the post-founding defenses of
the American political order. Together, these essays
provide a broad though far from complete-discussion
of all of the aspects of the founding principles.

PART I

The Founding Principles

CHAPTER 1

"The Federalist: Governmental Power and Individual Rights."

Robert Webking

Upon reading The Federalist Papers George Washington remarked that "that work will merit the notice of Posterity; because in it are candidly discussed the principles of Freedom and the topics of government, which will always be interesting to mankind so long as they shall be connected in Civil Society."[1] Washington's use of the word "candidly" suggests that there is something not obvious about the principles of freedom and the topics of government. That is to say, while it may be a self-evident truth that governments exist to secure individual rights, it is perhaps not at all self-evident what the best organization of government ought to be to secure them effectively. Indeed, it may be that investigation and experience show that, to paraphrase Machiavelli, those things which would appear to secure liberty will in fact lead to ruin, and those things which would appear to threaten liberty will in fact secure it. I believe that careful investigation of the argument of The Federalist substantiates this suggestion, and my purpose here is to consider those difficult points in the argument where the authors seek to explain the complex relationships between the organization of government and the security of individual rights.

Given the circumstances surrounding the production of The Federalist it is somewhat surprising that the work has remained the rich source that Washington believed it would be. The eighty-five essays that make up the work were written by three men, Alexander Hamilton, James Madison, and John Jay (who wrote only five of the essays) over a period of only eight months in 1787 and 1788. Their purpose was to examine and explain the proposed Constitution with the goal of persuading, in the first instance the citizens of New York (where most of the essays were printed in newspapers), and in the second instance the citizens of other states (where the work was circulated in book form), that the Constitution ought to be ratified. While the work owes its existence to three men, it was presented as the work of a single author, "Publius." For present purposes it will be sufficient to treat the argument as it was presented, leaving aside questions about differences that might have existed between Madison and Hamilton and concentrating on

1

their unified argument about the virtues of the Constitution.

Publius was engaged in a strong debate over an immediate political decision. Yet Publius' arguments are on a level that transcends the immediate political issue so that they remain a source of political wisdom "so long as men are connected to Civil Society." At least two reasons can be offered for the high level of The Federalist. First, there is the nature of the issue--a debate about society's fundamental law ought to bring forth consideration of fundamental political questions. Second, there is the nature of the authors--James Madison had been the most influential delegate to the Constitutional Convention because he had studied thoroughly and thought carefully about the problems involved in governing human beings. Alexander Hamilton had also attended the convention and would demonstrate his brilliant political mind in the first years of the Constitution's operation. John Jay was an eminent lawyer and statesman who had authored the 1777 Constitution of New York.

Although The Federalist transcends its immediate political context, we can nonetheless gain some perspective upon its general argument from a brief discussion of the arguments made by the opponents of the Constitution, the Antifederalists. The Federalists and Antifederalists based their arguments upon the same fundamental question. In the words of the Anti-federalist "Agrippa,"

> All the defenders of (the Constitution) undertake to prove that the rights of the states and the citizens are kept safe. The opposers of it agree that they will receive the least burden-some system which shall defend those rights.
> Both parties therefore found their arguments on the idea that these rights ought to be held sacred.[2]

The goal to be sought was clear. The purpose of government was what the Declaration of Independence had claimed: to secure people's inalienable rights. The dispute lay over the means. The Antifederalists argued many specific points, but in general it can be said that each particular objection they raised was designed to show that individual rights would be insecure under the Constitution. It is possible to make a more specific generalization about the Anti-federalists' arguments: they claimed that rights would be insecure under the Constitution because the central government created by the document would invade those rights.[3] They feared the national government's power.

Publius' explanation of the Constitution is an attempt to show that the Antifederalists' objection is not warranted. In response to the vast assortment of Antifederalist arguments tending to the conclusion that the new government would take away people's rights Publius makes two general arguments. First, and I shall argue more importantly, Publius contends that the extensive powers of the central government are necessary for the security of citizen liberties. Second, Publius argues that sufficient safeguards are included within the Constitution to prevent the infringement of individual rights by the government.

II

Certainly it is true that recent scholarship has concentrated upon the second of these two arguments. The argument that the Constitution provides adequate safeguards against the government's violating individual rights occurs primarily in The Federalist Numbers 10 and 51, the two numbers which have received by far the most attention from scholars in recent years. Douglas Adair points out that Number 10, at least, was barely mentioned until this century when it began to serve a prominent place in the arguments of those who attack the Constitution.[4] The Tenth Federalist has also achieved additional notice in recent years due to Martin Diamond's efforts to rescue it from the faulty interpretations of others and to show the insights that this "most important original political writing by an American"[5] can generate about the nature of the American regime.[6] The interest in Federalist 51 in recent years has also been sparked by criticism of the institutional arrangements it defends as necessary to the preservation of the people's liberties.[7] The arguments in these two papers are indeed of seminal importance for understanding a part of the founders' plan for securing citizen liberties, specifically for securing those liberties from violation by rulers.

3

The issue in <u>Federalist</u> 51 is exactly the issue of the danger to individual rights prevented by government officials. Any decent government must prevent those who exercise its powers from using those powers to reach their own private goods at the expense of the citizens. Publius explains that the expedient designed to prevent that kind of abuse of power by government officials is separation of powers. Simply stated, the whole power of government is divided up into three parts, and each part is given to a separate branch. By this means the government has the powers it needs to govern but no single official or branch has sufficient constitutional power in and of itself to become tyrannical.

The difficulty that the authors of the Constitution faced, Publius tells us, was not with the general principle of separation of powers, but with its practical implementation. It is one thing to tell an official that he may have this much power and no more, it is quite another to make sure that the official stays within that boundary.

> After discriminating, therefore, in
> theory, the several classes of power,
> as they may in their nature be
> legislative, executive, or judiciary,
> the next and most difficult task is
> to provide some practical security
> for each, against the invasion of
> the others.[8]

The most difficult task is to keep separated powers separate. A people cannot count upon "parchment barriers" to hold back the assaults of ambitious men for power. It is to supplement these, indeed to replace them as "the great security against a gradual concentration of the several powers in the same department"[9] that checks and balances are employed. The expedient operates by giving to the officers of each branch enough of a share in the powers of the other branches to enable them to defend themselves against attempts by the others to assume extra powers. The separated powers overlap a little so that each branch has the "constitutional means" to secure its borders. But even that is not enough, for it was not sufficient for the founders to provide each branch with the weapons necessary to prevent the others from gaining enough power to become tyrannical unless they

4

could make certain that the weapons would actually be used. For this additional requirement the founders count upon personal motives. "Ambition must be made to counteract ambition. The interest of the man must be connected with the constitutional rights of the place."[10] The force to be controlled if tyranny is to be prevented is individuals' desire for power. Those desires are effectively controlled when the institutions are fashioned in such a manner that whenever one government officer attempts to take power to which the Constitution does not entitle him he runs into another official to whom the power rightfully belongs. The ambition of that second official can be counted upon to lead him to use the weapons the Constitution gives him to protect his power. Thus a government full of selfish ambitious people is prevented from becoming a tyrannical government since "the private interest of every individual" becomes "a sentinel over public rights."[11]

The issue in The Federalist Number 10 is a different one.[12] The danger to individual rights under discussion here comes not from the officers of government themselves, but from those who hold the ultimate power of government, the power to appoint those officers. The problem of government being dominated by a particular faction is one which threatens governments of all descriptions, but as Publius writes, it is a problem which has been particularly troublesome for popular governments.

Publius defines a faction as a group held together "by some common impulse of passion or of interest, adverse to the rights of other citizens, or to the permanent and aggregate interests of the community."[13] He writes that "the latent causes of faction are . . . sown in the nature of man."[14] And hence the problem of faction is ubiquitous. In popular governments, however, one particular source of faction, "the most common and durable source," predominates. That source is economics. Always and everywhere societies seem to divide themselves up into two major economic groups: the haves and the have-nots (or have-lesses). Each of these groups would like to have political power so that it could pillage the other and improve its economic condition. If government is to be just, to secure the rights of all, it must prevent such happenings. "Is a law proposed concerning private debts?" Publius asks. "It is a question to which the creditors are parties on one side and the debtors on the other. Justice ought to hold the balance between them."[15]

Unfortunately the circumstance that ought to obtain did not typically obtain with popular governments. The history of popular governments indicated that the majority faction of the have-nots would usually use government for their own partial good at the expense of both the public good and minority rights. Furthermore, this historical tendency could be seen immediately in the behavior of majorities in many of the states in the 1780's. Publius writes of the common complaint that in many states "measures are too often decided, not according to the rules of justice and the rights of the minor party, but by the superior force of an interested and overbearing majority."[16]

If the government was to do its job, therefore, some way to avoid the government's being controlled by a faction must be found. Publius considers and rejects the two methods commonly used by governments of all descriptions for removing factions. The first is the method used by despotic governments. It consists of taking away the liberty of people to form groups, or, stated another way, in using force to forbid the formation of factions. This alternative is rejected out of hand by Publius because the end of government is to secure liberty, and although the maintenance of any government requires some surrender of liberties from the citizens, such a total surrender would be unacceptable if another way could be found to control faction.

The second traditional method for removing the danger of factions is through education. Publius explains that people form factions because they have different opinions, passions, and interests. Those differences result in different citizens being moved by different desires and competing with one another to satisfy those desires. Factions would not form if citizens could be taught to have the same opinions, passions and interests. This alternative of teaching people to want the public good was usually employed by non-despotic regimes. Publius does not say that it would be wrong to teach people to want the common good, but only that it is "impracticable." The impracticality, however, appears to be related to the

6

need to secure liberty. One of the major factors that leads to the formation of differing interests is the "diversity in the faculties of men." That diversity leads to the possession of "different degrees and kinds of property." Now if the diversity in human abilities could be supressed then the inequalities could be prevented. Yet Publius writes that "The protection of these faculties is the first object of government,"[17] which is to say that government's job is to secure people's liberty to develop themselves and to be as successful as their abilities and efforts will allow. If government secures equal opportunity and liberty, the diversity in human faculties means inequality will result. To teach people, especially those who have less, to respect those inequalities and to understand that they exist by right of superior ability is, Publius says, impractical. You cannot be sure of success.

The rejection of these two traditional methods of removing the causes of faction leaves Publius with no alternative but to live with factions and to control their bad effects. Now controlling the effects of minority factions is not difficult with popular government. The simple fact of majority rule prevents any minority from using the government for unjust purposes.[18] The difficulty with majority rule is the majority itself. The great advantage of majority rule lies in the calculation that the majority is a more safe depository for the public good and private rights than any majority. The commonly experienced disadvantage of majority rule is that the majority, like most minorities, tends to use power to further its own interest at the expense of the public good and private rights.[19]

Publius' original argument about how a people can secure the advantage and avoid the disadvantage of majority rule rests upon a distinction between species of popular government. In a pure democracy, where people gather to rule themselves directly, he writes, the danger of majority faction is unavoidable. Such a form of government can exist with only a small territory, and in a small community it is virtually certain that there will be a majority with the same partial interest. In a republic, however, the problem can be avoided. The difference between a pure democracy and a republic is that in the latter the people do not rule directly, but through representatives. Representation yields a number of happy advantages for Publius, but the decisive one is size. A republic can be very much larger than a pure democracy, and because it is larger it can include a great variety of people with many different kinds of economic activities and, hence, a multiplicity of interests. The existence of many distinct interests means the existence of many interest groups or factions. The existence of many factions rather than merely two makes it likely that there will be no majority faction. All factions will be minority factions and each faction will be prevented from using the government unjustly by the fact of majority rule. "Extend the sphere," Publius writes, "and you take in a greater variety of parties and interests; you make it less probable that a majority of the whole will have a common motive to invade the rights of other citizens."[20]

Thus the dangers of majority faction can be avoided _without abandoning majority rule_. Indeed, the solution to the problem of faction depends upon the presence of majority rule. Majority rule secures the citizens from oppression by minority factions and a large republic insures that all factions will be minority factions. "A well-constructed Union," then, can secure the advantages and avoid the disadvantages of popular government. Publius summarizes the argument well in another place:

> In the extended republic of the United States, and among the great variety of interests, parties, and sects which it embraces, a coalition of a majority of the whole society could seldom take place on any other principles than those of justice and the general good.[21]

Thus the rights of all are made secure from invasion by those who hold the ultimate authority of government.

III

In the very essay in which the primary means for insuring that government officials do not abuse power is explained, Publius makes this important comment:

> In framing a government which is to be administered by men over men, the great

8

difficulty lies in this: you must
first enable the government to control
the governed; and in the next place
oblige it to control itself.[22]

Thus the problem of protecting the people from government is only of secondary importance. If it is true,
as Publius writes, that the general object of government is the happiness of citizens,[23] then this
statement from Federalist 51 indicates that the most
serious barriers to that happiness do not come from
government. Furthermore, the implication is that
government exists precisely to overcome those barriers.

The argument that the most important consideration
in evaluating governments is not whether the government
itself violates citizen rights appears very early in
The Federalist. In a series of essays beginning with
the second Federalist Publius considers the advantages
of maintaining the Union and the disadvantages of
allowing it to divide up into several smaller confederacies. The first of the advantages is the
increased safety from foreign attack that comes with
Union. "Among the many objects to which a wise and
free people find it necessary to direct their attention,
that of providing for their safety seems to be the
first."[24] Other nations must be prevented from having
just causes for warring with the Americans and they
must also be discouraged from attacking injustly on
the pretext of trumped up charges. With the Union the
Americans will be less likely to present just causes
for war to foreign nations because there will be a
single interpretation of the law of nations and of
treaties. That single interpretation will not be
dominated by the unjust desires of any part of the
Union. Moreover, should the national government
provide a just cause for war to a foreign nation it
is far more likely that the dispute will be settled
without recourse to war with one large nation than it
would be with several smaller confederacies. Publius
notes the reality that "acknowledgements, explanations,
and compensations are often accepted as satisfactory
from a strong united nation" when they would not be
accepted from a weaker power.[25]

This recognition of the importance of national
power in preventing foreign attack becomes more clear
when the thought turns to the danger of war without
just causes. "It is too true," Publius writes,

"however disgraceful it may be to human nature, that nations in general will make war whenever they have a prospect of getting anything by it."[26] Thus it appears that the first consideration, that of not giving just causes for war, is not of great importance since justice is not foremost among the motives of most human beings. The desires for gain, glory, power, and ambition are all more prominent. The safety of citizens from foreign attack depends most decisively, then, upon having a government with a system of defense strong enough to make rulers of other nations believe that they would have no easy prospect of victory in war. Such a strong defense can be offered by a united national government, Publius argues, but not by several smaller confederacies. Such confederacies could not be counted upon to come to one another's assistance in war if only because the duty of each government would be to pursue its own citizens' welfare and not that of the citizens of the rest of the continent. And again, one is not entitled to count upon rulers' being moved by good motives. The more likely occurrence, Publius writes, is that "envy and jealousy would soon extinguish confidence and affection, and the partial interest of each confederacy, instead of the general interests of all America, would be the only objects of their policy and pursuits."[27] Foreign nations could be expected to understand this reality, to act to encourage divisions, and then to take advantage of them. For security from foreign attack, then, a Union is more useful than several smaller confederacies.

We have seen Publius' statement that the first object of any government is to provide for the safety of the citizens. One threat to that safety comes always from foreign attack, but another threat, of perhaps greater importance for the Americans, came from their fellow Americans. Publius argues that were the Union to be dissolved into several confederacies one could expect not only that those three or four confederacies would not unite to defend each other, but also that they would be positive threats to each other.

> One must be far gone in Utopian
> speculations who can seriously doubt
> that, if these States should either
> be wholly disunited, or only united
> in partial confederacies, the sub-
> divisions into which they might be

thrown would have frequent and
violent contests with each other.
To presume a want of motives for
such contests as an argument against
their existence, would be to forget
that men are ambitious, vindictive,
and rapacious.[28]

The same fact that makes strength rather than just
conduct the principal deterrent to foreign attack,
then, leads to the conclusion that several confederacies in America would pose constant threats of attack
to each other. The "accumulated experience of the
ages,"[29] Publius tells us, is that men cannot be
counted upon for affection and trustworthiness, but
that they may be counted upon for ambition, rapacity,
and greed. Therefore, were the Union to be divided,
those new political units would, before very long, be
at one another's throats. Attacks would be inspired
by motives of collective greed, by a collective desire
for safety, as well as by a collective desire for power
or dominion. In addition, hostility could originate
in the private passions of rulers. The important fact
is that history shows that "momentary passions, and
immediate interests, have a more active and imperious
control over human conduct than general or remote
considerations of policy, utility, or justice."[30]

The wars that would unavoidably take place between
the States or confederacies left from the division of
the Union would, Publius continues, be more devastating
to the citizens of those confederacies than most wars,
especially European wars, are to the citizens of the
countries involved. This effect would follow from the
fact that the Americans did not have the fortifications
and professional armies that moderate the effects of
armed conflicts upon the civilians in the countries
involved, even when the countries are of significantly
different size in population. These particularly
devastating wars would lead to even more serious consequences. "Safety from external danger is the most
powerful director of national conduct. Even the ardent
love of liberty will after a time, give way to its
dictates."[31] Separate confederacies with liberal
governments would soon be found unable to secure the
lives and properties of their citizens from attack by
other confederacies. Publius argues that no matter
how strong the dedication to liberty is, the need for
security is stronger, and that in order to get that,

11

therefore, "To be more safe, they at length become willing to run the risk of being less free."[32]

Specifically, frequent war between bordering confederacies and the constant fear of war would lead the citizens to support the institution of standing armies. Furthermore, the citizens would be led by the need for safety to grant more and more power to the executive branches of government since it is the executive that is responsible for defense. Thus were the Union to be divided its parts would soon develop the "engines of despotism which have been the scourge of the Old World."[33] Not only would the institutions of despotism be established, however, for those institutions together with the ever-present danger of attack that makes them necessary, would combine to instill in the citizens the habits of despotism. From necessity, people would become used to granting pre-eminence to the executive and to the military and would become unused to asserting civil and political rights:

> The inhabitants of territories, often
> the theatre of war, are unavoidably
> subjected to frequent infringements
> on their rights, which serve to
> weaken their sense of those rights;
> and by degrees the people are brought
> to consider the soldiery not only as
> their protectors, but as their
> superiors.[34]

Hence disunion, combined with the fundamental human desire for self-preservation and the unavoidable human tendency to selfishness, would result in a slavish population.[35]

Publius' argument that Union is necessary to prevent the picture of "liberty everywhere crushed between standing armies and perpetual taxes"[36] bears a noteworthy resemblance to the argument made by Thomas Hobbes in his _Leviathan_. Hobbes' argument is essentially this: that citizens should obey the laws of their political communities since if they do not, and if they escape detection and punishment by the government, the laws will cease to have force and the order they impose will be replaced by a circum-stance where there is no government capable of imposing order, that is, by a state of nature. Now any reason-able human being in almost any political situation should want to avoid a state of nature, for in such a state life is "solitary, poore, nasty, brutish, and short."[37] Unless there is a power capable of over-awing all men in the community and enforcing peace, human nature will lead each man to be in a constant state of war with every other man. Human beings will invade for gain, to get things useful for the satis-faction of their desires; they will invade from diffidence, from fear that others will attack them; and they will invade for glory, for the feeling of pleasure that comes from contemplating their own power. Each is on his own and since every man is a constant threat to every other man, each must spend all of his efforts in the struggle to stay alive. This constant struggle leaves no time for the development of industry, agriculture, knowledge, or art. It makes the develop-ment of the faculties of men impossible. Therefore, Hobbes argues, it is reasonable for men to support almost any government because no matter how much a government may restrict liberty, it is bound to provide for more security, and hence for a greater possibility of the realization of the blessings of liberty, than will a state of nature.

Publius too presents the danger of a state of nature. The difference is that where Hobbes is speak-ing primarily of a state of nature between individuals, Publius is discussing the dangers of allowing a state of nature to exist between the States. Yet the prospects appear to be the same. It has been noted that Publius' argument is that without the Union the States of Confederacies would attack each other from a desire for gain, a desire for safety, or a desire for power. These are the same as the causes Hobbes points to as the reasons for the war of each against all in the state of nature. Hobbes' argument that in a state of nature there are no resources that may safely be devoted to anything but self-preservation is also paralleled by Publius who writes that in the event of disunion "our liberties would be a prey to the means of defending ourselves against the ambition and jealousy of each other."[38] And just as Hobbes argues that virtually any government is better than no government, Publius argues that the liberties of Americans require the Union for their security.

Yet the great difference between Hobbes and Publius must not be overlooked. Physical security, self-preservation, is far and away the principal object

13

of government for Hobbes. As long as government
provides for that object it does its job. Liberty is
a thing which may or may not be allowed by government,
but that government is not to be judged good or bad
according to the amount of liberty it provides, but
only according to whether it secures life. Thus
Hobbes does not hesitate to prefer monarchy over rule
by the few or the many since a single ruler is able to
enforce laws and maintain order more efficiently than
are many rulers sharing power.[39]

On the other hand we have seen how easily Publius
rejects the idea of removing the liberty of citizens
in order to prevent the violence of faction.[40] Publius
recognizes the importance of safety not by calling it
the object of government, but by calling it the first
of many objects of government.[41] Elsewhere he writes
that the protection not of the lives of men, but of
their diverse faculties, is the first object of
government.[42] And still elsewhere Publius writes that
the object of government, an object to which most
governments are insufficiently faithful, is the
happiness of the people.[43] There is, in fact, no
careful, sustained discussion of the ends of government in The Federalist for the reason that Publius
knew of the general agreement among the members of
his audience about the end of government. What is
apparent, however, is that Publius is much more concerned with the liberties of the citizens than was
Hobbes. He agreed that if it were impossible to obtain
both liberty and security that men would ultimately opt
for security,[44] but he did not agree with Hobbes that
the question of liberty was unimportant relative to
the question of security. Unlike Hobbes, Publius is
always aware of a need to construct government in such
a way as to allow as much liberty as possible.

Still, Publius shares Hobbes' realization that
complete liberty is not possible. Because of the
selfishness inherent in human nature men will abuse
liberty to the point where they take away each others'
liberties. The absolute liberty of the state of nature
is in reality no liberty at all since each must spend
all his efforts on the goal of staying alive and none
has the freedom to develop his faculties or to pursue
happiness. At one point Publius notes, in passing,
that even the strong choose to give up the absolute
liberty of the state of nature because of the uncertainty that obtains therein.[45] And in another place

14

he writes that governments are necessary because "the passions of men will not conform to the dictates of reason and justice, without constraint."[46] Indeed, as the argument against disunion has shown, there is a very strong connection between security and liberty. The argument was that the Union ought to be supported since it can provide security to life and property more easily than could several confederacies. It allows laws to be instituted to constrain the passions of men, and thereby allows the citizens of each state to be more secure from invasion by each other and consequently more secure in their liberties. In order for some liberty to be secure some liberty must be given up.

> Nothing is more certain than the
> indispensable necessity of govern-
> ment, and it is equally undeniable,
> that whenever and however it is
> instituted, the people must cede to
> it some of their natural rights,
> in order to vest it with requisite
> powers.[47]

The argument for Union is that were the Americans to divide themselves into several confederacies they would need to cede more liberty to their governments than with the Union.

But there is no denial by Publius that effective government under the Union requires a significant cession of liberties. To the contrary, he argues consistently the other side: that if some liberty is to be secure the government must have extensive power to rule. The Federalist is replete with passages wherein Publius charges that the great defect of American governments and especially of the Articles of Confederation is that their creators have not given them enough power to control the governed. He writes, for example, that "liberty may be endangered by the abuses of libery as well as by the abuses of power . . . and that the former, rather than the latter, are apparently most to be apprehended by the United States."[48] Thus there are times when Publius argues that the danger of abuse of powers must be accepted when a power is essential for the government to provide security.

The most fully discussed case where Publius claims

the need for security concerns to predominate has to do with the standing army. Recall the argument made in the early numbers of The Federalist that disunion would be disadvantageous because each separate state or confederacy would be forced by necessity to maintain an extensive standing army in order to defend its citizens from neighboring states or confederacies. Such armies could be expected to crush citizen liberties. Yet the Constitution allows the national government to maintain a standing army, and Publius defends that fact.

When he was arguing against disunion Publius argued that the great danger to liberty would arise from each confederacy's having a standing army. He did not argue, however, that such confederacies should not maintain standing armies. To the contrary, he argued that the fundamental need for each government to protect its citizens from foreign attack would make a standing army something that no good government could be without. That same necessity applies to the Union. It is of great importance, Publius writes, to understand that the security problems of the Union will be less severe than the security problems of several confederacies would be, but it is of great importance also to realize that the Union once firmly established must be able to protect itself and its citizens from foreign attack.

Publius discusses the issue of a standing army in the forty-first Federalist as part of a general discussion of the powers of the national government. He introduces this discussion with the observation that all political advantages bring with them certain inconveniences, usually in the form of potential abuses of power. Publius reminds his readers that "the purest of human blessings must have some alloy in them; that the choice must always be made, if not of the lesser evil, at least of the GREATER, not the PERFECT, good."[49] In creating governments the application of this observation means that in order to get the security to life and liberties that can be created only by governmental power one must often accept the risk that liberty will be curtailed by abuses of that power.

Publius continues to say that a decision about whether to grant a power to the government must rest on the answer to one question: Is the power necessary for the public good? If the answer here is yes, Publius

suggests, then the power must be granted, but granted
with such safeguards against abuse as it is possible
to devise without negating the effectiveness of the
power. Notice the difference between this calculus
and that used on the one hand by Hobbes and on the
other hand (according to Publius) by the Americans
before 1787. Hobbes would not appear concerned enough
about liberties to be willing to restrict power at all
in the name of preventing abuse. The Americans would
have asked first whether the power was dangerous and
not whether it was necessary.

This process is easily applied to the problem of
whether to allow the power to have a standing army.
"How," Publius asks, "could a readiness for war in
time of peace be safely prohibited unless we could
prohibit, in like manner, the preparations and establishments of every hostile nation?"[50] The government
must be allowed to adapt its security measures to
particular circumstances or be unable to protect its
citizens. This is clearly a case, Publius writes,
where "it is better to hazard the abuse of that
confidence than to embarass the government and endanger
the public safety by impolitic restrictions on the
legislative authority."[51] Necessity requires the
power. But having said that, Publius notes that it
remains possible to take measures to make abuse less
likely. The most important such measure in the case
of the standing army is the general one of maintaining
the Union. In addition, the Constitution provides that
no appropriation of money for the raising and supporting
of armies may be for a period of over two years, thus
forcing relatively frequent legislative deliberations
about the need for military forces, and keeping the
executive from having exclusive control of the armies.
But, thus controlled, the power of necessity remains,
and with it some possibility that a standing army would
be used to restrict rather than to protect citizen
liberties.

Publius' argument that good governments must
restrict liberty in order to protect life and liberty
appears also in the discussions of the characteristics
of the institutions created by the Constitution. The
calculation that was commonly accepted in 1787 was that
a popular form of government would be most likely to be
interested in securing citizen liberties. A strong
connection between political liberty and the security
of individual rights was assumed. Publius shares that

assumption, although the connection was so taken for granted that it was never really argued in The Federalist.[52] What Publius did have to argue is that the security of individual rights requires that some limits be placed upon political liberty, or upon the immediacy of the people's rule, if government is to govern effectively. The point recalls Hobbes. Hobbes' argument was that the best form of government is a monarchy since such a government can act more efficiently to protect citizens from one another and from foreign attack. Publius does not defend monarchy because he, like his fellows, is concerned with securing both safety and liberty, not merely safety. But because liberty requires safety, Publius is concerned with the government's having sufficient ability to protect its citizens, i.e., to govern.

In the thirty-seventh Federalist Publius discusses the difficult problem of reconciling the things needed for safety with the things needed for political liberty. On the one hand, he writes, there is a need for energy and stability in government. Energy is "essential to that security against internal and external danger, and to that prompt and salutary execution of the laws which enter into the very definition of good government."[53] Stability is necessary to secure the advantages of national character, meaning, presumably, the ability to exercise one's rights or to develop one's faculties with some assurance that government won't change so much as to make one's labors fruitless by the time their object is completed. On the other hand, it is imperative not to slight "the inviolable attention due to liberty and the republican form."[54] The problem is that the concern for liberty and the republican form and the concern for energy and stability lead to differing conclusions about how the institutions of government ought to be fashioned. If the only goal were republican liberty, the government would be characterized by many officials elected very frequently so as to reflect more accurately public sentiment. But the more people who must agree for government to act the more difficult it becomes for government to act, and the more frequently the officers of the government are elected the more likely it becomes that government measures will often be changed. Indeed, if the only goals were energy and stability the government, if not a monarchy, would have as few officers as possible, and those officers it had would serve very long terms.

The problem, thus, is that the general goal of securing individual rights requires the use of means that are opposed to each other because of the different sources from which threats to those rights might arise. Publius usually emphasizes the threat from foreign attack and from one's fellow citizens rather than the threat from government since he believed that Americans were likely to provide almost exclusively for the latter threat and to overlook the former. The American "zeal for liberty," he writes, has been "more ardent than enlightened."

> The circumstances of a revolution
> quickened the public sensibility
> on every point connected with the
> security of popular rights and in
> some instances raised the warmth of
> our zeal beyond the degree which
> consisted with the due temperature
> of the body politic.[55]

Publius' task is to cure the fever for the unlimited exercise of rights by reminding his readers that any security of rights depends upon the citizens' giving up enough rights to allow the government to govern effectively. He tries to draw the line where the surrender of rights should stop in this passage:

> It was a thing hardly to be expected
> that in a popular revolution the
> minds of men should stop at that
> happy mean which marks the salutary
> boundary between POWER and PRIVILEGE,
> and combining the energy of govern-
> ment with the security of private
> rights.[56]

The balance between measures that promote security and measures that preserve republican liberty should be struck at the point where additional measures would be absolutely unrepublican.[57] The government should be as powerful as possible while still being able to reflect popular sentiment and to respond to popular accountability.

The institution most clearly designed with the need for energy in mind is the presidency. The sub-stantial constitutional power of the office is held by one person who serves a long term of office, is eligible for reelection, who has a mode of election separate from the legislature, and whose powers are constitutionally protected from the legislature. Publius makes this clear in the first paragraph of The Federalist Number 70 when he once again alludes to the need to balance the requirements of safety with those of republican liberty:

> There is an idea, which is not without its advocates, that a vigorous Executive is inconsistent with the genius of republican government. The enlightened well-wishers to this species of government must at least hope that the supposition is destitute of foundation; since they can never admit its truth, without at the same time admitting the condemnation of their own principles. Energy in the Executive is a leading character in the definition of good government.[58]

Publius reiterates the point made in the argument for Union. However much a people may desire liberty, safety must come first. And if they cannot have the energy in government necessary for safety and republican liberty at the same time, it is ultimately the liberty that will fade. To give the Executive great power and independence is to court a danger of abuse, but to fail to give the Executive the requisite power and independence is to make a government that will fail in the most basic way to secure private rights.[59]

The question of the critical importance of energy in the executive allows us to see separation of powers in a somewhat different light. Ordinarily, separation of powers and checks and balances are seen as an institutional feature designed to make the people safe from government and tyranny. The price for this safety is often seen to be paid in efficiency, for the system of checks and balances yields a government whose parts are disposed to compete rather than to cooperate.[60] But separation of powers and the checks and balances that maintain it also contribute mightily to the energy and efficiency of the government as a whole. They do so primarily by securing the independence of the Executive in his proper sphere of activity, and, thus, allowing the President to act quickly and decisively when necessary without the interference of the

20

legislature. Were it not for separation of powers the
energy of the executive and with the government's
ability to secure individual rights from foreign
attack and domestic invasion would be seriously,
perhaps fatally, threatened.61

The institution which most clearly represents a
sacrifice of political liberty in the name of stability
is the United States Senate. Its members serve six
year overlapping terms, they were appointed by state
legislatures, and ordinarily they come from large
districts. Publius writes that the Senate, which is
clearly designed in such a way as to allow it to
overlook short term popular desires, was designed as
it was to give stability to the government's measures.

It is in the discussing the Senate that Publius
engages in his most lengthy discussion of the need for
stability in government. A mutable government, he
argues, "forfeits the respect and confidence of other
nations."62 With those goes support and perhaps all
unwillingness on the part of some other nations to
attack. Instability then, is a danger to safety. It
also appears to be a danger to happiness and the
development of human faculties: "it poisons the blessing of liberty itself"63 by making citizens unsure of
the benefits of their industry and ultimately making
them unwilling to risk their labors and the fruits of
those labors on the hope for future benefits. The
Senate is an institution less immediately controlled
by the people than republican liberty alone would
warrant, but that dilution of immediate popular control
is necessary for the effective exercise of private
rights in the longer run.

The need to sacrifice political liberty for
stability is reflected in another feature of the
Constitution discussed in Federalist 49. Publius
confronts Thomas Jefferson's argument that there
should be frequent conventions for the revising of
the Constitution (whenever two of the three branches
call for such a convention). Publius notes that from
the point of view of republican liberty the proposal
is sensible. "As the people are the only legitimate
fountain of power . . . it seems strictly consonant
to the republican theory, to recur to the same original
authority"64 whenever it might appear necessary to
alter the government. Nonetheless, Publius argues,
Jefferson's idea must be rejected.

21

Publius writes that the greatest objection to
Jefferson's argument is that frequent conventions
would be dangerous for the system of separation of
powers. It is another objection, however, that is of
more interest here. Frequent conventions would
threaten the government's stability. Each appeal to
the people, he writes, would imply some defect in the
Constitution. Frequent appeals would indicate a
general defectiveness and lead people to withhold "that
veneration which time bestows on every thing, and
without which perhaps the wisest and freest governments would not possess the requisite stability."[65]
The government is more stable when people are of the
opinion that it is good. People develop such an
opinion when the government has stood essentially
unchanged for a long time. The prejudice that the
government is good creates stability because it translates into a general law-abidingness. Without it the
government would have to depend upon either reason or
force to secure obedience. Publius writes that one
could depend upon reason if the nation were "a nation
of philosophers."[66] Since it is not, no matter how
good the government is, it stands to benefit much from
having the people's prejudices on its side. Otherwise,
in order to secure its rule and the safety that rule
provides, the government would have to use more force
and be more harmful to citizen liberties. It is a
choice between surrendering more liberty to the government at the outset by not providing for frequent appeals
to the people on the worthiness of the Constitution
itself and surrendering even more liberty to the
government as the years progress so that it will have
the ability to enforce its decrees upon a people disposed to have contempt for it.

The discussion of the importance of stability in
government points to another perspective from which the
argument in Federalist 10 can be viewed. It is worth
noting that the argument that a large republic will
control the harmful effects of faction immediately
follows the argument that the Union is necessary to
prevent wars between the states that would be devastating to life, property, and liberties. When the
discussion turns to the question of how the Union will
prevent the "violence of faction" Publius lists three
specific evils that may be attributed to faction:
"injustice, instability, and confusion."[67] Ordinarily
discussions of Publius' solutions to the problem of
majority faction center around the problem of injustice,

22

of the majority's violating the rights of minorities.
But it is important to keep in mind that of equal
importance is the danger of instability. Indeed, when
the issue of faction is first raised it is raised with
this sentence: "A firm Union will be of the utmost
moment to the peace and liberty of the States, as a
barrier against domestic faction and insurrection."[68]
Thus the harm of faction is identified first not as a
problem of minority rights, but as a problem that could
threaten the peace and therefore the liberty of the
whole. Majority faction is a threat to stability in
democracies primarily because the rich minority often
objects to having its property removed by an unjust
majority faction. Their objection can end in insurrection, and whatever the outcome, the liberties of
all are curtailed.[69] Just majority rule, however, need
have less fear that economic minorities will appeal to
the sword for the obvious reason that there would
normally be enough to be gained by working within the
system to further one's economic position that the risk
of losing that position through revolt would not be
worth taking so long as one could be certain of maintaining the fruits of his labor. As the threat of
insurrection lessens government needs to curtail fewer
citizen liberties than it would if it had to be constantly fearful of rebellion. The argument in Federalist 10, then, is not simply an argument for the rights
of the minority. It is an argument that by not allowing any faction to control government the large republic
secures the rights of all its citizens from insurrection
and from the more despotic sort of government that
would be required to provide against the threat of
insurrection by a powerful and oppressed minority.

IV

"If men were angels, no government would be
necessary."[70] Because human beings are insufficiently
angelic, however, they pose a danger to one another.
Before any person can move to develop his faculties
he must provide against that danger. Government is
the tool that men use to protect themselves from each
other, to secure the opportunity to exercise their
rights. In order to do its job effectively government
must be strong. The stronger a government becomes
the more likely it becomes that government itself will
become a danger to individual rights. Yet this fact
does not constitute an argument against strength in

23

government, only an argument against unnecessary strength in government. It is difficult to draw the line between necessary and unnecessary strength, but this much can be said: The rights of human beings are more secure when government has too much power than when government has too little. This is the principle of freedom that George Washington found candidly discussed in The Federalist.

NOTES

[1]George Washington to Alexander Hamilton, August 28, 1788, in Harold C. Syrett, ed., _Papers of Alexander Hamilton_ (New York: Columbia University Press, 1962), Vol. V., p. 207.

[2]Paul Leicester Ford, ed., _Essays on the Constitution of the United States_ (Brooklyn: Historical Printing Club, 1892), pp. 61-62.

[3]See Cecilia M. Kenyon, _The Antifederalists_ (Indianapolis: The Bobbs-Merrill Company, Inc., 1966), pp. xlii-xlvi, lxii-lxix.

[4]Douglas Adair, _Fame and the Founding Fathers_ (New York: W. W. Norton and Company, 1974), pp. 75-76. See also Gary Wills, _Explaining America_ (Garden City: Doubleday and Company, Inc., 1980), pp. xiv-xv.
The most important critic of the American Founders who uses _Federalist_ 10 to buttress his argument that the Constitution was a coup engineered by the wealthy for the wealthy is Charles Beard. Beard's interpretation of the founding was the dominant one throughout most of the century. For a recent restatement of Beard's argument see Michael Parenti, "The Constitution as an Elitist Document," in Robert A. Goldwin and William A. Schambra, eds., _How Democratic is the Constitution_? (Washington: American Enterprise Institute for Public Policy Research, 1980), pp. 39-58.

[5]Martin Diamond, "The Declaration and the Constitution: Liberty, Democracy, and the Founders," in Nathan Glazer and Irving Kristol, eds., _The American Commonwealth--1976_ (New York: Basic Books, 1976), p. 52.

[6]See especially Martin Diamond, "Ethics and Politics: The American Way," in Robert H. Horwitz, ed., _The Moral Foundations of the American Republic_ (Charlottesville: University Press of Virginia, 1979), p. 52.

[7]The criticisms come from those who argue that separation of powers and checks and balances are designed to prevent majority rule. For example, see James MacGregor Burns, _Deadlock of Democracy_ (Englewood Cliffs, New Jersey: Prentice-Hall, Inc., 1963),

pp. 8-23; and Robert A. Dahl, <u>A Preface to Democratic Theory</u> (Chicago: The University of Chicago Press, 1956), pp. 4-34.

The fundamental confusion about the purpose of separation of powers that exists in these and similar works is very well explained by George W. Carey, "Separation of Powers and the Madisonian Model: A Reply to the Critics," <u>American Political Science Review</u> 72 (March, 1978), pp. 151-164.

[8]Alexander Hamilton, John Jay, and James Madison, <u>The Federalist</u> (New York: The Modern Library, 1937), Number 48, p. 321.

[9]<u>The Federalist</u> Number 51, p. 337.

[10]<u>Ibid.</u>

[11]<u>Ibid.</u>

[12]I have discussed <u>Federalist</u> 51 before discussing <u>Federalist</u> 10 in order to demonstrate that the argument in the former is not simply a continuation of the argument in the latter, but is, instead, about a separate problem. See the authors cited in note 7 above.

[13]<u>The Federalist</u> Number 10, p. 54.

[14]<u>Ibid.</u>, p. 55.

[15]<u>Ibid.</u>, pp. 56-57.

[16]<u>Ibid.</u>, p. 54.

[17]<u>Ibid.</u>, p. 55.

[18]Publius was not unconcerned with injustices that might be perpetrated by minority factions. He simply understood that minority factions would be prevented from assuming control of the government by the fact of majority rule. Parenti's statement that "There was, then, no need to impose constitutional checks upon the haves," misrepresents Publius' thought. Parenti, p. 48. The great constitutional check of majority rule was designed to control the haves.

[19]James Madison, who, as Publius, presents the famous argument in the tenth <u>Federalist</u>, first

articulates that argument in a memorandum written in
the spring of 1787 entitled "Vices of the Political
System of the United States." In that memorandum we
find the statement that the injustice of the laws
passed by many state legislatures due to the pressure
of factious majorities is a great evil "because it
brings more into question the fundamental principle
of republican Government, that the majority who rule
in such Governments, are the safest Guardians both of
public Good and of private rights." Robert A. Rutland,
ed., The Papers of James Madison (Chicago: The University
of Chicago Press, 1975), Vol. 9, p. 354. The
great problem, then, is to keep the principle that
recommends republican government from being overcome
by majority faction.

[20] The Federalist Number 10, p. 61.

[21] The Federalist Number 51, pp. 340-341.

[22] Ibid., p. 337.

[23] See The Federalist Number 62, p. 404, Number 1,
p. 6, and Number 43, p. 287.

[24] The Federalist Number 3, p. 13 (emphasis in the
original).

[25] Ibid., p. 17.

[26] The Federalist Number 4, p. 18.

[27] The Federalist Number 5, p. 24.

[28] The Federalist Number 6, p. 207.

[29] Ibid.

[30] Ibid., p. 30.

[31] The Federalist Number 8, p. 42.

[32] Ibid.

[33] Ibid., p. 44.

[34] Ibid., p. 45.

[35] The same argument is made later by Publius in

The Federalist Number 41 where he writes that "This picture of the consequences of disunion cannot be too highly colored, or too often exhibited," p. 264.

[36] The Federalist Number 41, p. 263.

[37] Thomas Hobbes, Leviathan, Ch. 13.

[38] The Federalist Number 8, p. 46.

[39] See Hobbes, Leviathan, Chs. 21 and 19.

[40] The Federalist Number 10, p. 55 and p. 17 above.

[41] The Federalist Number 3, p. 13.

[42] The Federalist Number 10, p. 55.

[43] The Federalist Number 62, p. 404.

[44] The Federalist Number 8, p. 42.

[45] The Federalist Number 51, p. 340.

[46] The Federalist Number 15, p. 92.

[47] The Federalist Number 2, p. 8.

[48] The Federalist Number 63, p. 413. See also Number 26, p. 159 and Number 62, p. 404.

[49] The Federalist Number 41, p. 260.

[50] Ibid., p. 262.

[51] The Federalist Number 26, p. 159.

[52] See, e.g., The Federalist Number 30: "It is evident that no (form of government other than the republican) would be reconcilable with the genius of the people of America; with the fundamental principles of the Revolution; or with the honorable determination which animates every votary of freedom, to rest all our political experiments on the capacity of mankind for self-government." p. 243.

[53] The Federalist Number 37, p. 227.

[54] Ibid.

[55] *The Federalist* Number 26, p. 159, 161.

[56] *Ibid.*, p. 159.

[57] See Publius' definition of a republic in *The Federalist* Number 39, pp. 243-244.

[58] *The Federalist* Number 70, p. 454.

[59] On Alexander Hamilton's argument for energy in the Executive see the article by David Marion in this volume.

[60] See, for example, Burns, *The Deadlock of Democracy*, pp. 20-23.

[61] See Martin Diamond, "Conservatives, Liberals, and the Constitution," in Robert A. Goldwin, ed., *Left, Right and Center* (Chicago: Rand McNally and Company, 1965), p. 67; Gary Wills, *Explaining America* (Garden City: Doubleday and Company, 1981), pp. 109-110; and James Madison to Caleb Wallace, August 23, 1785, in *The Papers of James Madison*, Vol. 8, p. 352.

[62] *The Federalist* Number 62, p. 405.

[63] *Ibid.*, p. 406.

[64] *The Federalist* Number 49, p. 327.

[65] *Ibid.*, pp. 328-329.

[66] *Ibid.*, p. 329.

[67] *The Federalist* Number 10, p. 53.

[68] *The Federalist* Number 9, p. 47.

[69] See *The Federalist* Number 43 where Publius notes that the minor party "may possess such a superiority of pecuniary resources, of military talents and experience, or of secret success from foreign powers, as will render it superior in an appeal to the sword," p. 284.

[70] *The Federalist* Number 51, p. 337.

CHAPTER 2
"Alexander Hamilton On The Spirit and Form of a
Responsible Republican Government"
David E. Marion

Recent developments involving the apparent
enlargement of the authority and prerogatives of the
national executive together with the popularization of
the idea of an emerging American bureaucratic state
have contributed to a resurgence of interest in the
political thought of Alexander Hamilton. The prevailing tendency, however, is to magnify the significance of decidedly discrete elements in Hamilton's
thought at the expense of the overarching concerns
that render intelligible the entire corpus of his
political reasoning. Thus, for example, it is not
uncommon for commentators on Hamilton to advance the
accusation that he championed an illiberal, if not
"imperial," presidential establishment. It is the
Hamiltonian model of the executive that is singled out
as the historical paradigm for such reforms as the
plan for an "administrative presidency" that was adopted
by the Nixon White House.[1] More generally, Hamilton's
endorsement of an energetic executive and a strong
national administration is cited as evidence of his
impatience with democratic constitutionalism. Witness
the observation by Henry Cabot Lodge late in the 1890's
that Hamilton "believed in class influence and representation, in strong government, and in what, for want
of a better phrase, may be called an aristocratic
republic."[2] What is missing from much of the literature is an appreciation of the relationship between
Hamilton's perception of the ends or purposes of a
liberal republic and his commitment to competent and
effective government. In short, the substantive side
of Hamilton's understanding of "good government" is
too frequently lost from sight.

Significantly, the weaknesses that mark the
literature on Hamilton are reflective of the generally
unsatisfying character of the contemporary scholarship
on the nature and purposes of the American national
government. The persistence of disagreement on the
intended form and spirit of the American regime prompts
a review of the writings and teachings of those persons
who were responsible for shaping the constitutional
order. This exercise necessarily involves an examination of the Constitution itself. Considering its
formative influence, the Constitution may well be
expected to supply indispensable clues to the character

of, say, the executive power and the federal system of administration. It is after all to the Constitution that we look in order to decide the eminently political question having to do with who rules and in what fashion. Needless to add, in order to be effective this exercise requires an acquaintance with the intentions of the framers who drafted the Constitution. To put this differently, there is no better way to appreciate the American constitutional order than to reflect on the thought and practices of the founders. Precisely this enterprise constitutes the prolegomena to a recovery of the motives behind the establishment of the national government.

With respect to Hamilton in particular, a restoration of his classic defense of the Constitution should enable us to better appreciate how the American regime attempts to reconcile the competing claims raised on behalf of the principle of liberty and the requisites of capable and effective government. This, indeed, is the principle theme that unifies his contribution to The Federalist. It was, after all, as a self-proclaimed "friend of liberty" that Hamilton sought to persuade Americans of the virtues of a government that possessed both a capacity for vigor and competence on the one hand, and a commitment to the preservation of liberty on the other. In this connection, the contrast between Hamilton's defense of the Constitution and conventional opinion of his political thought is instructive. As will become evident in the course of this examination of his work, Hamilton's decisive concern was to defend limited government and the regime of liberty, not 'positive' government and a regime of perfect equality, nor a monocratic government and a regime based on wealth and power. Hamilton regarded himself as defending neither an aristocratic republic nor a pure democracy whose weaknesses should ever be corrected by extending the popular democratic characteristics of the government, but a democratic republic capable of reconciling and accommodating the competing requisites of liberty and competence as well as of equality.

Hamilton's defense of the American Constitution in The Federalist begins with the observation that it had fallen to the American people to decide whether a community can govern itself competently and still remain faithful to republican principles. Acknowledging that competence in governance and the

31

commitment to preserve private rights are the principal ingredients of "good" government, Hamilton insisted that it remained for the Americans to demonstrate the possibility of embracing and maintaining the requisites of effective republican government as a result of reflection and deliberate choice. The decisive test involved the ratification of the Constitution. Hamilton did not quibble about his conviction that the adoption of the Constitution represented "the safest course for liberty, dignity and happiness."[3] The task undertaken by Publius is to convince the people by way of argument of the merits of the proposed system of government. This is significant, for Hamilton implicitly invites us to assess the reasonableness of his arguments and, in turn, the soundness of the proposed Constitution itself. That is to say, Hamilton's defense of the capacity of the Constitution to promote "good" government provides an excellent basis for examining the nature and purposes of the American constitutional order.

It is perhaps to reverse the conventional wisdom on Hamilton to observe that what is frequently lost from sight is the connection in his thought between the energetic executive and defensible republican government. The Jeffersonian charge that Hamilton was a monocrat at heart has not only had a powerful effect on popular attitudes, but seemingly has obscured, and dampended interest in, Hamilton's republican credentials. In point of fact, both in his contribution to The Federalist Papers and elsewhere in his correspondence Hamilton acknowledged that what distinguishes and, indeed, recommends modern republican government is its rootage in the popular will. By its nature, the modern liberal republic rests on the elevation of the public will as the sovereign principle of governance. But just the proposition that popular consent supplies political legitimacy and forms the irreducible core of liberal republicanism was not contested by Hamilton. The following passage from a speech he delivered at the New York Ratifying Convention demonstrates that Hamilton had no quarrel with the republican principle of rule based on consent that figures prominently in the Declaration of Independence:

> All governments, even the most
> despotic, depend, in a great degree,
> on opinion. In free republics, it
> is most peculiarly the case: In

these, the will of the people makes
the essential principle of the
government; and the laws which
control the community, receive
their tone and spirit from the
public wishes.[4]

Hamilton clearly understands the essence of republican
government. Like John Marshall, Hamilton's endorsement of republicanism is based on the recognition that
underlying the dependence of modern republican government on popular consent is a commitment to the pre-
eminence of individual rights and the safety and
happiness of the people among the ends of legitimate
government. Significantly, it is as a self-proclaimed
friend of liberty and defender of the security and
prosperity of the people that Hamilton praises the
virtues of republican government.[5]

But Hamilton understands well that the virtues
which recommend republican government may easily be
neutralized by the characteristic problem that marks
all popular regimes. In a capsule statement, the
modern republic is plagued by the constant probability
that the people will not recognize or embrace "right"
opinion, understood as opinion that promoted the safety
and prosperity and secures the liberties of the people.
This is the characteristic problem of republican
government precisely because of the rootage of republican systems in the popular will. As a species of
popular government, a democratic republic is at its
best when informed by enlightened public opinion or the
deliberate will of the community. Especially at the
founding, but not confined to the formative period, the
presence of "right" opinion in the citizen body is
crucial. Unless it is to be left to accident or chance,
the choice of a decent and defensible republican system
depends on informed deliberation by the citizen body.
That this was not lost on Hamilton is evident from the
significance attached by him to convincing the people
through reasoned arguments of the utility of the Constitution, and the strong national government promised
by the Constitution, to the ends of a liberal and
prosperous civil society. This was the task undertaken
in The Federalist Papers. But what bears emphasizing,
precisely because it is frequently lost from sight,
is Hamilton's acknowledgment that a government can be
republican only so long as its principal guide is the
public will; while it can be a decent and defensible

republic only as long as the public will is informed. Thus as a friend of republican government, Hamilton is obliged to promote "right" public opinion.

To repeat, however, precisely because republican government rests on the principle of popular consent, it is peculiarly vulnerable to faltering whenever the people fail to appreciate the demands of the common good. It was with the intent of compelling the people to consider their best interests and, thus, to make republican government equal to its ends that Hamilton endeavors in The Federalist to instruct the popular will as he was later to instruct the legislative will in his reports as Secretary of the Treasury.[6] Now to succeed in this exercise, Hamilton recognizes that appeals must be made to the interests of the people. More precisely, the desideratum is to confront the people on the level of their interests with reasoned arguments. This exercise, when undertaken seriously, requires that you have some faith in the capacity of the people for reflection on the true nature of their interests. In fact, Hamilton recognizes that republican government, more than any other political system, presumes the presence of self-discipline and a capacity to form judgments based on enlightened self-interest in the citizen body. Hamilton's defense of the American constitutional republic is evidence of his belief that there is more knowledge and decency in the people than ignorance and perversity.

Hamilton's faith in the capacity of men to respond to reasoned arguments appealing to their best interests translates into the conviction that democratic government can be decent and defensible. But experience reveals that not all persons will be equally open to such arguments. Hence, Hamilton's specific appeal in The Federalist for the support of the unprejudiced and the sincere friends of liberty.[7] Appeals to the interests of such citizens through reasoned arguments are most likely to prompt judgments based on a due regard for the security of private rights and the advancement of the general welfare. By contrast, the best that can be done in the case of persons given to unreflective or impractical views and prejudiced political opinions is to diminish their influence on the citizen body. Accordingly, in the case of the most prejudiced critics of the Constitution, Hamilton can expect to quiet them at best, and must dull their effect on the general public at the least. Hamilton's strategy is to address those persons whose opposition to a strong central government is based less on a commitment to the moral and public virtues than on the protection of private rights. With persons of this persuasion, Hamilton can make a convincing defense of the Constitution in terms of security and prosperity.

It is instructive that Hamilton begins and ends his contribution to <u>The Federalist</u> with appeals to good judgment and a prudent regard for what is possible. Hamilton recognized as well as any of the Founders that what is possible is far more modest than what might be desirable. What is possible is the establishment of a liberal republic that rests on the personal interests of the people and offers protection for their private rights. These are hardly the lofty and ennobling aims of classical political philosophy. Nor did these goals satisfy the desire on the part of some Anti-Federalists for securing the moral and public virtues. But Hamilton is confident that the government established by the Constitution can satisfy the expectations of men of good judgment who have a sensible appreciation for the advantages as well as the characteristic weaknesses of the modern republic and for the limits to what can be accomplished through political arrangements.[8] To paraphrase Madison, the Constitution can survive examination by persons who recognize that men are not angels and that securing comfortable self-preservation in a regime of rights is hardly a negligible accomplishment. For Madison and Hamilton, the extended liberal commercial republic could be expected to promote greater justice than the older orders and would be far easier to establish and maintain than the ideal regimes of antiquity. Hamilton's political wisdom is marked by a fixed attention to the limits of political action. This "political realism" bore heavily on his conduct as a public servant and, more generally, as a political thinker. His distrust of messianic philosophies and "speculative" reformers is nowhere better evidenced than in a letter addressed to the Marquis de Lafayette in the year of the Constitution's ratification: "... I dread the reveries of your Philosophic politicians who appear in the moment to have great influence and who being mere speculatists may aim at more refinement than suits either with human nature or the composition of your Nation."[9]

Not surprisingly, the most controversial elements
in Hamilton's vision of a defensible republican system
are connected to the probability that appeals even to
the best interests of most of the people will not
always be successful in generating "right" opinion.
Here is the rub and the basis of Hamilton's defense
of a strong national government. This, in turn, has
spawned the accusation that Hamilton preferred an
"aristocratic" republic to one that was democratic in
nature.[10] It is, in fact, the constant probability
that popular opinion will not coincide with the best
national interest that leads Hamilton to attach
considerable importance to devices that enable the
government to refine and moderate, and indeed to check
when necessary, popular opinion. It is to meet the
demands of the common good when the citizen body does
not recognize its best interests that Hamilton proposes the strong and independent executive armed with
a capable administration. As Hamilton demonstrates in
Federalist 71, implicit in the trust with which the
president is charged is a responsibility to discriminate between informed and uninformed public opinion:

> The republican principle demands that
> the deliberate sense of the community
> should govern the conduct of those to
> whom they intrust the management of
> their affairs; but it does not require
> an unqualified complaissance to every
> sudden breeze of passion, or to every
> transient impulse which the people
> may receive from the arts of men, who
> flatter their prejudices to betray
> their interests.... When occasions
> present themselves in which the
> interests of the people are at vari-
> ance with their inclinations, it is
> the duty of the persons whom they
> have appointed to be the guardians
> of those interests to withstand the
> temporary delusion in order to give
> them time and opportunity for more
> cool and sedate reflection.[11]

Now without doubt, Hamilton's energetic executive
is the most distinctive ingredient in his conception
of "good" government or moderated democratic government, that is, a popular government committed to
securing the private rights and promoting the

comfortable preservation of the citizen body.
Hamilton's consideration in The Federalist of the
"real nature and form" of the executive commences
with the observation that the difficulties which beset
agreement on the constitutional form appropriate to
this department could hardly be exaggerated.[12] Just
this remark sets the tone for his apology, in the
truest sense of a definitive defense, for the Convention's plan for an independent executive. As the
first major theme in the series of nine papers on
the executive, Hamilton considers the compatibility
of vigor in that department with the principles of
republican liberalism. In short, Hamilton set out
to rescue strength in the executive from the oppro-
brium under which it labored. To this end he proceeds
to demonstrate that both the appointment formula and
the grant of powers affixed to the presidency were
consistent with the demands of republican government.

With regard first to the appointment of the
president Hamilton commends the decision to rest his
selection with a group of electors, rather than with
the national legislature, on the grounds that this
arrangement would mute the disruptive effects of
"cabal, intrigue, and corruption" on the office, the
very vices associated in later papers with election
by the Congress. Significantly, Hamilton argues that
the "intrigue and corruption" which is likely to
attend selection by the legislature would interfere
with the "sense of the people" determining choice of
a chief magistrate in whom the "public trust" will be
confided.[13] Plainly, this argument goes a long way
towards recommending an independent mode of appointment for the president. But this is not all that
Hamilton found to be salutary about the electoral
college system. To the extent that electors are free
of ulterior motives of a pernicious sort, the system
would lend itself to the selection of persons of the
first character.[14]

> This process of election affords a
> moral certainty that the office of
> President will seldom fall to the
> lot of any man who is not in an
> eminent degree endowed with the
> requisite qualifications... It
> will not be too strong to say that
> there will be a constant proba-
> bility of seeing the station filled

by characters pre-eminent for
ability and virtue.[15]

By connecting this claim to his insistence that the
electoral college system would be attuned to the
"sense of the people," Hamilton is in a position to
declare that the appointment formula adopted by the
Framers reconciles the democratic principle of consent
with the principle of selection based on fitness of
character.[16] Thus he addresses the concerns of those
persons who questioned the republican credentials of
the Convention's plan for the executive without losing
sight of the necessity for assuring the requisite
personal motives and capacity in the office.

By way of further disarming the opinions and
prejudices that pose a threat to the creation of an
energetic executive, Hamilton reviewed the powers and
responsibilities that were to be entrusted to that
department. In the process, he responds to the
apprehension that the executive might aggradize
influence and privileges in a manner and to a degree
that would permit the office to approach the conditions
of a monarchy in practice if not in name.[17] Regarding
such fears, Hamilton reminds his reader that a president is accorded only a concurrent authority to
appoint persons to high offices and could confer no
formal privileges whatsoever.[18] This observation is
of more than incidental importance. It is addressed
to the specific fear that the appointment power lends
itself to the establishment of a special class of
dignitaries and, hence, could serve as a device for
insulating the president from the citizen body.[19]
Thus, in the course of distinguishing the proposed
executive from the British monarch, Hamilton places
the president's control over the administration in the
context of the separation of powers doctrine in
particular, and of republican constitutionalism in
general. Again we have evidence of Hamilton's intent
to establish the republican credentials of the independent executive.

Hamilton's understanding of the proper character
of a republican executive also surfaces in his
thoughts on the confusion and irresponsibility that
would attend plurality in that office. It is
significant that among the defects in the case for
plurality in the executive Hamilton emphasizes the
probability that different factions would attach

themselves to the various magistrates and, thereby,
generate dangerous divisions within the presidential-
administrative province.[20] Here, again, he recurs to
the distinctive requisites of an effective and
responsible executive. While Hamilton concedes that
party divisions might prove useful in the legislature,
he pointedly declares that their presence in the
executive department could incite conflicts which
would "lessen the respectability, weaken the authority,
and distract the plans and operations of those whom
they divide."[21] With this defense of the single,
energetic executive, Hamilton affirms his commitment
not only to "good" administration but to "respectable"
government. More importantly, he defines his criteria
according to republican principles. Plurality in the
executive is shown to corrupt the accountability which
is essential to republican government. Public opinion,
for example, loses its capacity to restrain to the
extent that the responsibility for government action
is masked by the interaction of numerous parties or
interests.[22] In the case of the presidency, the
importance of this thought was magnified during the
founding period by the prevailing suspicion of
executive authority. For his part, Hamilton duly
cautioned that "every magistrate ought to be personally
responsible for his behavior in office.[23] Under the
constitutional system defended by Hamilton, the "trust"
lodged in public officers is regulated procedurally by
legal and institutional prescriptions and substantively
by the competition of men of ambition whose personal
interests are connected to the responsibilities of
their public offices. And it was precisely in this
setting that Hamilton rested his defense of the single
executive. This is plainly visible in a related
critique of the plurality scheme.

The ill effects of factious competition and the
resulting enervation of the government and loss of
accountability were not the only charges laid against
plurality in the executive by Hamilton. At the end
of Federalist 70 he introduces a criticism based on
the dangers to liberty that would result should the
energies of the various office-holders be joined to
secure ignoble ends. He spoke as a "friend to
liberty:"

> The united credit and influence of
> several individuals must be more
> formidable to liberty than the credit

and influence of either of them
separately. When power, therefore,
is placed in the hands of so small
a number of men as to admit of
their interests and views being
easily combined in a common enterprise, by an artful leader, it
becomes more liable to abuse, and
more dangerous when abused, than
if it be lodged in the hands of one
man, who, from the very circumstance
of his being alone, will be more
narrowly watched and more readily
suspected, and who cannot unite so
great a mass of influence as when
he is associated with others.[24]

Hence, in a very real sense the single executive is
presented by Hamilton as a mean between the danger of
creating either a hydra-like tyrant on the one hand,
or an inept and irresponsible government on the other.[25]
To put this differently, plurality in the executive is
doubly stigmatized as being liable to issue either in
illiberal and oppressive rule, or in the breakdown of
governance altogether. Accordingly, the argument on
behalf of the single executive points to the coinci-
dence of the requisites of both responsible and
competent government.

The preceding review of Hamilton's response to
the detractors of the Convention's plan for the
presidency clearly reveals that his characterization
of the responsible executive centered on a well
defined doctrine of official responsibility. Broadly
conceived, the doctrine holding public office to
constitute a "public trust" may be said to rest on a
dual understanding of political responsibility of
which one view figured prominently in Hamilton's
thought. On the one side, common usage equates governmental responsibility with responsiveness. This construction takes its bearings from the literal
understanding of what it means to be a "public
servant."[26] The emphasis is on the obligation to
heed the wishes and pleas of those persons to whom
one ministers and at whose "pleasure" one serves.
Thus a relationship of strict dependence is construed
to exist between government personnel and the public
at large. This perspective corresponds to conventional
democratic opinion which places a premium on responsive-

ness to popular demands. There is, however, another
understanding of political responsibility which is
rooted in the claim that official authority ought to
be guided by the legal and constitutional duties of
the office.[27] This 'Burkean' construction stresses
the obligation of the officer to render independent
judgments regarding the security of the interests
entrusted to his care. Significant in this regard is
the president's oath to "faithfully execute the Office
of President of the United States," and to the best of
his ability to "preserve, protect and defend the
Constitution."[28] The president is independently
responsible for advancing the ends of the constitutional order. It is undeniably this view of the high
responsibilities of the executive that informed
Hamilton's treatment of that department. Along with
magnanimity, Hamilton singles out courage as a virtue
especially to be desired in persons who are entrusted
with the presidential powers.[29]

In the context of this understanding of official
responsibility the president must have the confidence
and security to mobilize the resources of his office,
to include the national administration, to the end of
promoting the general welfare.[30] It is not mere
exaggeration to suggest in this regard that Hamilton
considers the capabilities of the executive and the
qualities of the federal administration to be mutually
dependent. Thus, for instance, duration in the
executive contributes to constancy in the mode and
system of administration. Re-eligibility and an
independent grant of power allow for the formulation
of long-range plans and policies calculated to advance
the best interests of the republic. In effect, they
establish the conditions for both "energy in the
administration" and "good" government. Significantly,
on one occasion during the New York Ratifying Convention, Hamilton quite revealingly referred to "energy
in the administration" and "strength of government"
as seemingly interchangeable objectives.[31] It took
virtually no explanation for him to make the
transition from this thought to the claim that the
government would share in the assessment of the
federal administration by the citizen body. Thus he
declared, "The confidence of the people will easily
be gained by a good administration. This is the true
touchstone."[32] It was Hamilton's belief that a
properly ordered administration would generate support
for the central government and offset the natural

41

affection shown the states.[33] At the same time, the
prestige of the national government would be likely
to diminish whenever the people considered the management of public affairs to be illiberal, illicit or
ineffective. On the basis of reasoning it is not
difficult to appreciate the attention and prominence
assigned to "good administration" in Hamilton's
defense of the plan for a national executive.

Hamilton's thoughts on the substantive connection
between energy in the executive, "good administration,"
and republican government can be gleaned from his
passing reference in Federalist 68 to Alexander Pope's
melodic couplet from Epistle III of the Essay on Man:
"For forms of government let fools contest; what'er is
best administered is best."[34] Hamilton freely admits
that Pope's counsel constituted a species of "political
heresy."[35] This comment on the couplet has been
rendered largely hollow, however, by the attention
that is given to Hamilton's subsequent insistence in
Federalist 68 that as a matter of practical wisdom "we
may safely pronounce that the true test of a good
government is its aptitude and tendency to produce a
good administration."[36] Just this declaration is
commonly construed in a fashion that neutralizes his
disagreement with Pope. That is to say, the tendency
has been to separate out and exaggerate the importance
of Hamilton's contention that energy in the executive
and administration is a "leading character" or a "true
test" of a "good government."[37] The upshot of this
exercise is to obscure Hamilton's appreciation of the
formal constitutional dimension of the American
republic. But not only did he refrain from branding
executive or administrative energy as the necessary
and sufficient cause of "good government," Hamilton's
charge of "political heresy" against Pope itself
renders suspect the accusation that he disregarded the
formal side of the political order that establishes
its character as a regime committed to the protection
of private rights. Indeed, it is precisely the
defender of republican principles who would find Pope's
couplet to be "heretical." As has been already noted,
it was as a self-styled "friend to liberty" that
Hamilton undertook to defend the credibility of what
was perhaps the most suspected feature of the proposed
constitutional system, that is, the compatibility of
an independent and active executive and administration
with republican principles.[38]

Considering the emphasis that has been given to
Hamilton's appeal for a strong national administration
it is eminently important that his credentials as a
"friend to liberty" be firmly established. In this
regard, what is striking in Hamilton's political
thought is his concern to achieve the proper blend
of governmental power and limits that are appropriate
to a commercial republic. Thus during the New York
Ratifying Convention he reasoned that a system of
government ought to be "so skillfully contrived, that
it is next to impossible that an impolitic or wicked
measure should pass the great scrutiny with success."[39]
This statement exposes a sensitivity not often
associated with Hamilton to the need for arrangements
which will promote decent government. In point of
fact, his formula for "good government" contains an
appeal not merely for energy in the executive province
but also for the security of private rights:

> There are two objects in forming
> systems of government--Safety for
> the people, and energy in the
> administration. When these objects
> are united, the certain tendency of
> the system will be to the public
> welfare. If the latter object be
> neglected, the people's security
> will be as certainly sacrificed,
> as by disregarding the former. Good
> constitutions are formed upon a com-
> parison of the liberty of the indi-
> vidual with the strength of government:
> If the tone of either be too high,
> the other will be weakened too much.[40]

Far from endorsing unlimited executive authority,
Hamilton proceeds to declare that through the "opposition and mutual control" of the departments of
government it is possible to create "the perfect
balance between liberty and power."[41] Here, surely,
is convincing evidence of his regard for constitutional
forms and of his commitment to a regime of liberty.
Liberty emerges as the comprehensive good to be secured
through a proper configuration of governmental powers
and institutions. Hamilton's treatment of the executive, and of the administration of the government
generally, becomes fully intelligible only in light
of this perspective. To summarize, the strength in
the executive that he considers to be "essential to

43

the security of liberty" must be toned and directed by
the proper constitutional forms. Admittedly, Hamilton
wanted to go "as far in order to attain stability and
permanency, as republican principles would admit."[42]
But what is instructive is his reluctance to exchange
the requisites of republican constitutionalism for the
demands of "necessity or utility."[43]

This concern for responsible republican government
is prominent in Hamilton's views on the relationship
that ought to obtain between the president and
administrative officials. The reflections in _Feder-
alist_ 76 on the appointment of persons to serve in
administrative posts are characteristic of Hamilton's
political counsel. As with the power to grant pardons,
he argues that the chief magistrate is "better fitted
to analyze and estimate the peculiar qualities adapted
to particular offices than a body of men of equal or
perhaps even of superior discernment."[44] Underlying
this argument was the opinion that the special
constitutional place of the executive would dispose
him to select persons whose character and conduct
would lend credit to his administration. He has, in
other words, a vested interest in the reputation of
the administrative service. True to the modern
liberal tradition, Hamilton formulates his recommendations with an eye to tapping the force of self-interest
in human affairs. This is of no mean importance. It
appears as well, although in a far more complex form,
in the thought that merit would be a more formidable
factor in the selection process if the choice was left
to an agency that was generally free of the vicissitudes
of party agitation and division to which political
bodies composed of numerous members are most prone.[45]
To a remarkable degree Hamilton anticipates the
patronage abuses that were most pronounced during the
periods of executive dormancy in the nineteenth century
and which took the form of the spoils system. As
commonly practiced, the spoils system involved the
liberation of self-interest in the public domain in
a manner and to a degree that threatened competent and
impartial governance. In terms of Hamilton's argument,
it is the possibility of party intrigues that vitiates
the selection of administrative personnel by the
legislature. He had no scruples in declaring that it
would "rarely happen that the advancement of the public
service will be the primary object either of party
victories or of party negotiations."[46] This defect is
decisive for Hamilton. By contrast, he expected that

the president would be beholding to fewer persons and
interests for his appointment and, hence, would not
be handicapped by the numerous political debts
accumulated by the members of the legislature.
Despite the fact that this description passed over
the demands of high-powered presidential campaign
politics, what cannot be discounted is the emphasis
on the "advancement of the public service." To
restate Hamilton's position, selection by the
executive establishes an immediate connection between
his legal obligations and the conduct of administrative officials; thereby making explicit his obligation
to promote the general welfare or suffer popular dis-
favor or legal penalties for want of proper supervision
of the public's affairs. In short, administrative
efficiency as well as the principle of official
responsibility are shown to be best satisfied by
executive selection of federal administrative functionaries.

When all of these observations are synthesized
it is apparent that for Hamilton a stable, efficient,
and highly qualified public service is indispensable
to "good" republican government. His concern for the
integrity of the national administration is strikingly
evident in Federalist 77. There he advances the
desirability of institutional devices that might
diminish the effects of executive ineptitude and
corruption on the administration of the government.
In this regard Hamilton particularly approves that
provision of the Constitution which entrusts the
confirmation of superior executive officers to that
branch of the Congress which is least subject to
inconstancy due to the length of the tenure of its
members, that is to say, to the Senate.[47] Thus the
Senate is depicted as having an implicit responsibility for promoting the stability and integrity of
the federal administration by discouraging appointments
based on ignoble motives, to include mere favoritism.
Surely revealing of the significance that Hamilton
attributes to this oversight function is his
insistence that even a change in magistrates need
not occasion a wholesale removal of administrative
officials so long as the Senate refuses to ratify
nominations of persons to displace officers who
demonstrate fidelity and fitness of character.[48]
By way of an aside, it is of more than passing interest
that a similar desire to protect the integrity of the
federal public service promoted the plea during the

later part of the nineteenth century for a career
civil service based on merit principles and supervised
by a separate Civil Service Commission.[49] In much the
same spirit as the civil service reformers, Hamilton
saw in the Senate an institutional device for guarding
the administrative service against the worst effects
of illiberal or illicit impulses or of "favoritism"
in the executive. Here again is evidence that his
gaze was not fixed on unbridled executive vigor or
energy, but fully embraced the advantages of a system
of "checks and balances" that was fashioned to secure
liberty through respectable government. To put this
in a slightly different form, he never forgot the
requisites of republican constitutionalism. And as
an ingredient of his understanding of responsible
republican government he never lost sight of the
qualities of "good administration." Hence, although
he considers officials who are involved in administrative affairs to be deputies of the president and
"subject to his superintendence," a thought not unlike
that expressed by Gouverneur Morris during the Federal
Convention, Hamilton expects them to be chosen for
their "intrinsic merit" and not on the basis of
personal affection.[50] He discourages any system of
selection that presumes that appointees ought to
possess "the necessary insignificance and pliance to
render them the obsequious instruments of (the
executive's) pleasure."[51] The true test of fitness
is not a naive or fawning devotion to a superior
according to Hamilton, but the capacity to discharge
the duties of one's office. This should not be construed as an endorsement of an independent administrative order, however; rather it is further confirmation
of his commitment to guarding the federal administration against the debilitating prejudices of facious or
personal politics. While fully acknowledging his
abiding interest in "good administration," it would
be a caricature of Hamilton's political thought to
suggest that it lends itself to liberating administrative personnel entirely from executive supervision
or to removing them altogether from the demands of the
constitutional order. His object was to reconcile the
demands of republican constitutionalism and competent
government. And with respect to administration, this
exercise issued in the thought that official conduct
ought to be dynamic, but not reckless or irresponsible;
it ought to be innovative, while mindful of the ends of
limited government.

Surely the integrity and cohesiveness of the administrative fabric is of considerable significance to a system of effective and, as well, decent government. Internal dissension might easily transform the executive department into a mass of jarring and competing interests. Thus Hamilton's rebuke of Jefferson in 1792. Throughout his writings, Hamilton was ever attentive to the need for a proper conformity to the shared responsibilities of the federal administration. Disagreements not only work a hardship on accountability in the executive, but lack of confidence on the part of the president in his subordinates invites loss of vigor and direction. When fitted together, these observations depict a political system that is constituted not merely by structure, but by human judgment and action; and, to be sure, by judgment and action of a political character.

In the context of this review of Hamilton's defense of the plan for an independent executive armed with administrative authority, and in view of the contemporary scepticism regarding the republican credentials of Hamilton's political thought, it is instructive to recall his characterization of the formidable task that confronted the delegates at the Federal Convention of 1787. In what is still stirring language, he reminded them that they were "to decide for ever the fate of Republican Government; and that if (they) did not give to that form due stability and wisdom, it would be disgraced and lost among (themselves), disgraced and lost to mankind for ever."[52] It was in this spirit that Hamilton pressed the virtues of a competent federal executive order that was free of the debilitating effects of facitous intrigues and internal dissensions.

To repeat, for Hamilton a strong executive is a "leading character" in the definition of "good" government.[53] The energetic executive enables republican government to be equal to the ends of "good" government in the sense of providing the capacity for decisive action necessary to all government and the wherewithal to adjust the competition of rival rights and interests in a democratic system where men are least habituated to accept restraints and most disposed to press their claims. It is this view of the necessity for a strong executive that compels his response in Federalist Papers 68 and 70 to the proposition that a vigorous executive is inconsistent with republican government. If this proposition is correct, or if the people are led to believe that it is correct, then republican government will be ill prepared to satisfy the requirements of "good" government. This theme is bluntly addressed in Federalist 70 when Hamilton insists that a feeble executive is a bad executive and that such an executive invariably issues in bad government.[54] Notice, however, that Hamilton never proclaims the energetic executive to be the necessary and sufficient cause of "good" government, only a "leading character" of "good" government. Still, he reserves his fiercest criticism for those persons who maintain that the strong executive is incompatible with republican government. If the critics of the strong executive succeed in persuading the people to weaken the vigor or independence of the president, they would effectively undermine an important device for moderating popular opinion and, accordingly, diminish the defensibility of the republican system in this nation.

To restate Hamilton's thesis, the proper form and spirit of the federal administration are in the service of effective government and republican constitutionalism in the broad sense of protecting the political order generally, and its members in particular, against the prejudices that easily beget incompetence, illiberality, and injustice. Along with Madison, Morris and Wilson, to cite only the leading nationalists of the period, Hamilton believed that through a vigorous and just administration of national affairs and assurances for the security of private rights the central government could inspire the confidence and allegiance of the people. These properties in the government were valued by the framers in part for the "habitual sense of obligation" to the new constitutional order that they were likely to generate among its members.[55] By enabling the government to act with "dispatch, method and system," a proper executive and system of administration would contribute to the capacity of the regime to satisfy its ends or purposes, foremost among them being the protection of the private rights and the liberty of the people. And in this regard, it is undeniable that linking Hamilton's political thought with the plan for a national government drafted at the Federal Convention was the conviction that administration and government become "good administration" and "good government" only when informed by the principles of a responsible

republican political order. To neglect this fact is
to obscure the motives that gave form to the Constitution of 1787, and that presided over its defense.

Briefly summarized, Hamilton's commitment to an
energetic executive is only intelligible in the context
of his understanding of the purposes and the peculiar
dangers of the modern republic. Rather than leave the
safety and happiness of the people and the security of
private rights to the chance that the people will
embrace "right" opinion or that foreign threats will
never demand the attention that prompted Locke to
argue for entrusting "prerogative" powers to the
executive, Hamilton recommends the inclusion in the
formal constitutional order of "devices of prudence"
for neutralizing the dangers to which republican
governments are especially prone. This thought can
be traced to an important dimension of the modern
liberal tradition, that is, to the claim that government by consent means government by the consent of
men who are enlightened about their rights and able
to choose a government protective of those rights.
Consider in this connection the fact that the
American Constitution requires that amendments to
the fundamental law be ratified or defeated by
representative agencies of the people and not by the
people directly.[56] In keeping with this same principle, Hamilton's plan for a strong executive is
intended to afford protection for the decisive ends
of republican government, that is, for the rights and
safety, along with the happiness and prosperity of the
people.

By promoting government that is guided by the
deliberate and informed will of the community, an
energetic executive and an efficacious administration
increases the likelihood that the republic will be
equal to its own ends. An executive capable of
temporarily checking misguided popular or even legislative majorities, and able to avoid the temptation to
serve the people's inclinations rather than their best
interests, is an essential ingredient of a republican
system that is preservative of the equal rights of all
of its members. Admittedly, the emphasis must be on
the temporary nature of the executive check. In a
democratic republic, checks on the popular or legislative will by the president ought to be only such as
will promote deliberation, not such as will fundamentally change the nature of the political system.

Nor should it be forgotten in this regard that Hamilton's executive represents the national popular will at the pleasure of the people themselves. Hence in a fundamental respect Hamilton's treatment of the responsibilities of the republican executive preserves the distinction between "ruling" and "governing." Consider in this context Hamilton's insistence that the single executive not only provides for decisiveness and vigor, but promotes accountability in government.[57] In short, his is a model of institutionalized or confined and responsible leadership. The necessity to balance the strong executive with proper safeguards for the safety and liberty of the people was freely acknowledged by Hamilton at the time of the New York Ratifying Convention:

> There are two objects in forming
> systems of government--Safety for
> the people, and energy in the ad-
> ministration. When these objects
> are united, the certain tendency of
> the system will be to the public
> welfare. If the latter object be
> neglected, the people's security
> will be as certainly sacrificed, as
> by disregarding the former. Good
> constitutions are formed upon a
> comparison of the liberty of the
> individual with the strength of
> government: If the tone of either
> be too high, the other will be
> weakened too much.[58]

The great claim that can be made on behalf of Hamilton's political thought is that it brings together the requisites of competent and effective government and the principles of constitutional republicanism.

[1]Consider in this connection, Richard P. Nathan, The Plot That Failed: Nixon and the Administrative Presidency (New York: John Wiley and Sons, 1975), p. 91. Also see Jacob Cooke, "The Hamiltonian Presidency: A Model For Our Time?" Paper delivered at the White Miller Burkett Center, University of Virginia, April 4, 1978.

[2]Henry Cabot Lodge, Alexander Hamilton (Boston: Houghton, Mifflin and Co., 1898), p. 278, also see p. 138.

[3]Hamilton, Madison and Jay, The Federalist Papers (New York: The New American Library, 1961), p. 36. Hereafter cited as The Federalist.

[4]Alexander Hamilton, The Papers of Alexander Hamilton, ed. Harold C. Syrett, 26 vols. (New York: Columbia University Press, 1960-78), Vol. 5, p. 37. Hereafter cited as Hamilton, Papers.

[5]In a letter to LaFayette, dated October 6, 1789, Hamilton declares himself to be "a friend to mankind and to liberty." Ibid., Vol. 5, p. 425.

[6]See, for example, the opening paragraphs of the report on the national bank. Ibid., Vol. 7, pp. 256-57.

[7]The Federalist, No. 23, p. 153; also No. 36, p. 224; No. 61, p. 372; and No. 85.

[8]During the New York Ratifying Convention, Hamilton expressed confidence that "prudent men will consider the merits of the plan in connection with the circumstances of our country...." Hamilton, Papers, Vol. 5, p. 71.

[9]Ibid., Vol. 5, p. 425.

[10]Lodge, p. 278.

[11]The Federalist, No. 71, p. 432. Also consider in this regard the following observation by Tocqueville: "... it is this clear perception of the future, based on judgment and experience, which must often be lacking

in a democracy. The people feel more strongly than they reason; and if present ills are great, it is to be feared that they will forget the greater evils that perhaps await them in case of defeat." Alexis deToucqueville. Democracy in America, trans. George Lawrence (New York: Doubleday and Co., 1969), p. 223.

[12] Ibid., No. 67, p. 407.

[13] Ibid., No. 68, p. 412.

[14] Ibid., No. 68, p. 414.

[15] Ibid., No. 68, p. 414.

[16] Ibid., No. 58, p. 412. Hamilton unequivocally acknowledged during the debates at the New York Ratifying Convention that a provision for popular participation in the choice of representatives is of the essence of republican government: "After all...we submit to this idea, that the true principle of a republic is, that the people should choose whom they please to govern them. Representation is imperfect in proportion as the current of popular favor is checked. This great source of free government, popular election, should be perfectly pure, and the most unbounded liberty allowed." Jonathan Elliott (ed.), The Debates in the Several State Conventions on the Adoption of the Federal Constitution (1888 ed., New York: Burt Franklin), Vol. II, p. 257.

[17] Ibid., No. 69, pp. 415-23. Gordon Wood draws attention to the colonial suspicion of governors in general by quoting a Delaware Whig who characteristically described executive power as being "ever restless, ambitious, and ever grasping at encrease of power." Gordon Wood, The Creation of the American Republic, 1776-1787 (New York: W. W. Norton and Co., 1969), p. 135.

[18] Ibid., No. 69, pp. 420-22.

[19] For a consideration of the prevailing colonial views on the appointment power, see Wood, pp. 143-50.

[20] The Federalist Papers, No. 70, p. 426. In an earlier paper Hamilton had declared that the likelihood of improprieties increases when decisions are left to bodies of numerous men: "Regard to reputation has

a less active influence when the infamy of a bad action is to be divided among a number than when it is to fall singly upon one. A spirit of faction, which is apt to mingle its poison in the deliberations of all bodies of men, will often hurry the persons of whom they are composed into improprieties and excesses for which they would blush in a private capacity." Ibid., No. 15, p. 111.

[21]Ibid., No. 70, p. 426. It is instructive to note that Montesquieu defended the place of the monarch in the English system in part on the basis of his capacity for momentary action: "The executive power ought to be in the hands of a monarch, because this branch of government, having need for dispatch, is better administered by one than by many...." Montesquieu, II, p. 156.

[22]Consider Hamilton's remarks on this subject at the New York Ratifying Convention. Jonathan Elliot (ed.), The Debates in the Several State Conventions on the Adoption of the Federal Constitution (Philadelphia: J. B. Lippincott, 1901), Vol. II, p. 257. Madison broached this matter as well at the Virginia Ratifying Convention. See Ibid., III, p. 487,

[23]The Federalist Papers, No. 70, p. 429.

[24]Ibid., No. 70, p. 430.

[25]Hamilton did not quibble about the significant objectives to be secured by the American Constitution. He shared his thoughts on the purposes of the Constitution with the delegates at the New York Ratifying Convention. "I trust that the proposed Constitution affords a genuine specimen of representation and republican government, and that it will answer, in an eminent degree, all the beneficial purposes of society." Elliot, 1901 edition, II, p. 259.

[26]Here we might usefully recall Franklin's characterization of public officers in free government as "servants" of the people. Farrand, II, p. 120.

[27]Hamilton was emphatic in declaring that public officials assume an obligation to promote the interests of the political community as a whole. Thus, for example, he considered Senators to be representatives of the Union, and not merely delegates of local

constituencies: "That a man should have the power,
in private life, of recalling his agent, is proper;
because in the business in which he is engaged, he
has no other object but to gain the approbation of
his principal. Is this the case with the senator?
Is he simply the agent of the state? No: He is an
agent for the union, and he is bound to perform
services necessary to the good of the whole, though
his state should condemn them." Hamilton, Papers,
V, p. 85. Anticipating Hamilton, Edmund Burke had
insisted in 1774 that a member of the English Parliament owe a special commitment to the public good
comprehensively understood: "Parliament is not a
congress of ambassadors from different and hostile
interests; which interests each must maintain, as
an agent and advocate, against other agents and advocates; but parliament is a deliberative assembly of
one nation, with one interest, that of the whole;
where, not local purposes, not local prejudices ought
to guide, but the general good, resulting from the
general reason of the whole." The Works of Edmund
Burke (Rivington ed.; London , 1803-27), Vol. III,
p. 20.

[28]U.S. Constitution, Art. II, sec. I.

[29]The Federalist Papers, No. 71, p. 432. In his
disquistion on the proper attributes for a statesman,
Sir Henry Taylor singled out a "strong conscience" as
being indispensable to good governance: "The conscience
of a statesman should be rather a strong conscience
than a tender conscience. For a conscience of more
tenderness than strength will be liable in public life
to be perverted in two ways: lst. By reflecting responsibilities disproportionately to their magnitude, and
missing of the large responsibilities whilst it is
occupied with the small. 2nd. By losing in a too
lively apprehension of the responsibilities of action,
the sense of responsibility for inaction." Sir Henry
Taylor, The Statesman (Cambridge: W. Heffer and Sons
Ltd., 1957), p. 32.

[30]It bears mentioning that the obligation to
protect the public interest brings with it a duty to
inform and direct the collective opinion of the
community; that is to say, to shape, and when appropriate, to restrain public opinion. But the executive's
check in this regard can only be temporary. He retains
no absolute negative over the preferences of the people

or of their representative in Congress. The sovereign status of the popular will is a fundamental principle in the modern liberal political tradition which Hamilton embraced. See Elliot, 1901 edition, II, p. 257.

[31]Ibid., II, p. 316. Emphasis in the original.

[32]Ibid., II, p. 316.

[33]Hamilton addressed this issue in Federalist 46: "If, therefore...the people should in future become more partial to the federal than to the State governments, the change can only result from such manifest and irresistible proofs of a better administration as will overcome all their antecedent propensities." The Federalist Papers, No. 46, p. 295; see also Ibid., No. 27, pp. 174-75.

[34]Ibid., No. 68, p. 414.

[35]Ibid., No. 68, p. 414.

[36]Ibid., No. 68, p. 414.

[37]See Frisch, pp. 1-2.

[38]See The Federalist, No. 9, p. 72; Farrand, I, p. 304.

[39]Hamilton, Papers, V, p. 95; also, Ibid., V, p. 97.

[40]Ibid., V, p. 81.

[41]Ibid., V, p. 81.

[42]Farrand, I, pp. 289, 308.

[43]Hamilton, Papers, VIII, p. 104; also Ibid., V, p. 97.

[44]The Federalist, No. 76, p. 455.

[45]Ibid., No. 76, pp. 455-57. Similar thoughts on the significance of the location of the appointment power can be found in Sir Henry Taylor, p. 109.

[46]The Federalist, No. 76, p. 456.

[47]Ibid., No. 76, p. 457. Edward Corwin has argued that Hamilton expected that the Senate "would concern itself only with the merits of suggested appointees." Actually this has not historically been true, as Corwin was quick to point out. The evidence indicates, however, that Hamilton expected the Senate to assume a broader role than that portrayed by Corwin in his description of Hamilton's political thought. Edward S. Corwin, The President: Office and Powers (New York: New York University Press, 1957), p. 74.

[48]The Federalist, No. 77, p. 459.

[49]See David E. Marion, "Towards a Political Theory of Public Administration: The Place and Role of Federal Public Service Personnel in the American Democratic Republic (unpublished dissertation; DeKalb: Northern Illinois University, 1977), pp. 4-15.

[50]The Federalist, No. 76, p. 456.

[51]Ibid., No. 76, p. 458.

[52]Farrand, I, p. 424.

[53]The Federalist, No. 70, p. 423.

[54]Ibid., No. 70, p. 423.

[55]Farrand, I, p. 305. Hamilton was scrupulously attentive to the need to impart to the government those qualities that will command the respect of the people: "The manner in which a thing is done has more influence than is commonly imagined. Men are governed by opinion; this opinion is as much influenced by appearances as by realities; if a Government appears to be confident of its own power; it is the surest way to inspire the same confidence in others; if it is diffident, it may be certain, there will be a still greater diffidence in others, and that its authority will not only be distrusted, controverted, but con- temned." Hamilton, Papers, II, p. 417. Related comments by Madison appear in The Federalist, No. 46, p. 295. Also see Ibid., No. 27, p. 176.

[56]On this question, see the decision of the United States Supreme Court in Hanke v. Smith, 253 U.S. 221 (1920).

[57] The Federalist, No. 70, pp. 427-28.

[58] Hamilton, *Papers*, Vol. 5, p. 81; also Vol. 5, pp. 94-95.

CHAPTER 3

"Jefferson's Rational Religion"
Sanford Kessler

Writers seeking to strengthen the role of traditional Christianity in America generally turn for
support to the works of the Founding Fathers. In a
recent article defending public assistance to religion,
for example, Terry Eastland claims that the Founders
intended Protestantism to be "our established religion"
in all but the strictly legal sense. Reverend Jerry
Falwell, who goes further, asserts that the United
States "was founded by godly men upon godly principles
to be a Christian nation." The Founders' Christian
orientation, in Falwell's view, justifies current
attempts by fundamentalists to establish "the authority
of Bible morality" as the "legitimate guiding principle"
of our common political life.[1]

There is considerable evidence that the Founders
saw a link between religion, morality, and the public
good (and even sought to provide some public support
for religion). But to infer that they saw religion as
playing a leading role in American political life is to
misread their words and deeds. In fact, as Walter
Berns has shown, the Founders intended America to be
a secular polity in which religion holds an important,
but subordinate place. The Founders also had a clear
sense of the type of religion most appropriate for the
United States and this religion was not fundamentalist
Protestantism or any other form of traditional Christianity. As Berns points out, these men held certain
key Christian doctrines at least partially responsible
for a wide variety of political evils including tyranny
and religious persecution. One of their political goals
was to insure that religion in America was compatible
in all respects with the values and needs of a free
society.[2]

The purpose of this essay is to illuminate contemporary discussions on the role of religion in American
life by exploring the thought of Thomas Jefferson, the
most authoritative spokesman for the Founders on
religious-political matters. Jefferson was the author
of a "rational" verson of Christianity which he hoped
would gradually supplant traditional Christianity as
the chief American faith. Although his religious views
differ from the views of other Founders in some respects
and have never been as popular in America as he hoped
they would be, they have deeply influenced the dogma

of most American churches. Jefferson was also the
author of a "bill for Establishing Religious Freedom"
which instituted the principles of religious freedom
and the separation of church and state in Virginia,
and served as the prototype for the religion clauses
of the First Amendment. His aim in promoting these
principles was to establish secular supremacy over
religion while protecting the rights of conscience.
In the Preamble to the Bill, Jefferson taught that God
seeks to "extend" religion "by its influence on reason
alone" indicating that in his mind institutional and
theological reform were closely interrelated.[3]

     Jefferson also believed that the establishment of
religious freedom and the separation of church and
state were essential to free government. He illustrated the link he saw between these principles and
political freedom in a letter he wrote two weeks before
his death commenting on the significance of the Declaration of Independence:

          May it be to the world, what I believe
          it will be (to some parts sooner, to
          others later, but finally to all), the
          signal of arousing men to burst the
          chains under which monkish ignorance
          and superstitition had persuaded them
          to bind themselves, and to assume the
          blessings and security of self-
          government. That form which we have
          substituted, restores the free right
          to the unbounded exercise of reason
          and freedom of opinion. All eyes are
          opened, or opening, to the rights of
          man. The general spread of the light
          of science has already laid open to
          every view the palpable truth, that
          the mass of mankind has not been born
          with saddles on their backs, nor a
          favored few booted and spurred, ready
          to ride them legitimately by the grace
          of God.

     In this passage, Jefferson connects a particular
form of government with a particular religious understanding. Despotic governments in Christian Europe
were based on the premise that a king or a "favored
few" were superior to the people, and could rule them
legitimately "by the grace of God." These arrangements

were supported by established churches and accepted by the people themselves whose eyes were clouded by "monkish ignorance and superstition." They enabled those in power to persecute and punish critics of their regimes as well as dissenters from the prevailing orthodoxies.

Jefferson held that the Bible itself was the source of the ideas that political power comes "by the grace of God" and that the "favored few" could use religion for illicit ends. Divine revelation was opposed on principle to the "light of science" and prevented the mass of mankind from learning the truth about their rights. According to Jefferson, the Declaration of Independence was the "signal of arousing men to burst the chains" of religious despotism and to "assume the blessings and security of self-government." To do this successfully it was necessary to overturn the existing alliances between church and state. It was also necessary to establish religious freedom so that the "monkish ignorance and superstition" supporting these alliances could be destroyed and his new, more "reasonable" form of religion could emerge.

The "Bill for Establishing Religious Freedom" was the end result of a fierce struggle to disestablish the Anglican church in Virginia and to free the state from what Jefferson called a "spiritual tyranny." Although the Virginia constitutional convention of May, 1776, declared "it to be a truth, and a natural right, that the exercise of religion should be free," the efforts of those supporting religious freedom for the next ten years were only partially successful. Prior to the passage of the Bill, for example, a person "brought up in the Christian religion" residing in Virginia could be subject to increasingly harsh penalties for "deny(ing) the Christian religion to be true, or the scriptures to be of divine authority." According to the common law still in effect at the time, he could also theoretically be burned for heresy.[5]

When the bill was finally passed, however, Jefferson could write to James Madison that the Virginia assembly was the "first legislature" to liberate the human mind from the "vassalage" imposed by "kings, priests, and nobles" and to declare "that the reason of man may be trusted with the formation of his own opinions." He considered his authorship of the Bill so important that he wished it recorded on his tombstone as one of the three greatest accomplishments of his

60

political career (along with the writing of the Declaration of Independence and the founding of the University of Virginia).[6]

The Virginia law itself provides that:

> no man shall be compelled to frequent or support any religious worship, place, or ministry whatsoever, nor shall be enforced, restrained, molested, or burthened in his body or goods, nor shall otherwise suffer, on account of his religious opinions or belief; but that all men shall be free to profess, and by agreement to maintain their opinions in matters of religion and that the same shall in no wise diminish, enlarge or affect their civil capacities.[7]

Stated simply, no one in Virginia after the passage of the Bill could be forced to attend religious services, to support a church financially, or to suffer any civil loss because of his religious beliefs. Despite an attempt in the legislature to limit the religious freedom provided to Christians, the Bill as passed was "meant to comprehend, within the mantle of its protection, the Jew and the Gentile, the Christian and Mahometan, the Hindoo, and Infidel of every denomination." This "universal...protection of opinion" was based on the premise that the sacred and secular realms are separate and distinct. "Our civil rights have no dependence on our religious opinions," Jefferson wrote in the preamble to the Bill, or as he put it more pungently in the Notes on the State of Virginia, "it does me no injury for my neighbor to say there are twenty gods, or no God. It neither picks my pocket nor breaks my leg."[8]

For Jefferson, political power comes from the people rather than from God and the purpose of government is to protect certain natural rights which they are unable to enjoy fully in their prepolitical condition. These rights include the rights to "life, liberty, and the pursuit of happiness" enumerated in the Declaration of Independence. In order to better "secure these rights," people surrender a portion of their natural freedom which becomes the source of the civil rights mentioned above.[9]

Since the powers of government "extend to such
acts only as are injurious to others," the state must
not attempt to enforce religious orthodoxy or to interfere with religion in any way. While the government
may "beget habits of hypocrisy and meanness" through
the use of force, it can never induce sincere religious
belief. God has provided that this be acquired through
"free argument and debate" and in religious matters we
are answerable to Him alone. Furthermore, the danger
of suffering "the civil magistrate to intrude his
powers into the field of opinion" always outweighs the
potential benefits for magistrates are "fallible men;
men governed by bad passions, by private as well as
public reasons." Such a man, vested with power over
religious doctrines would most likely "make his opinions the rules of judgment, and approve or condemn
the sentiments of others only as they shall square with
or differ from his own."[10]

While Jefferson barely discusses the role of
churches in his writings, he seems to consider them
purely voluntary societies which cannot be supported
by force or legitimately use force for any reason.
Churchmen who "have assumed dominion over the faith of
others" have not served the cause of faith, but, like
their secular counterparts, have "established and maintained false religions over the greatest part of the
world and through all time." Furthermore, "to compel
a man to furnish contributions" to any church fosters
"indolence" in its clergy. The only way to guarantee
the "earnest and unremitting labours" of the clergy
"for the interest of mankind" is through "temporary
rewards" which proceed from "an approbation of...per-
sonal conduct."[11]

Although the major premise of the "Bill for Establishing Religious Freedom" seems to be that church and
state are by nature completely separate and equal, it
becomes clear when closely examining Jefferson's arguments that the relationship he envisioned between the
two bodies was one of neither complete separation nor
complete equality. While Jefferson adheres to a strict
interpretation of the principle of separation by denying
religion its traditional influence over politics, he
violates this principle by giving government significant
authority over the rights of conscience and enabling
government to aid religion under certain circumstances.

We shall consider the issue of political support

62

for religion first. While Jefferson as President vigorously opposed any national aid to religion (arguing that the First Amendment created a "wall of separation" between church and state), he was at least in his later years willing to allow state governments to provide religion with some public assistance. During his retirement, for example, he authored an "Act for Establishing Elementary Schools" (1817) in Virginia which allowed for religious activity in the classroom, and as founder of the University of Virginia was willing to have the government aid religion in a variety of ways on campus. These ways included requiring courses which teach certain elements of religion (such as "proofs of the being of a God" and the "moral obligations" in which "all sects agree") and encouraging, or perhaps compelling, students to attend religious services at sectarian schools established within the confines of the university. On the basis of this evidence, some commentators suggest that his attempt to prevent the national government from aiding religion as President was more the result of his concern for the prerogatives of the states than of a desire to create an absolute breach between religion and government.[12]

While insisting that the free exercise of religion is a natural right, Jefferson also allows government to limit the scope of religious freedom for the public good. His general principle is that "operations of the mind" are free, but "acts of the body" are "subject to the coercion of the laws." Thus, "overt acts against peace and good order" may be outlawed by the government regardless of whether or not they are religiously motivated. Even Jefferson's distinction between belief and action was not that rigid, however, and he allows government some control over religious doctrines that have political significance. The most precise statement of his position on this matter occurs in a footnote to his private notes on a passage from John Locke's A Letter on Toleration:

> Will not h is own excellent rule be
> sufficient here too; to punish these
> as civil offenses. e.g.r. to assert
> that a foreign prince has power within
> this commonwealth is a misdemeanor,
> the other opns. may be despised.
> Perhaps the single thing which may be
> required to others before toleration
> to them would be an oath that they

would allow toleration to others.[13]

The "excellent rule" Jefferson tentatively recommends is the Lockean principle clearly establishing the supremacy of the public good over the right to express religious opinions. These opinions are to be tolerated by the government only if they do not harm secular interests which the government is obliged to defend. In terms of Locke's categories as listed above, it seems that Jefferson, at least in 1776, would have allowed state governments to punish the expression of seditious opinions no matter how religious. When he wrote two drafts of a constitution for Virginia during this time, for example, he qualified the provision for "full and free liberty of religious opinion," by stating that "this shall not be held to justify any seditious preaching or conversation against the authority of the civil government." He also appears willing to proscribe all religious doctrines justifying persecution for heterodoxy. This prohibition seems a necessary corollary to the pledge of toleration he would possibly require of all churches.[14]

Jefferson favored a high degree of religious freedom because he believed that "education and free discussion" would expose and discredit harmful religious doctrines and pave the way for beneficial reform. Despite his optimism with regard to popular enlightenment, however, he did not think the "spirit of the poeple," even in an age of reason, could be relied on by itself to protect the rights of individuals against religious tyranny. Although the "spirit of the times" in late eighteenth-century Virginia made it unlikely that "the people...would suffer an execution for heresy, or a three years' imprisonment for not comprehending the mysteries of the Trinity," this spirit, Jefferson wrote, may alter, will alter." The people can become "careless" over time if their freedom is not overtly endangered and "forget themselves, but in the sole faculty of making money." Under these circumstances, they "will never think of uniting to effect a due respect for their rights." Because the progress of reason is sometimes precarious, "every essential right" must be firmly protected by law.[15]

Although Jefferson publicly argued that truth is "the proper and sufficient antagonist to error" and "will prevail if left to herself," he deeply believed that in order to eliminate the conditions which had

"made of Christiandom a slaughterhouse," it was necessary to reform Christianity in decisive respects. In
his later years, therefore, Jefferson devoted a significant portion of his time to stripping the traditional
faith of its "artificial scaffolding" and to depicting
the remnant as "a religion of all others most friendly
to liberty, science, and the freest expansion of the
human mind." To this end, he corresponded at length
on religious matters with such "reasonable" men as
Benjamin Rush, Joseph Priestly, and John Adams, wrote
a "Syllabus of an estimate of the Merits of the Doctrines of Jesus" during his first term as President
(which he considered "the result of a life of inquiry
and reflection"), and began work during the same
period on a revised verion of the New Testament called
The Life and Morals of Jesus of Nazareth which he completed in 1819.[16]

In his attack on traditional religion, Jefferson
sought to discredit the authority of revelation, to
debunk Judaism as well as all prevailing versions of
Christian orthodoxy, and ultimately to subjectivize
all religious belief. He disguised his assault as
an attempt to rescue "primitive Christianity" or "the
genuine system of Jesus" from the "artificial structures" erected by priests. True Christianity, he argued, was not responsible for the persecution of untold
"millions of innocent men, women, and children," but
was rather "the most sublime and benevolent code of
morals which has ever been offered to man."[17]

One of the boldest statements of Jefferson's
"rational" approach to Christianity appears in a letter
he wrote to his nephew, Peter Carr, instructing him on
how to study religion. In this letter Jefferson develops the idea first expressed in the "Bill for Establishing Religious Freedom" that reason rather than
revelation is the standard by which religious beliefs
are to be measured. In examining the subject of religion, he advises Carr, a careful student must divest
himself of "all bias in favor of novelty and singular-
ity of opinion" as well as "all the fears and servile
prejudices, under which weak minds are servilely
crouched." "Every fact, every opinion" is to be brought
before the bar of reason. This includes "even the
existence of a God," Jefferson asserts, "because, if
there be one, he must more approve of the homage of
reason, than that of blindfolded fear." For Jefferson,
divine favor depends not on the "rightness" but the

"uprightness" or sincerity of one's beliefs.[18]

We can clearly see the unorthodox nature of Jefferson's advice to his nephew in his discussion of the Bible. Jefferson advises Carr to "read the Bible... as you would read Livy or Tacitus," that is as an historical work of human rather than divine origin. Those facts "which are within the ordinary course of nature" may be believed "on the authority of the writer," but anything which "contradict(s) the laws of nature" must be viewed with the utmost suspicion. If, for example, the Book of Joshua in the Old Testament tells us that the "sun stood still several hours," this should not be accepted as truth unless the "evidence is so strong...that its falsehood would be more improbable than a change in the laws of nature." The same procedure must be adopted in scrutinizing the New Testament. One must not believe that Jesus "was begotten by God, born of a virgin, suspended and reversed the laws of nature at will, and ascended bodily into heaven" unless these things are "within the law of probabilities." Indeed, in the final accounting Jefferson believed that the truth or falsity of revelation must be determined by the private, rational judgment of each individual:

> Whether the particular revelation which you suppose to have been made to yourself were real or imaginary, your reason alone is the competent judge. For dispute as long as we will on religious tenets, our reason at last must ultimately decide, as it is the only oracle which God has given us to determine between what really comes from Him and the phantasms of a disordered or deluded imagination.[19]

Since Jefferson viewed the Bible as a human rather than a divine creation, he generally adopted the standard of political utility when evaluating Biblical doctrines and attacked the authority of those he considered harmful to civil society. He sought to discredit the Old Testament, for example, because he believed that Judaism was a source of the zealotry and fanaticism that characterized traditional Christianity. "The fumes of the most disordered imaginations," he wrote to William Short, "have not only preserved their credit with Jews of all subsequent times, but are the

66

foundation of much of the religion of those who have
schismatized from them." Most baneful for Jefferson
was the Hebrew notion that Jehovah was a "Being of
terrific character, cruel, vindictive, capricious, and
unjust," who punishes the "sins of the fathers upon
their children, unto the third and fourth generation."
It was this conception of the deity, in Jefferson's
view, which provided a theological basis for intolerance and religious persecution.[20]

In Jefferson's account, Christ was "the great
Reformer of the Hebrew code of religion" whose mission
was to transform Judaism into a faith "more worthy,
pure, and sublime." Unfortunately, however, Jesus
wrote nothing, and the task of transmitting his teaching fell on "unlettered and ignorant men; who wrote...
from memory, and not till long after the transactions
had passed." Entrusted with a task "far beyond the
power of their feeble minds," his biographers placed
the "splendid conceptions" of Jesus in "a groundwork
of vulgar ignorance, of things impossible, of superstitions, fanaticisms, and fabrications." Hence, we
have "fragments only of what he did deliver," and
these "have come to us mutilated, misstated, and often
unintelligible."[21]

The greatest crime against Christianity in Jefferson's eyes, came shortly after the death of Christ
when those "who professed to be his special servants"
intentionally "disfigured" his teachings "into various
forms" to serve as "instruments of riches and power"
for themselves. The primary means by which the clergy
transformed Christianity into "an engine for enslaving
mankind" was by infusing the simple faith with the
doctrines of Plato. Jefferson accused Plato, whom he
neither fully understood nor appreciated, of providing
the basis for "endless systems of mystical theology"
which are "incomprehensible" to common sense and without any foundation in the words of Christ. Plato was
"all but adopted as a Christian saint" by the priests
because they found in his "foggy conceptions" a "basis
of impenetrable darkness" on which to build their
"fabrications." These "fabrications" or "artificial
systems" as Jefferson liked to call them, included
most of the basic tenets of Christian orthodoxy.
Among them are, in his words, the "immaculate conception of Jesus," "His deification,". . . "His miracu-
lous powers," "His resurrection and visible ascension,"
and "His corporeal presence in the Eucharist." It was

doctrines such as these which, in Jefferson's eyes, divided the church "into castes of inextinguishible hatred to one another."[22]

Jefferson's most radical departure from traditional Christianity was to deny that Christ was divine. In his view, only those incidents in Jesus' life "which are within the ordinary course of nature" deserve to be reported and these alone are mentioned in The Life and Morals of Jesus of Nazareth. In the Gospel rightly understood, "Jesus did not mean to impose himself on mankind as the Son of God, physically speaking." Although "He might have conscientiously believe(d) Himself inspired from above," this was due either to the teachings of Judaism which were "founded in the belief of divine inspiration," or perhaps to the misguided "enthusiasm of a warm and pure heart." Whatever the cause of these "marks of weakness in Jesus," they ought, in Jefferson's opinion, to carry "no more personal imputation, than the belief of Socrates, that himself was under the care and admonition of a guardian Daemon."[23]

Jefferson also believed that the circumstances under which Jesus lived and taught accounted for certain difficulties in his doctrines. Because of the animosity of the Jews, his work was fraught with constant peril. "The office of reformer of the superstitions of a nation," Jefferson remarked, "is ever dangerous."

> Jesus had to walk on the perilous confines of reason and religion; and a step to the right or to the left might place Him within the grasp of the priests of the superstition. . . . They were constantly laying snares, too, to entangle Him in the web of the law.[24]

In order to defend himself, Jesus linked his teachings to the Old Testament "by evasions, by sophisms, by misconstructions and misapplications of scraps of the prophets," and these tactics, although entirely "justifiable," resulted in weak and defective "passages in the Gospel." In addition to detracting from the "pure and perfect" doctrines which he preached, they failed to prevent His suffering martyrdom--"the ordinary fate of those who attempt to enlighten and reform mankind."[25]

Stripped of its "artificial scaffolding," Jefferson's Christianity is a monotheistic faith in which morality rather than dogmatic belief is the chief criterion for salvation. "He who steadily observes those moral precepts in which all religions concur," he wrote to William Conby, "will never be questioned at the gates of heaven, as to dogmas in which they all differ." These "moral precepts" include:

> universal philanthropy, not only to
> kindred and friends, to neighbors and
> countrymen, but to all mankind,
> gathering all into one family, under
> the bonds of love, charity, peace,
> common wants and common aids.[26]

The strong emphasis in this enumeration on general benevolence and material improvement derives from Jefferson's belief that "utility to man is the standard and test of virtue." Indeed, the traits of character Jefferson sought to foster through religion are more compatible with the secular goals of enlightenment philosphy than with the ascetic and otherworldly orientation of the New Testament. One indication of Jefferson's preference for enlightenment over New Testament thought appears in his famous account of a conversation with Alexander Hamilton about extraordinary individuals. Although Jefferson had the highest regard for Jesus of Nazareth, it was Locke, Bacon, and Newton who, according to this account, formed his "trinity of the three greatest men the world had ever produced."[27]

Although Jefferson hoped that "rational" Christianity would help foster popular morality in America, he did not believe it would ever be its primary source. This role he reserved for a "moral instinct" which "nature hath implanted in our breasts." This "moral principle," he wrote in a letter to Thomas Law in 1814, is "so much a part of our constitution" that "no errors of reasoning or of speculation might lead us away from its observation in practice." Religion is needed, however, to strengthen our innate moral sense against self love, its "sole antagonist" and an ever-present threat. Also, there is a "want or imperfection of the moral sense in some men," and "the prospects of a future state of retribution for the evil as well as the good done while here" can serve as a significant

69

corrective for those "whose disparity is not too profound to be eradicated."[28]

Perhaps the most noteworthy example which Jefferson gives of the positive role religious belief could play in influencing morality concerns the institution of slavery. Jefferson thought that the operation of the moral instinct in man was vitally affected by the nature of his political relationships. In the case of the master-slave relationship, the moral sense of both blacks and whites was adversely affected. The "disposition to theft," for example, which could be observed among slaves was due to their condition of bondage rather than to innate depravity. "The man in whose favor no laws of property exist," he writes, "probably feels himself less bound to respect those made in favor of others." Far more serious in Jefferson's eyes, however, was the evil effect of slavery on the morality of masters. "There must doubtless be an unhappy inflence on the manners of our people produced by the existence of slavery among us," he wrote.

> The whole commerce between master and slave is a perpetual exercise of the most boisterous passions, the most unremitting despotism on the one part, and degrading submissions on the other.

In addition to nourishing the most evil dispositions of the masters and adversely affecting their desire to work, slavery corrupts the minds of their children who, while watching its operations, are "nursed, educated and daily exercised in tyranny."[29]

Although Jefferson was not sanguine about the possibilities for voluntary emancipation under any circumstances, he hoped that religious belief could bolster the moral sense of his countrymen and at least provide the basis for movement in that direction. In order to do this, such belief must teach that the "liberties of a nation. . . are of the gift of God," which "are not to be violated but with his wrath." While this doctrine does not explicitly appear in Jefferson's "rational" version of Christianity, it is part of a non-sectarian creed which he developed in the Declaration of Independence and other public documents. We learn in the Declaration, for example, that the "Creator" endowed all men with their "unalienable rights" and, as "Supreme Judge of the world," He aids those legitimately fighting to preserve their rights against despots. Although Jefferson was not the author of the latter reference, he did adopt as the motto for his own seal the phrase, "Rebellion to Tyrants is Obedience to God." We may assume, therefore, that the notion of a deity who supports legitimate rebellion is not inconsistent with his thoughts.[30]

Jefferson also taught that the United States and God are bound together by a special covenant analagous to the covenant made between God and the Jews at Mount Sinai. In his "Second Inaugural Address," for example, God appears to the nation as the "Being in whose hands we are, who led our fathers, as Israel of old, from their native land, and planted them in a country flowing with all the necessaries and comforts of life." In contrast to the old covenant, however, which required the Jews to foster religious orthodoxy in exchange for God's blessings, Americans are required to follow and further the principles of the Declaration.[31]

Jefferson's religious-political principles became a fundamental part of the American regime when the First Amendment to the Constitution was adopted in 1791. This amendment, which forbids Congress from making any law "respecting an establishment of religion" or "prohibiting the free exercise thereof" established both the separation of church and state and religious freedom on the national level. These principles were also made binding on the states when incorporated into the due process clause of the Fourteenth Amendment by the Supreme Court in 1940. For much of our history, they have helped to eliminate religious discord and protect the interests of civil society while at the same time guaranteeing the rights of conscience. Jefferson could write as early as 1808 in a letter to a group of Virginia Baptists:

> We have solved by fair experiment, the great and interesting question whether freedom of religion is compatible with order in government, and obedience to the laws. And we have experienced the quiet as well as the comfort which results from leaving everyone to profess freely and openly those principles of religion which are the inductions of

his own reason, and the serious convictions of his own inquiries.[32]

Jefferson's best hope for "rational" religion in this country was expressed in his "First Inaugural Address" where the great American statesman eloquently set forth some of the basic tenets of his creed. "Having banished from our land that religious intolerance under which mankind so long held and suffered," he wrote, the United States will be

> enlightened by a benign religion, professed, indeed, and practiced in various forms, yet all of them including honesty, truth, temperance, gratitude, and the love of man; acknowledging and adoring an overruling Providence which by all its dispensations proves that it delights in the happiness of man here and his greater happiness thereafter.[33]

While the First Amendment has allowed American churches to practice the Biblical (and non-Biblical faiths) "in various forms," most religious bodies place political freedom at the center of their creed, teaching that "an overruling Providence" blesses only those nations which foster the rights of self-government. No American church teaches that a "favored few" are superior to the people, and can rule them legitimately "by the grace of God." Most churches also stress the shared moral virtues mentioned in the passage above while downplaying the divisive doctrinal differences traditionally considered most important by orthodox Christians. Finally, American clergymen generally allow their flocks "to regulate their own pursuit of industry and improvement," perhaps because Jefferson's God, in contrast to the Biblical God, "delights in the happiness of man here" even more than "his greater happiness hereafter."[34]

The widespread acceptance of these elements of Jefferson's religion has contributed to the relative harmony existing among our theologically diverse population. This population now includes a large number of Christian fundamentalist groups seeking to restore the Bible as the touchstone for all human affairs. If Jefferson's principles are to continue governing American religious-political life, these groups must continue to enjoy the freedom which is theirs by natural right. At the same time, however, their energetic piety must respect the limits Jefferson prescribed.

NOTES

[1]Terry Eastland, "In Defense of Religious America,"
Commentary, 71 (June, 1981), 39-45, 39; Jerry Falwell,
Listen America! (New York: Doubleday Publishing
Company, 1981), pp. 25, 233.

[2]See, for example, the Northwest Ordinance of
1787 and George Washington's "Farewell Address."
Walter Berns, "Religion and the Founding Principle,"
in The Moral Foundations of American Politics, ed. by
Robert H. Horwitz (Charlottesville, Virginia: University Press of Virginia, 1977), pp. 164-178 (hereafter
cited as Berns, "Religion"). Berns' essay as well as
Jeffrey M. Burnam, "Religion and American Political
Society: The Contemporary Supreme Court and the
American Founding" (unpublished M.A. thesis, Uni-
versity of Chicago, 1964) are the sources for much
of my understanding of Jefferson's thoughts on reli-
gion and politics. Burnam's work will hereafter be
cited as Burnam, "Religion and American Political
Society." See also Michael J. Malbin, Religion and
Politics: The Intentions of the Authors of the First
Amendment (Washington, D. C.: American Enterprise
Institute for Public Policy Research, 1978), pp. 29-
36 (hereafter cited as Malbin, Religion and Politics).
For the latest treatment of Jefferson's religious-
political thought from a different perspective see
William B. Huntley, "Jefferson's Public and Private
Religion," The South Atlantic Quarterly, 79 (Summer,
1980), 286-302.

[3]Berns, "Religion," p. 170. Thomas Jefferson,
The Writings of Thomas Jefferson, ed. by Andrew
Adgate Lipscomb and Albert Ellery Bergh (20 vols.;
Washington, D. C.: The Thomas Jefferson Memorial
Association, 1905), XV, 323 (hereafter cited as
Jefferson, Writings). The 1779 text of the Bill
appears in Thomas Jefferson, Papers, ed. by Julian
P. Boyd (vols.; Princeton: Princeton University
Press, 1950-), II, 545-547 (hereafter cited as
Jefferson, Papers).

[4]Thomas Jefferson, The Life and Selected Writings
of Jefferson, ed. by Adrienne Koch and William Peden
(New York: Random House, 1944), pp. 729, 730 (hereafter cited as Jefferson, Life and Selected Writings).
My analysis of this passage is indebted to Harvey C.

Mansfield, Jr., "Thomas Jefferson," in American Political Thought: The Philosophic Dimensions of American Statesmanship, ed. by Morton J. Frisch and Richard G. Stevens (New York: Charles Scribner's Sons, 1971), pp. 28, 29.

[5]Thomas Jefferson, The Complete Jefferson, ed. by Saul K. Padover (New York: Tudor Publishing Company, 1943), pp. 1142, 674 (hereafter cited as Jefferson, The Complete Jefferson). See also Berns, "Religion," pp. 172, 173.

[6]Jefferson, Life and Selected Writings, p. 409; Jefferson, The Complete Jefferson, p. 1300.

[7]Jefferson, Papers, II, pp. 546-547.

[8]Ibid., pp. 545, 546; Jefferson, The Complete Jefferson, pp. 675, 1147.

[9]See the Declaration of Independence.

[10]Jefferson, Papers, II, pp. 545-546; Jefferson, The Complete Jefferson, p. 675.

[11]Ibid., Jefferson, Papers, II, p. 545.

[12]Jefferson, Life and Selected Writings, p. 332; Jefferson, The Complete Jefferson, pp. 412, 1076. See David Lowenthal, "Connecting Religion and Government Constitutionally," in The Alternative: An American Spectator, May, 1977, pp. 19, 20, 30 (hereafter cited as Lowenthal, "Connecting Religion").

[13]Jefferson, The Complete Jefferson, p. 675; Jefferson, Papers, II, 546, I, 551. For an extended discussion of Locke's influence on Jefferson's religious-political thought see my article, "Locke's Influence on Jefferson's "Bill for Establishing Religious Freedom," Forthcoming in the Journal of Church and State.

[14]Jefferson, Papers, I, p. 353. See also Burnam, "Religion and American Political Society," p. 58, and Malbin, Religion and Politics, p. 35.

[15]John Adams and Thomas Jefferson, The Adams-Jefferson Letters, ed. by Lester J. Cappon (New York: Simon and Schuster, 1971), pp. 484, 485 (hereafter

cited as Cappon, Adams-Jefferson Letters); Jefferson, The Complete Jefferson, p. 676.

[16]Jefferson, Papers, II, 546; Jefferson, Writings, XV, 374, X, 237; Cappon, Adams-Jefferson Letters, pp. 594, 368, 384n; Jefferson, Life and Selected Writings, pp. 556-570; Thomas Jefferson, The Life and Morals of Jesus of Nazareth (St. Louis: N. O. Thompson Publishing Co., 1902). Hereafter cited as Jefferson, Life and Morals.

[17]Jefferson, Writings, XIV, 233; XV, 391; Jefferson, The Complete Jefferson, p. 676; Cappon, Adams-Jefferson Letters, p. 384.

[18]Jefferson, Life and Selected Writings, pp. 431-433.

[19]Ibid., pp. 431, 432; Jefferson, Writings, XIV, 197.

[20]Jefferson, Writings, XV, 260, 261, 203.

[21]Ibid., XV, 244, 259; Cappon, Adams-Jefferson Letters, p. 593; Jefferson, Life and Selected Writings, p. 569.

[22]Cappon, Adams-Jefferson Letters, p. 384; Jefferson, Life and Selected Writings, pp. 693, 694n; Jefferson, Writings, XII, 345, XV, 258, 373, 374.

[23]Jefferson, Life and Selected Writings, p. 431; Jefferson, Writings, pp. 261, 262. While there are several references to Jesus' healing in the Life and Morals, there is no mention of events such as the virgin birth or the resurrection. See, for example, Jefferson, Life and Morals, pp. 19, 20, 29, 168.

[24]Jefferson, Writings, XV, 260, 261.

[25]Ibid., Jefferson, Life and Selected Writings, pp. 569, 570. Because of the unorthodox nature of Jefferson's attempted reforms, it is not surprising that he was "averse to the communication of his religious tenets to the public" while he was alive. Despite his caution, however, he was widely denounced for his religious views at various points in his career, and was never able completely to "erase from the public mind, the conviction of his hostility to

revealed religion." Jefferson, Life and Selected Writings, p. 567; "Boston Columbia Centinel," August 22, 1801, cited in Dumas Malone, Jefferson and His Time, Vol. IV: Jefferson the President (Boston: Little, Brown, and Company, 1970), p. 195.

[26]Jefferson, Life and Selected Writings, pp. 703, 704, 570; Jefferson, Writings, XIII, 377.

[27]Jefferson, Life and Selected Writings, pp. 609, 639 (emphasis in the text).

[28]Ibid., pp. 639-640.

[29]Jefferson, The Complete Jefferson, pp. 664, 677.

[30]Ibid., Declaration of Independence; Jefferson, Papers, I, 679.

[31]Jefferson, The Complete Jefferson, p. 414.

[32]The religious parts of the First Amendment were absorbed into the Fourteenth Amendment by the Supreme Court in Cantwell v. Connecticut, 310 U.S. 296 (1940). Jefferson, The Complete Jefferson, pp. 538, 539. One reason for this success of the "fair experiment" is that American courts have traditionally used Jefferson's belief-action distinction to proscribe religiously motivated behavior which conflicts with secular law. Recently, however, the Supreme Court has sought to balance the behavior in question against the secular interest involved, tilting the balance in favor of freedom unless the state interest was of the "highest order." In Wisconsin v. Yoder (1972), the Court for the first time in its history exempted a particular religious group, the Amish, from the requirements of a valid criminal statute on First Amendment grounds, or, to use Jeffersonian terms, required the state to tolerate a religious practice which it believed contrary to the public good. Perhaps the most serious shortcoming of the Yoder decision from a Jeffersonian perspective is not the exemption granted to the Amish, who are generally recognized as a productive and law-abiding people, but rather the damage done to the principle of secular supremacy. See Gerald Gunther, Cases and Materials in Constitutional Law (Mineola, New York: The Foundation Press, 1975), pp. 1505 ff. Wisconsin v. Yoder 406 U.S. 205 (1972).

[33]Jefferson, The Complete Jefferson, pp. 385-387.

[34]Ibid., Jefferson, Life and Selected Writings, p. 730. For a description of the ways in which American religion has conformed to the Jeffersonian guidelines set forth in this essay see Seymour Martin Lipset, "Religion and American Values," in The First New Nation: The United States in Historical and Comparative Perspective (New York: Basic Books, 1963), pp. 140-169, and Will Herberg, "The Religion of Americans and American Religion," in Protestant Catholic Jew (Garden City, New York: Doubleday and Company, Inc., 1960), pp. 72-98.

PART II

Democracy Defined and Redefined

CHAPTER 4
"Democracy In America and Tocqueville's New Science:
Civic Virtue In A Commercial Republic"*
Edmund D. Carlson

The first of the duties that are at this time imposed
upon those who direct our affairs is to educate
democracy, to reawaken, if possible, its religious
beliefs; to purify its morals; to mold its actions;
to substitute a knowledge of statecraft for its
inexperience, and an awareness of its true interest
for its blind instincts, to adapt its government to
time and place, and to modify it according to men and
to conditions. A new science of politics is needed
for a new world. (Democracy in America, Author's
Introduction, emphasis added)

* * *

The science of politics, however, like most other
sciences, has received great improvement. The efficacy
of various principles is now well understood, which
were either not known at all, or imperfectly known to
the ancients. (The Federalist, No. 9, emphasis added)

I

Theories of Modern Virtue

A new view of nature, man and history marks the
dawn of the modern age. Many believe this dawn to
have enlightened mankind and to have dispelled the
previously authoritative superstitions underlying
traditional religion, political authority, and ancient
philosophy. In this view the ascending light of a
reformed reason illuminates new modes and orders--new
scientific and social horizons.[1] The promises made
on behalf of modernity have included the following:
to relieve man's earthly estate,[2] to free men from
destructive religious passions--deliberately finding
political uses for religious "fears of power invisible"[3]--and to secure comfortable self-preservation by
safeguarding life, liberty and property as natural
rights.[4] Men such as Machiavelli, Bacon, Hobbes and

*This paper was written while the author was enjoying
a National Endowment for the Humanities Fellowship in
Residence at Princeton University.

Locke have made profound contributions toward forming the modern perspective. Modern political philosophy and its step-child, modern social science, have time and again reaffirmed similar promises while continuing the struggle to overcome the vestiges of the same classical and medieval adversaries. In spite of some five centuries invested in the effort, modern men somehow have not completely fulfilled those promises.

The eighteenth century Italian philosopher, Giambattista Vico, exemplifies both the promises and the problems accompanying such modern views in his greatest work, Principles of New Science of Giambattista Vico Concerning the Common Nature of the Nations.[5] A new world is revealed by a new science; the heavenly city of God no longer simply dominates the earthly city: ". . .the world of civil society has certainly been made by men, and. . . its principles are therefore to be found within the modifications of our own human mind."[6] Vico unfolds a view of nature rejecting ancient essences; he turns toward historical origins as the true "nature" or genesis of religion, politics and science. Vico's new science centers on human "poetry" or creativity as the primitive basis for human institutions. For example, great poet-founders of the past had to labor "to invent sublime fables" which would help "teach the vulgar to act virtuously."[7] The new science--to be useful--seeks to mold common men with common vices into happy members of society.

> To be useful to the human race,
> philosophy must raise and direct
> weak and fallen man, not rend his
> nature or abandon him in his cor-
> ruption. . . .Legislation considers
> man as he is in order to turn him
> to good uses in human society. Out
> of ferocity, avarice, and ambition,
> the three vices which run throughout
> the human race, it creates the
> military, merchant, and governing
> classes, and thus the strength,
> riches, and wisdom of commonwealths.
> Out of these three great vices, which
> could certainly destroy all mankind
> on the face of the earth, it makes
> civil happiness.[8]

Understanding nature as origins, man as creator, and politics as malleable helped set the stage, as it were, for later ideas--such as progress in history--which influenced such men as Paine, Marx and Engels.[9]

The past few centuries have seen the modern science of politics recur in various ways; two strands of that science, of great importance to the American regime, have been liberalism and constitutionalism. The modern thrust of such doctrines implies that the new political world be established by human, and not divine, creativity. In this light, Alexis de Tocqueville's call for a new science of politics for a new world can be seen in two ways: 1) as his response to the emerging humanistic tradition of modern political thought, and 2) as his attempt to shape and improve that world.

"Considering man as he is in order to turn him to good uses in society" is a vision close to the heart of the modern democratic enterprise. Legislating such a "turnabout" raises an abiding question for the new science in all its various forms: to what extent can man be molded into a citizen without losing his natural freedom?[10] Democracy in America leads the student of constitutional republics into a more thoughtful awareness of that transformation. In part Tocqueville proposes to explain and, ultimately, to foster free citizenship in modern democratic societies. His statesmanlike new science seeks to weave together a practicable theory of individual freedom that can survive the pressures of mass democracy. To this end he gleans non-utopian lessons from his visit to the United States in the early 1830's. These lessons do not pretend to dispell--as if by magic--the riddle of "man and citizen" which has intrigued western thinkers from Aristotle to Rousseau. Rather than a magic potion, these sober lessons suggest a comprehensive pathology for democracy.

To see the full importance of Tocqueville's thought, then, one should never bifurcate its philosophic context from the political one; Montesquieu and Rousseau have at least as much to do with our understanding Tocqueville's new science as do the circumstances he observed in nineteenth century France or America. However, our purpose here is at once less grand and more specific: namely, what is this new science in Tocqueville's Democracy in America and what can it teach us about the American polity?

Tocqueville's observations on American democracy give insights into a youthful, expansive regime working out the somewhat problematic implications of its founding principles. He finds as an example the implied tension between human equality and liberty-- the core American dilemma pitting majorities against individual and minority rights.[11]

The theme of fostering democratic civic virtue or healthy citizenship emerges as one approach to resolve this dilemma by moderating the citizens likely to constitute future majorities. Informing the character and molding the souls of democratic citizens through a variety of public and private institutions constitutes the main political task of the new science. Yet how is it possible to foster a moderate species of public-spiritedness in a regime most strongly promoting the opinions, passions, and interests of the marketplace? How is it possible "to educate democracy and purify its morals" without denying freedom, that is, without resorting to the harshness of ancient religious orthodoxy, to the unacceptable inequality of a feudal aristocracy, or to the "imaginary" virtue of classical philosophy?

II

New Devices for a New World

Tocqueville divides science into three parts: abstractly theoretical science, theoretical science with direct applications, and methods of application.[12] Americans, he notes, "admirably understand" the purely practical or technological aspect of science while virtually ignoring abstract philosophy. Hence, ". . . in no country in the civilized world is less attention paid to philosophy than in the United States."[13] Americans apparently live their philosophic or scientific method--often called pragmatism today--rather than reflect on it. This celebrated Yankee ingenuity is tied closely to the emancipation of traditionally discouraged commercial appetites or passions. The bourgeois profit motive usually underlies the American "pursuit of happiness" so nobly proclaimed as a natural right in the Declaration of Independence. In this respect the American commercial republic

epitomizes for Tocqueville a new, democratic age; the
virtues it unconsciously fosters and the habits it
engenders are not classically political: "the passions
that stir Americans most deeply are commercial and not
political ones, or rather they carry a trader's
habits over into the business of politics."[14]

Ingenious acquisitiveness, however, is a mixed
blessing. On the positive side it certainly spawns
a new commercial empire based on an expanding middle
class enjoying, for the most part, Lockean "comfortable
self-preservation." But, on the negative side,
Tocqueville warns that commercial democracy may decay
into a new, insidious form of slavery which, unfortunately for most men, appears benign. That new
slavery--majority despotism--hastens a philistine
barbarism devoid of true philosophy or science in
the highest sense. Hence, to avoid an obscurantist
and egalitarian slavery, democratic statesmen must
devise ways of coercing or leading the human mind into
theoretical studies toward the contemplation of primary
causes.[15] It is clear, then, that Tocqueville's new
science of politics--his "art of being free"[16]--aims
less at merely reflecting the new age than at elevating
and healing it.

Only on the surface to the "tools" or lessons of
the new science offer a one dimensional political
technology, using private passions to attain a kind of
public good (very similar to Mandeville's "private
vice, public virtue" in The Fable of the Bees or Adam
Smith's liberal capitalism in The Wealth of Nations).
But these lessons also teach more thoughtful students
something concerning the genuinely philosophic, root
problems of American liberal democracy. Consequently
each of Tocqueville's following three practical recommendations also contains the seeds of such theoretical
problems: 1) foster a new, more realistic morality
which he calls "self-interest rightly understood" to
replace the fast-vanishing traditional virtue; 2) teach
the sanctity of human rights and the love of freedom
to mitigate the all-consuming "passion for equality"
likely to dominate politics in the democratic age; and
3) strive to "make great men" more than merely "to do
great things with men."[17]

Various devices to ground these recommendations
compose the bulk of the two volumes in Tocqueville's
work. For our purposes these devices may be placed in

five categories: first, American legislators must recognize the importance of unpretentious forms and rituals (especially found in moderate religions) which help inculcate crucial dogmas knitting society together. Second, the moral and intellectual faculties of citizens should be encouraged through free educational and journalistic institutions. Third, organizational skills derived from citizen participation in a host of salutary private and political associations should emerge from vigorous municipal institutions and administrative decentralization. Fourth, an additional hortatory means to qualify self-interest, sanctify human rights, and, perhaps, promote human greatness stems from an independent and assertive legal system composed of non-partisan courts, citizen juries and a learned class of lawyers. And fifth, the coaxing of basically sound habits of mind and spirit from democratic citizens may well result from well-framed laws on the constitutional level (such as separation of powers or the indirect election of some officials) or on the level of ordinary legislation (such as the abolition of primogeniture or of slavery in the Northwest Territories).

    1) Tocqueville's well-stressed warning against the spreading "inordinate love of material pleasure" which threatens to isolate and brutalize men as well as to atomize society in the new democratic age is the context for his recommending forms and rituals as remedies. Such ceremonies gently congregate otherwise selfish men into a more enlightened, tolerant society. A healthy modern society is held together by the use of humanizing and charitable dogmas--what we might well call moderated religious opinions. Moderated religious beliefs should avoid the opposite dangers of fanatical enthusiasm and bland religious indifference. The new science relies on the political unity of religions while remaining largely silent as to the ultimate truth behind the forms and rituals of various sects. Many commentators rightly underscore the key role played by religions in the origin and maintenance of healthy democracy in America.[18]

    Fanatical enthusiasm must not become the engine of religious oppression; hence, freedom is negatively buttressed by a careful separation of church and state--avoiding dangerously partisan political involvement by churches or clergy. On the other hand, tolerant religion solidly supports political liberty in a _positive_ way by edifying citizens, that is, by elevating their sights above the crassest love of comforts and the narrowest passions for gain. Gentle dogmas teaching a belief in the soul and human responsibility can act as a subtle check on the pervasive love of the body and material well-being. In these two ways, non-militant or non-traditional religious opinion ". . . best teaches the Americans the art of being free."[19]

The helpful forms or "exterior ceremonies" of religion, however, would be "particularly dangerous to multiply. . . beyond measure, indeed (it is important) that they should be limited to such as are absolutely necessary to perpetuate dogma itself, which is the essence of religions." Tocqueville's sober expectations for the political utility of moderated religions--somewhat secularized versions of Christianity safely subdivided into a variety of demoninations--becomes evident when he admits the futility of completely eradicating the love of material pleasure.[20]

> The main business of religions is to
> purify, control and retain that
> excessive and exclusive taste for
> well-being which men acquire in times
> of equality, but I think it would be
> a mistake for them to attempt to
> conquer it entirely or abolish it.
> They will never succeed in preventing
> men from loving wealth, but they may
> be able to induce them to use only
> honest means to enrich themselves.

Whether such a low but solid view of religion is sufficient to restrict even most citizens to _honest_ enrichment is not altogether clear; it is much clearer that such minimal decency or honesty, however realistic it may be, falls short of traditional civic virtue-- say as discussed in Book III of Aristotle's _Politics_-- or even traditional Christian virtue--say as found in Chapter 28, Boox XIV of Augustine's _City of God_. "Honest enrichment" is not the same as courage in the face of death when defending one's country. Common decency is necessary but not sufficient to support a republic. Uncommon nobility of spirit or--in Tocqueville's own words--"great men" cannot realistically be expected from the rather tame and simple platitudes of secularized Christianity. Hence Tocqueville looks beyond the newer form of religion toward a newer form of patriotism--a species of civic religion--to move men to higher actions. "Americans rightly think that patriotism is a sort of religion strengthened by practical service."[21]

This new patriotism is less instinctive, less ardent, and less generous than the older one; yet, for all its limitations, it comes closer to addressing the problem of civic virtue than does "honest enrichment." For Tocqueville this new love of country, perhaps like the new religion itself, ". . . is more creative and more lasting, it is engendered by enlightenment, grows by the aid of laws and the exercise of rights, and in the end becomes, in a sense, mingled with personal interest."[22] A new civic spirit arises from this new civic religion, mixing what formerly were regarded as opposites: love of one's own rights and interests with love of country. Virtue is no longer its own reward; patriotism no longer, as it were, altruistic. The new science assumes a modern and liberal definition of virtue. "Next to virtue as a general idea, nothing, I think, is so beautiful as that of rights, and indeed the two ideas are mingled. The idea of rights is nothing but the conception of virtue applied to the world of politics."[23]

"Forms and rituals" then, prudently applied, politicize virtue by teaching individuals self-discipline and majorities self-government--the only solid bases for democratic justice. For example, formal procedures reinforce the discipline of patience and may help inculcate the collective habit of de-liberating before taking action. Habitual deliberation in small groups may then instill in individuals a disposition to rational forethought rather than im-pulsive selfishness. These are examples of the moral and intellectual faculties Tocqueville's new science urges democratic leaders to coax from the citizenry.

2) Three additional devices he envisions to develop citizenship are: a free press, mass public education, and liberal education for the few most talented.[24] The press functions to raise public issues, encourage the formation of civic groups or associations and to act as a check upon the actions of government officials. Tocqueville well realized, however, that such functions can and probably would be abused leading to the danger of misinforming the

public, creating factious special interests and even, on occasion, libeling public officials. While he does not lightly dismiss such dangers, Tocqueville does reject any notion of political censorship as inimical to free popular government.[25] His new science nevertheless is not without any remedy for those likely abuses; in an argument reminiscent of the Tenth Federalist he notes that ". . . it is an axiom of political science there that the only way to neutralize the effects of newspapers is to multiply their numbers."[26] A multiplicity of news sources vastly lessens the chance that any one will unjustly influence public opinion.

While a search for American scholars of the first rank would not bear much fruit in Tocqueville's opinion, a search for literate and capable, ordinary citizens would lead one toward thinking ". . . the Americans the most enlightened people in the world."[27] These qualities bear witness to the success of American mass education. The new morality based upon self-interest rightly understood may be realistic but is clearly not automatic; it does not spring naturally into the souls of democratic men. Consequently, Americans have braced public education as one means of teaching valuable moral lessons remedying the defects of the older morality and patriotism.

> I do not think that the doctrine
> of self-interest as preached in
> America is in all respects self-
> evident. But it does contain many
> truths so clear that for men to see
> them it is enough to educate them.
> Hence it is all-important for them
> to be educated, for the age of
> blind sacrifice and instinctive
> virtues is already long past, and
> I see a time approaching in which
> freedom, public peace, and social
> stability will not be able to last
> without education.[28]

Yet mere literacy is not enough; ". . . I would not exaggerate this advantage and am very far from thinking. . . that to teach men to read and write is enough to make them good citizens immediately."[29] Americans are educated not so much by books as by "taking a share in legislation. . . it is by governing

87

that he becomes educated about . . .government.
. . . .In the United States, education as a whole is
directed toward political life. . . ."[30]

Tocqueville's third goal of fostering great men
depends partially upon their receiving excellent,
liberal education including a study of Greek and Latin
classics. The insidious majoritarian pressures to
conform "enervate the souls" of the few naturally
most gifted. For "most people" he recommends a
"scientific, commercial, and industrial rather than
literary" education.

> Greek and Latin should not be taught
> in all the schools. But it is impor-
> tant that those who are destined by
> nature or fate to adopt a literary
> career or to cultivate such tastes
> should be able to find schools where
> the classics are taught and true
> scholars formed. A few excellent
> universities are better means to this
> end than a multitude of bad schools
> in which the classics are an ill-
> taught extra, standing in the way
> of sound instruction in necessary
> studies. . . .Not that I hold the
> classics beyond criticism, but I
> think they have special merits well
> calculated to counter-balance our
> peculiar defects (in democratic
> nations). They provide a prop just
> where we are most likely to fall.[31]

3) In the governmental sphere, <u>vigorous municipal
institutions serve in the new science of politics to
secure the political benefits of administrative decentralization.</u> Americans learn to be joiners and
organizers at the local level; citizen virtues are in
part the by-products of what Tocqueville calls the
"art of association." ". . .(T)he strength of free
peoples resides in the local community. Local institutions are to liberty what primary schools are to
science; they put it within the people's reach; they
teach people to appreciate its peaceful enjoyment and
accustom them to make use of it."[32]

Tocqueville carefully distinguishes between
"governmental centralization" which is vital for a

nation's prosperity and "administrative centralization" which ". . .only serves to enervate the peoples that submit to it, because it constantly tends to diminish their civic spirit."[33] It is his evident concern for civic spirit that leads him to espouse the new, realistic forms of religion and patriotism which are best fostered locally. America derives benefits from its governmental centralization--what the Founders called a "more perfect Union"--and its administrative decentralization--what the Founders called a "compound, extended republic." In a key chapter on townships in America, Tocqueville links the new religion and patriotism specifically to the benefits of administrative decentralization.

> In the United States the motherland's presence is felt everywhere. It is a subject of concern to the village and to the whole Union. The inhabitants care about each of the country's interests as if they were their own. Each man takes pride in the nation; the successes it gains seem his own work, and he becomes elated; he rejoices in the general prosperity from which he profits. He has much the same feeling for his country as one has for one's family, and a sort of selfishness makes him care for the state.[34]

Administrative decentralization means healthy "provincial institutions" for Tocqueville or what Americans call state and local governments.

Tocqueville's new "age of equality" tends to isolate and weaken each individual relative to the faceless and remote, but all-powerful, majority. Moral and intellectual freedom therefore becomes increasingly problematic ". . .unless each citizen learn(s) to combine with his fellows to preserve his freedom. . . ." Without the art of association, in part growing out of American experiences in local self-government, men in the United States could succumb to the new form of majority despotism which ". . .hinders, restrains, enervates, stifles and stultifies so much that in the end each nation is no more than a flock of timid and hardworking animals with government as its shepherd."[35] Learning to associate

within provincial institutions can give rise to a
multiplicity of other "secondary" or "intermediary"
powers--such as private associations--standing between
citizen and central government.

> The morals and intelligence of a
> democratic people would be in as much
> danger as its commerce and industry
> if ever a government wholly usurped
> the place of private associations.
> Feelings and ideas are renewed, the
> heart enlarged, and the understanding
> developed only by the reciprocal
> action of men upon one another. I
> have shown how these influences are
> reduced almost to nothing in demo-
> cratic countries; they must therefore
> be artifically created, and only
> associations do that. . . .If men
> are to remain civilized or to become
> civilized, the art of association
> must develop and improve among them
> at the same speed as equality of con-
> ditions.[36]

4) Additional devices contained in the new science
include an independent legal system composed of non-
partisan courts, citizen juries and a politically
active class of lawyers. "Private rights and interests
are . . .always in danger unless the power of the courts
grows and extends commensurately with the increase of
equality of conditions."[37] The peculiar power of
judicial review injects jurisprudence into the heart
of American constitutionalism. The rule of law applied
via the legal system can act to qualify and refine
democratic passions for equality; it teaches the love
of one's own rights, even if purchased only with
considerable effort, and the respect for the rights
of fellow citizens. Those lessons in Tocqueville's
opinion best reach American citizens through jury duty.[38]

> Juries . . .instill some of the habits
> of the judicial mind into every citizen,
> and just those habits are the very best
> way of preparing people to be free. It
> spreads respect for courts' decisions
> and for the idea of rights throughout
> the classes. . . .Juries teach men
> equity in practice. . . .Juries teach

each individual not to shirk responsibility for his own acts, and without
that manly characteristic no political
virtue is possible.

Finally one must note Tocqueville's view of lawyers.
As a very active political elite, they contribute to
American democracy a rare taste for formalities,
vigilance for procedures and habits of "directing the
blind passions" of their fellow citizens. Such tastes
and habits improve freedom's chances in American
democracy.

5) <u>Well-framed laws interact with social mores and
the physical conditions of American democracy to sustain freedom</u>. The legislative art must always work
upon given historical and physical materials; Tocqueville observes that the American regime has been
particularly fortunate to have had prudent Founders
meeting with abundant resources and geopolitical isolation. Yet neither a well-endowed continent open for
exploitation nor the absence of dangerous neighbors--
removing the cost and peril of a large standing army--
is enough to explain the success of American government.
Tocqueville cites Canada and South America to be lands
well-endowed with resources and similar geographic
assets but without the material and political success
of the United States.[39] This comparison suggests
the superiority of laws to mere physical circumstances
as likely causes for successful democracy.

The constitutional law of the United States, then,
must be considered a vital factor explaining the
success of the American experiment. Tocqueville
regards the national government--with longer terms for
its officers and greater independence for the executive
and judicial branches--to be superior to the respective
states.[40] On the other hand he is highly critical of
other American legal provisions--such as presidential
re-eligibility, annually elected state legislatures
or elected judges--which he understands to unduly
weaken public officials in the face of popular whims
or impulses.

In spite of his opinion that good laws contribute
more than mere physical circumstances to American
democracy, Tocqueville believes "mores" to be even
more important than laws. He defines mores (<u>moeurs</u>)
as "the whole moral and intellectual state of a

91

people."[41] Hence laws typically reflect underlying
mores. Nevertheless--in a way critical for the
success of Tocqueville's new science--laws and the
art of legislation may have long term influence on
the formation of mores. Such laws as the prohibition
against primogeniture, the disestablishment of any
religious denomination, the abolition of slavery, or
the public support for education may subtly yet power-
fully help remold the mores of a people in favor of
healthy democracy. In this way the legislative art
of the American Founders both reflected and, in turn,
sought to shape Anglo-American mores. The ubiquitous
commercialism of Americans did not just "grow" in a
totally mysterious flow of history. The peculiar
cultural mixture of the North American British colonies
almost unconsciously fostered such commercialism; but
it was the very conscious policy of American statesmen
like Madison and Hamilton to promote commercialism in
a continental republic precisely for the political
moderation they hoped it would induce. The legislative
art--the art of statesmanship at its best--has both an
active and passive aspect. The reciprocal influence
between laws and mores corresponds to those two aspects
and parallels the prescriptive and descriptive levels
of Tocqueville's political science.

III

Two Versions of the New Science

    Juxtaposing Tocqueville's new science with that
discussed by Madison and Hamilton--writing as Publius
some fifty years earlier--in The Federalist leads us
to certain lasting issues, such as the meaning of
"liberalism" or of "federalism," touching the health
of the American constitutional polity. Their differing
views on the proper size for a modern republic--at
heart the conflict between the respective merits of
participatory and representative democracy--divide
Tocqueville and Publius perhaps more than their views
on any other issue. In this regard, Tocqueville seems
to find more inspiration from Montesquieu and Rousseau
than did Publius who appears more related to such
thinkers as Locke and Hume.[42] While agreeing on the
inadequacy of traditional virtue for modern politics--
a failing Publius calls the "defect of better motives"--
these two versions of the new science emphasize divergent means to healthy popular government. The argument in

92

<u>Democracy</u> lays much greater stress on modern public-spiritedness derived from citizen participation.

In spite of Tocqueville's own disavowal of Aristotle's views, one is tempted to recall the Aristotelian overtones to this localistic stress in <u>Democracy</u>. It echoes the classical notions of man as a <u>polis</u> animal who only develops moral virtue in the context of a well-ordered city.[43] Of course Tocqueville's standard of what constitutes a "well-ordered" regime (regardless of its size) is decisively that of a modern liberal. Modern or liberal civic virtue is a <u>means</u> to sustain individual liberty in democracy in contrast to ancient moral virtue which is, at least in part, the <u>end</u> of the <u>polis</u>. The substitution of freedom for virtue as a political goal is one of the most important hallmarks of the modern perspective. In this light, Tocqueville's "great reformer" in history--presumably one who applies the new science--is much closer to Machiavelli's princely founder than Plato's famous, and illusive, philosopher-king.[44]

While equally sharing the modern perspective with Tocqueville, Publius clearly de-emphasizes the political virtues most citizens can only develop in small republics. <u>The Federalist</u> does not contain anything quite like Tocqueville's praise for participatory citizenship in townships. According to Martin Diamond, the ends of government associated with Publius' extended, commercial republic probably do not include the most noble--and explosive--political purposes of the ancient world:

> So far as concerns those ends of
> government on which <u>The Federalist</u>
> is almost wholly silent, it is
> reasonable to infer that what the
> Founders made no provision for they
> did not rank highly among the
> legitimate objects of government.
> Other political theories ranked
> highly, as objects of government,
> the nurturing of a particular
> religion, education, military
> courage, civic-spiritedness, mod-
> eration, individual excellence in
> the virtues, etc. On all of these
> <u>The Federalist</u> is either silent,

or has in mind only pallid versions
of the originals, or even seems to
speak with contempt. The Founders
apparently did not consider it
necessary to make special provision
for excellence.[45]

Civic virtue--even in its pallid "honest enrichment"
form--as an explicit concern for the new science is
clearly less central for Publius.

Publius does frankly admit that a "defect of
better motives"--too little "philantrophy" or
"patriotism"--is an all-too-common deficiency in
human affairs. This human failing is the reason why
constitutional "parchment barriers" are unrealistic
restraints on sovereignty.[46] To provide sufficient
precautions to insure non-tyrannical government,
Publius relies on his "improved science of politics"
outlined in the Ninth Federalist. His more practicable
barriers against tyranny include the following devices
(some of which correspond to Tocqueville's):[47]
1) separation of powers; 2) legislative checks and
balances (or bicameralism); 3) an independent judiciary
serving during good behavior; 4) the principle of popular representation; and, most importantly, 5) the
"extended and compound republic" giving the benefits
of a large, commercially developing society.[48]

This last device is the one most suspect for
Tocqueville. While he clearly accepts the military,
commercial and judicial advantages of an extended republic, he with equal clarity questions the ethical
effects of size, the growing threat of administrative
centralization, and the long-term erosion of patriotism
or civic spirit caused by commercial mores decaying
into a kind of selfish individualism.[49] The abiding
tension between the claims made on behalf of small
and large republics continues to be felt in American
federalism. Hence the ethical gains derived from
citizen participation must be balanced against the
danger of local majority factions Publius argues
inheres in small, homogeneous democracies.

Both Tocqueville and Publius rely on the political
utility of moderated religions as an essential basis
for liberal politics. Yet only in Democracy in America
does civic religion acquire a salient importance. A
liberal or "self-interested" public-spiritedness can

be found in both versions of political science, yet
Hamilton gives it the shape of noble political ambition
or a rare appetite for fame. The argument in Democracy, on the other hand, focuses on the more mundane
civic mores of ordinary citizens.[50] Publius envisions
a free republic wherein "the diversity in the faculties
of men" which eventuate in differing "degrees and kinds
of property" could be protected. No doubt on occasion
"better motives" and even higher virtues--possessed by
those "enlightened statesmen" at the helm from time to
time--were expected by Publius among those diverse
faculties. But the more common source of "opinions,
passions and interests" was not civic virtue but the
holding and desiring of property. Publius' new science
derives political moderation from the complex interaction of diverse commercial interests and competing
personal ambitions set against the backdrop of religious tolerance. The institutional expression of
such relatively peaceful competition filters and
refines the rule of democratic majorities and almost
always channels such rule through a series of deliberative compromises.

But, as Diamond reasons above, Publius is "almost
wholly silent" on the core problem of civic virtue in
a commercial republic. Consequently Diamond concludes
his essay with a question that opens the very issue
Tocqueville tries to understand: "Does not the
intensity and kind of our modern problems seem to
require of us a greater degree of reflection and
public-spiritedness than the Founders thought sufficient for the men who came after them?" Tocqueville's central focus on the problem of free citizenship in American democracy yields a somewhat equiovical
answer to this question. To a significant extent
Publius either takes for granted or less clearly
emphasizes certain elements in the American regime--
such as civic religion, the ethical benefits of private
associations, or the hortatory role of the legal
system--which Tocqueville magnifies in his new science.
In fairness, however, one should remember that Publius
faced the formidable constraints of securing mass consent to the novel idea of an extended republic; Tocqueville gazed upon the art of American statesmanship
more from the heights of theory than from the political
trenches.

IV

Man and Citizen

The modern art of legislation found in Democracy
in America paradoxically flirts with historical determinism in the name of human freedom. However seriously
Tocqueville wishes us to take his "inevitability
thesis" regarding the oncoming democratic age,[51] he
concludes his work by denouncing the crudely deterministic forms of modern thought stressing geographic,
racial or other causes underlying history--we might
well add economics and psychology--so prevalent in
what is now called social science.[52]

> These are false and cowardly doctrines
> which can only produce feeble men and
> pusillanimous nations. Providence did
> not make mankind entirely free or com-
> pletely enslaved. Providence has, in
> truth, drawn a predestined circle
> around each man beyond which he cannot
> pass; but within those vast limits man
> is strong and free, and so are peoples.
> The nations of our day cannot prevent
> conditions of equality from spreading
> in their midst. But it depends upon
> themselves whether equality is to
> lead to servitude or freedom, know-
> ledge or barbarism, prosperity or
> wretchedness.

Freedom as a goal for his science also means that
failure and slavery are very real possiblities for
American democracy. This helps to account for
Tocqueville's non-utopian sobriety; he does forecast
the likely decline of American democracy. The list
of possible causes for that decline is considerable:
race conflict; inept, democratically muddled foreign
policy; the growing enervation of the human spirit
meaning fewer great men; the decay of religious and
patriotic sentiments; the growing threat to freedom
from a stultifying and bureaucratic "administrative
centralization;" and, most importantly, the various
forms of majority tyranny.[53]

The new science does not rely on the "antique
virtue" of the Greeks, Romans, or Christian Patriarchs;
the old virtue is but a memory. Tocqueville admits,

96

in an unpublished fragment,[54] that "the Americans do not form a virtuous people and yet they are free." Their citizenship has low but solid roots nourishing freedom from qualified self-interest and mass participation. From a position transcending current American ideologies of the left or the right, Tocqueville's new science warns all sides against doing violence to the spirit of man either through an active, utopian egalitarianism or through a passive, atomistic libertarianism. Tocqueville does not simply resolve the tension between man and citizen--between freedom and duty--in American democracy. Whether his notion of a new civic spirit adequately balances the private and public needs of Americans or adequately preserves the possiblity of human greatness in an age of modiocrity is at least as uncertain in our day as it was in Tocqueville's.

NOTES

[1] Niccolo Machiavelli, The Prince and the Discourses (New York: The Modern Library, 1950), p. 103.

[2] Howard B. White, Peace Among the Willows: the Political Philosophy of Francis Bacon (The Hague: Martinus Nijhoff, 1968), p. 1.

[3] Thomas Hobbes, Leviathan, (ed.) C. B. Macpherson (New York: Penguin Books, 1978), pp. 682-715, 726.

[4] John Locke, Two Treatises of Government, (ed.) Peter Laslett (New York: The New American Library, 1965), pp. 309-44; and Leo Strauss, Natural Right and History (Chicago: University of Chicago Press, 1953), pp. 202-51.

[5] Thomas G. Bergin and Max H. Fisch (ed. and trans.), The New Science of Giambattista Vico (Ithaca: Cornell University Press, 1970), pp. xxi, 1.

[6] Ibid., pp. 52-53.

[7] Ibid., p. 75.

[8] Ibid., pp. 19-20, emphasis added.

[9] Hayden V. White, "Vico," International Encyclopedia of the Social Sciences, (ed.) David L. Sills, xvi (1968), pp. 315-16.

[10] Jean-Jacques Rousseau, On the Social Contract with Geneva Manuscript and Poltical Economy, (ed.) Roger D. Masters (New York: St. Martin's Press, 1978), pp. 46-52; 124-32.

[11] Alexis de Tocqueville, Democracy in America, (ed.) J. P. Mayer and Max Lerner, (trans.) George Lawrence (New York: Harper and Row Publishers, 1966), pp. 473-76. Hereafter cited as Democracy.

[12] Ibid., p. 426.

[13] Ibid., p. 393.

[14] Ibid., pp. 262-63.

[15]Ibid., pp. 430-31, and 510 where he notes: "No matter how a people strives for it, all the conditions of life can never be perfectly equal. Even if, by misfortune, such an absolute dead level were attained, there would still be inequalities of intelligence which, coming directly from God, will ever escape the laws of man."

[16]Ibid., pp. 221, 161.

[17]Ibid., pp. 497-501, 473-78, 219-21, 673-74, 676.

[18]Alfred Balitzer, "Politics and the 'Arts of Peace:' A Study of Religion in the Political Order Drawn from the Works of Alexis de Tocqueville." Unpublished doctoral dissertation in Government, Clarement Graduate School, Claremont, California, 1971; Max Lerner, "Tocqueville's Democracy in America: Reception and Reputation," Democracy, pp. lxxiv-lxxv; George W. Pierson, Tocqueville and Beaumont in America (New York: Oxford University Press, 1938), pp. 416, 418, 753; Marvin Zetterbaum, Tocqueville and the Problem of Democracy (Stanford: Standford University Press, 1967), pp. 109-24.

[19]Democracy, pp. 267, 408-14.

[20]Ibid., pp. 412-13, and 501 where he observes: "But preachers in America are continually coming down to earth. Indeed they find it difficult to take their eyes off it. The better to touch their hearers, they are forever pointing out how religious beliefs favor freedom and public order, and it is often difficult to be sure when listening to them whether the main object of religion is to procure eternal felicity in the next world or prosperity in this."

[21]Ibid., pp. 62, 84, 400; cf. Rousseau, Op. cit., p. 131 where he writes: "The dogmas of the civil religion ought to be simple, few in number, state with precision, without explanations or commentaries. The existence of a powerful, intelligent, beneficient, foresighted and providential divinity; the afterlife; the happiness of the just; the punishment of the wicked; the sanctity of the social contract and the laws. These are the positive dogmas. As for the negative ones, I limit them to a single one: intolerance. It belongs with the cults we have excluded."

[22] Ibid., p. 217.

[23] Ibid., p. 219, emphasis added.

[24] On a free press, see Ibid., pp. 166-73, 672; on the importance of education in America, pp. 38, 48, 83, 277-80; on liberal education, see pp. 444-45.

[25] Ibid., p. 167.

[26] Ibid., p. 170.

[27] Ibid., p. 277.

[28] Ibid., p. 499.

[29] Ibid., p. 279.

[30] Ibid., p. 280.

[31] Ibid., p. 445.

[32] Ibid., p. 55. For Tocqueville's views on the "art of association" and "administrative decentralization" see pp. 174 and 178.

[33] Ibid., p. 79.

[34] Ibid., p. 85, emphasis added.

[35] Ibid., p. 667.

[36] Ibid., pp. 487-88.

[37] Ibid., p. 673.

[38] Ibid., p. 252.

[39] Ibid., pp. 19-20, 258, 262-63, 281-82.

[40] Ibid., pp. 138-41.

[41] Ibid., p. 264.

[42] On the issue of size it is clearly the case that Tocqueville leans toward Montesquieu and Rousseau. For example, see Baron de Montesquieu, _The Spirit of the Laws_, (trans.) Thomas Nugent, (intro.) Franz Neumann (New York: Hafner Publishing Company, 1949),

pp. 120-22; Rousseau, Op. cit., pp. 71-72, 79-80,
82-85. On the other hand, Douglas Adair has shown
Hume's likely influence on Madison's large republic
position; see Douglas G. Adair, "That Politics May
be Reduced to a Science: David Hume, James Madison,
and the Tenth Federalist," The Reinterpretation of
the American Revolution, 1763-1789, (ed.) Jack P.
Greene (New York: Harper and Row, Publishers, 1968),
pp. 487-503. Finally both Tocqueville and Publius
offer a political science whose reliance on modern
commerce and commercial virtue may well have been
influenced by both Montesquieu and Locke; see Mon-
gesquieu, Op. cit., pp. 45-46; Locke, Op. cit., pp.
327-44; and Robert H. Horwitz, "John Locke and the
Preservation of Liberty: A Perennial Problem of Civic
Education," The Moral Foundations of the American
Republic, (ed.) Robert H. Horwitz (Charlottesville:
University Press of Virginia, 1977), pp. 129-56.

[43]Zetterbaum, Op. cit., pp. 56-57, 80. Also see
Aristotle, Nichomachean Ethics, (trans.) Martin Ostwald
(Indianapolis: The Bobbs-Merrill Company, Inc., 1962),
pp. 3-5, 14-15, 29-32.

[44]Democracy, p. 617n Cf. Machiavelli, Op. cit.,
pp. 104-05; and Allan Bloom, (trans.), The Republic
of Plato (New York: Basic Books, Inc., 1968), pp.
153-61, 389-97.

[45]Martin Diamond, "Democracy and The Federalist:
A Reconsideration of The Framers' Intent," Jack P.
Greene (ed.), Op. cit., p. 520.

[46]Alexander Hamilton, John Jay and James Madison,
The Federalist, (ed.) Jacob E. Cooke (New York:
Wesleyan University Press, 1961), pp. 3, 333, 349.

[47]Ibid., pp. 51-52.

[48]Ibid., pp. 351, 353.

[49]See above, notes 33 and 44.

[50]Compare Hamilton's praise for "the love of fame,
the ruling passion of the noblest minds" and Madison's
famous passages on "ambition counteracting ambition"
with Tocqueville's discussion of the new patriotism;
see Jacob E. Cooke, (ed.), Op. cit., pp. 349, 488; and
Democracy, pp. 217, 219.

[51] Zetterbaum, *Op. cit.*, p. 19.

[52] *Democracy*, p. 680.

[53] For specific examples of each problem facing American democracy see *Ibid.*, on race, pp. 291-373; on democractic foreign policy, p. 211; on great men, pp. 237, 617n; on religious and patriotic sentiments, pp. 275-76, 217-18; on administrative centralization and the bureaucratic state, pp. 79, 655-64; on majoritian tyranny, pp. 239-40, 665-69.

[54] *Ibid.*, p. 773.

CHAPTER 5

The Degradation Of The Democratic Dogma: Henry Adams
and the Death of the Democratic Ideal
Robert M. Gill

Turning and turning in the widening gyre
The falcon cannot hear the falconer;
Things fall apart; the centre cannot hold
Mere anarchy is loosed upon the world,
The blood-dimmed tide is loosed, and everywhere
The ceremony of innocence is drowned;
The best lack all conviction, while the worst
Are full of passionate intensity.

--Yeats, "The Second Coming"

Henry Adams was a varied and prolific writer. No
one of his books can be said to represent the essence
of his social and political thinking. The most
political of Adams' writings, The Degradation of the
Democratic Dogma, should be read together with Adams'
studies of history, art and architecture if one is to
understand his political thought. Even The Education
of Henry Adams gives only a fragmentary impression of
his thought if it is read without reference to his
other writings.

Taken together, Adams' writings reveal both the
progressive development of his thought and the underlying continuity which qualifies his writings as
political philosophy more than the works of most other
American political thinkers since The Federalist.
Like the authors of The Federalist, Adams was concerned with both the ends and means of politics and
government. While Adams was well aware of the
political problems of his time, his writings are not
simply a response to specific political problems.
Adams addressed the perennial questions of politics
and of human existence. Moreover, while not all of
Adams' writings are overtly political, they nonetheless
form a whole, one in which he presents a more comprehensive, explicitly stated view of history and the
polity than have most other American writers. Finally,
while the majority of American political thinkers have
tended to view the American polity in isolation, with
some going so far as to assert its uniqueness, Adams,
like the authors of The Federalist, takes a larger
view. In his writings Adams links the problems facing

democracy and constitutional government in America
with those facing the western world and mankind.

I

Henry Adams represents a tradition of western
moral, social and political philosophy which traces
its roots to Plato, but which has found itself increasingly on the defensive in the public life of
modern times. For Adams, the integrity and spiritual
vitality and worth of a society are the key to its
health and survival. Adams believes that the individual
can live well only when he is both contributing to and
drawing from the whole community. Thus, Adams shares
with modern conservatives a belief in the corporate
society, an ordered community from which the individual
members draw their identity and to which they owe their
being.

Throughout his writings Adams presents a vision
of unity said to have achieved its greatest realization
in the early thirteenth century as described in Mont-
Saint Michel and Chartres. Adams looks longingly at
an age in which all individuals possessed a profound
sense of predictability, of certainty, of oneness with
an identity in a larger society which was itself part
of an ordered universe. The age of the Virgin of
Chartres was, Adams notes, an age in which ideals were
shared while sectionalism and partisanship were ab-
horred.

For Adams, as for Plato, this sense of the corporate society can be secure only when it is based on
a goal or ideal, an end or purpose lying beyond the
individual. Only this universal ideal can sustain the
spiritual oneness of society, giving the individuals
within it a sense of duty and obligation, a feeling of
continuity and purpose, which cannot exist without it.

For Adams, in the thirteenth century all was united
in the service of the transcendent ideal. The writings
of St. Thomas Aquinas articulate the yearning to bring
both man and nature into a divine unity with the triune
God. In this age of social and intellectual oneness no
division was perceived to exist between faith and
reason, thought and action, theory and practice, aspirations and day-to-day activities, and public and private
life. Church and state, community and individual, and

government and society were one, united in the service
of the transcendent truth which gave meaning and purpose to all aspects of life. From this purposeful
unity, according to Adams, came the great creativity of
the age,[1] reflected in the cathedral of the Virgin at
Chartres.

In Adams' view, while all of the elements of the
thirteenth century were vigorous, its unity was of
necessity unconscious.[2] Any society which had to
search consciously for the transcendent could never
achieve it. It follows that for Adams, constitutionalism and limited government per se are never central
values of concerns, since in a corporate society
subject to natural law, constitutionalism can be
expected to take care of itself. In such a society
it is effectively limited as to both means and ends
by the natural law which is itself a reflection of the
transendent truth. Adams would argue that constitutionalism cannot be made to work in the absence of
such a vision.

For Adams, the unity of the thirteenth century
was in no sense analagous to the modern totalitarian
governments whose rise he foresaw. In thirteenth
century Europe government, like other institutions,
was effectively limited by acceptance of the transcendent ideal made manifest in the political realm as
natural law. In an age which accepted the concept
without question, natural law effectively limited
government by defining both its proper end and the
means permissible to achieve it.

In Adams' view, government is a reflection of
divine order, a moral agent whose proper end is the
promotion of virtu.[3] The role of the statesman is to
govern in accordance with natural law. The eternal
truths effectively limit both the ends and the means
of government.

For Adams, history since the Renaissance and
Reformation is the story of the slow death of the
notion of transcendent truth as the concept of natural
law--and thus of corporate unity--came to be disregarded or simply ignored in western thought. Adams
believed that with Aquinas reason had begun to predominate over faith in the working of the medieval
mind.[4] From that time forward, unreasoned acceptance
of transcendent truth became increasingly difficult

and ultimately impossible, as the Virgin of Chartres receded into the past as a symbol of unity.

The symbol of the new age would be the dynamo.[5] Unity would give way to multiplicity;[6] the corporate society would be split by the Reformation and the rise of nationalism. Ultimately, church and state would be separated, and arts and science would come to pursue different ends through different means. A gulf would appear between the good of the community and the good of the individual. Theory would be divorced from practice, faith from reason, thought from action, and public from private life. In public life at least, appearance would be the only "reality."

In these changes, Adams sees the collapse of medieval unity. For him the real importance of unity is its foundation, the idea of transcendent truth which is manifested in the political and social realm as natural law. While in the past different ages may have disagreed as to the exact nature of this truth, all shared some notion of its existence. Those individuals who did not were acting alone as isolated individuals apart from the societies in which they lived.

In the modern world, Adams argues, the notion of the existence of a transcendent truth--of a world of absolutes or reality apart from the everyday world of appearances--has all but disappeared from public life.[7] It follows that social unity and the corporate society have also disappeared since they had been the temporal manifestation of transcendence.

II

It is against this philosophical background that Adams examines what he perceives to be the historical failure of American constitutionalism and the American constitutional polity. He begins by noting that the Founders shared Locke's belief in the existence of a natural law.[8] In framing the Constitution, their intention was to confirm these laws by creating a government which would protect men's natural rights.

For Adams, as for the authors of The Federalist, constitutionalism and limited government are not ends in themselves, but are means to man's fulfillment and

106

and development as a citizen within a civic community.
Adams would agree with Chief Justice Marshall that
since the framers of the Constitution had definite
ends and objects in mind, one must distinguish between
the substance and the principles of the Constitution,
and that "judgment," not "will," must be exercised in
interpreting and applying it. Thus, Adams writes, John
Quincy Adams was primarily concerned with making
government "an efficient instrument for collective
administration."[9]

These distinctions are the more important for
Adams since he asserts that only by accepting the
existence of a higher law can government regulate the
competition between the few and the many, between man
and citizen, and between public and private life which
de Tocqueville had perceived in Democracy in America.
Like Justice Story, Adams perceives that only through
reverence for settled law could one preserve the
political understanding of the founding fathers in a
nation with crumbling social barriers and resting on
changeable public opinion.

In this sense, Adams would agree with Reinhold
Niebuhr that the means of the Constitution are no
substitute for its end. Unlike many contemporary
political thinkers, Adams realizes that no government
can rely solely on the equilibrium of opposing forces
to promote social unity where no common end or transcendent truth is perceived.

In his writings, Adams traces what he came to see
as the inevitable failure of American republicanism as
the ideal of the Founders came to be discarded in
American political life. The historical outline of
this development can be found in his History of the
United States during the Administration of Jefferson
and Madison, and his biographies of Albert Gallatin
and John Randolph, and his Degradation of the Democratic Dogma.

Adams notes approvingly that John Quincy Adams
had shared with others of his time an optimism based
on the assumption that ". . . man is a reasoning animal
and that there is a God . . . whom man can intelligently
serve and with whom he can covenant."[10] Moreover, he
continues,

Granting that there is a benign and

omnipotent Creator of the world, who
watches over the fate of men, (John
Quincy) Adams' sincere conviction was
that such a being thinks according to
certain fixed laws, which we call
scientific laws; that these laws may
be discovered by human intelligence
and when discovered may be adapted to
human uses. And if so discovered,
adapted and practiced they must lead
men certainly to an approach to perfection, and more especially to the
elimination of war and slavery.[11]

Henry Adams' conclusions are ironic for an Adams.
Adams asserts that while the Federalists argued that
government must be conducted according to circumstances, the Jeffersonians argued that government must
be conducted in accordance with immutable principles.
In his historical studies, Adams traces the initial
political triumph of the Jeffersonian-Republican view
and its ultimate betrayal by the Jeffersonians themselves.

Adams sees Republicanism as having been a national
ethos rather than merely the political beliefs of a
specific group of Americans. For Adams, the Jeffersonians were political idealists attempting through
concrete programs to realize their national goal.[12]
The Jeffersonians, Adams writes, had a sense of purpose
and a definite end toward which they felt the powers of
government should be used.

Adams concludes that all the experiments failed.
At the very outset, the moral imperative against
slavery had given way to the compromise necessary to
draft the Constitution. The optimist John Quincy
Adams lived to see the strengthening of slavery in the
United States because of the technology of the cotton
gin. In his defeat by Jackson, John Quincy Adams was
forced to acknowledge the eclipse of the corporate
society. It was this last event that was most bitter
for Henry Adams. For him, "Jackson embodied the
principle of public plunder."[13] By contrast, John
Quincy Adams had felt it possible to harness the
"energy" of the age to create a society of plenty,
thus avoiding the dangers which economic competition
poses for the constitutional polity:

108

. . .never since the world was made,
had any community been so favored as
was the American by the gift by
Providence of what was practically,
for them, an unlimited store of
wealth, which, for many generations
would raise them above the pressure
of any competition. . . The only
serious problem for them to solve,
therefore, was how to develop this
gift on a collective and not on a
competitive or selfish basis.

Dominant private interests as
a motor would be fatal . . . Were
a single capitalistic or speculative
class to get control, the interests
of the whole must be sacrificed to
the few and ancient injustice must
prevail.[14]

Adams was aware that no previous society had achieved
this goal:

. . . no code of human origin has
been satisfactory because it has been
the work of the strong and has consciously, for the most part, favored
their interests, at the cost of the
weak. Therefore, none has worked
justice.[15]

Ultimately the American experiment was bound to fail,
as had previous republican governments:

Democracy had failed to justify itself.
Man alone, unaided by a supernatural
power, could not resist the pressure
of self-interest and of greed. He
must yield to the temptation of competition. . . .

And so it has always been. Competition is the law of the flesh, and
in a contest between the flesh and the
spirit, in the end the flesh must prevail. . . .

Above this level of servitude to

"the flesh," or competition, democracy could not rise. On the contrary
democracy then deified competition,
preaching it as the highest destiny
and the true duty of man.[16]

The defeat of John Quincy Adams and the rise of the
spoils system and Jacksonian democracy were "all the
logical result of competition, of applied science,
and of education as stimulating social ambition, and
therefore greed."[17] The lesson is clear:

> . . . an education of conservation
> was contrary to the instinct of greed
> which dominated the democratic mind,
> and impelled it to insist on the
> pillage of the public by the private
> man.
>
> And it was precisely here that
> Mr. Adams fell a victim to that fallacy
> which underlies the whole theory of
> modern democracy--that it is possible
> by education to stimulate the selfish
> instinct of competition, which demands
> that each man should strive to better
> himself at the cost of his neighbor,
> so as to coincide with the moral prin-
> ciple that all should labor for the
> common good.[18]

For Adams, the defeat of what he terms "American
democratic idealism" is even more evident in the story
of Jeffersonian Republicanism. In his History, and in
his biographies of Gallatin and Randolph, Adams traces
the initial triumph of the Jeffersonians, with their
view that government must be conducted by principles,
and the ultimate betrayal of this view by the Jeffersonians themselves. In these works, Adams considers
the process by which the Republicans while in office
came to abandon their principles and at times to betray
openly their public promises. In the Republicans'
failure to meet their obligations and moral duties,
Adams sees the triumph of circumstances and events
over ideals. In Adams' view, necessitarianism had
vanquished idealism. Even Gallatin urged Jefferson,
the self-proclaimed strict constructionist, to ignore
the "constitutional difficulties" of the Louisiana
Purchase. And Randolph, his former idealism corrupted

by the desire to retain power as an end in itself,
turned the doctrine of states' rights into a divisive
theme. In Adams' view, this doctrine had originally
been a reflection of the idea of transcendent truth
and an effective limit to government power within a
larger framework of union.

In the political "victory" of the Republicans,
then, the historian Adams is forced to disagree with
Jefferson as to the basic goodness and perfectibility
of man and as to the "uniqueness" of the American
polity. Political problems remained essentially unchanged, and man's nature remained fixed, in America
as elsewhere.

Ultimately, Adams concludes that men's passions
and vices, and most especially their passion to acquire
or retain political power, can dominate their better
instincts and that a person's, or a society's, political
interests can win out over the real interests of the
citizen or community. In the absence of a transcendent
ideal, power becomes the end of politics and appearance
becomes the only political "reality."

"American democratic idealism" was dead and the
Republicans, once the voice of the American national
ethos, had become nothing more than another political
party. In his acceptance of these conclusions, Adams
finds himself at odds with the dominant intellectual
currents of his age. On the one hand, he remains
fascinated with the concept of determinism and at
times asserts that history and politics represent a
scientific progress governed by scientific laws.[19] On
the one hand, as a moralist Adams concludes that while
man's existence may be rigidly determined, it lacks an
ultimate purpose or end.[20] For Adams, the "forces of
energy" directing modern society, symbolized by the
dynamo, are essentially amoral.[21] As a moralist, then,
Adams is forced to reject the prevailing optimism of
his time.

III

Adams attributes the failure of American constitutionalism and the subsequent "degradation of
democracy" to the abandonment of any notion of underlying principles, that is, of an effective concept of
the transcendent truth manifested in politics as

111

natural law.[22] In Adams' view, this failure had
several results.

First, the vision of the unified, corporate
society governed in accordance with natural law has
been replaced by the actuality of a "polity" characterized by vitality and energy but also by a multiplicity and disunity which must ultimately prove fatal.
In the absence of any common sense of purpose, direction or design, modern society is characterized by a
lack of solidarity. With the eclipse of the notions
of commonality and national good, the civic community
has been replaced by a society of individuals. Individualistic society is characterized by a lack of
effective religious or social sanctions for individual
conduct. No restraints remain to temper the liberty
inherent in democracy. Partisanship and sectionalism
overcome citizenship, and private interests dominate
public principles.

Adams describes the political implications of the
new society as follows:

No man whose mind will not work on its
own independent pivot can escape being
drawn into the whirlpool of party
prejudices. Unless you can find some
theory of the progress of civilization,
which is outside and above all temporary
questions of policy, you must infallibly
think and act under the control of the
man or men whose thought . . . coincides
the most nearly with your prejudices.[23]

In this new society, "success" and "progress" are
measured in exclusively material terms. Men seek power
as an end in itself, with no ultimate purpose in view.
The "good" are demoralized; for the "bad" the end of
power is itself a suffcent motivation. Political
change, while rapid, is directionless; and the political
struggle, while continuous, is aimless:

Democracy is an infinite mass of conflicting minds and of conflicting
interests which, by the persistent
action of such a solvent as the modern
or competitive industrial system, becomes resolved into what is, in substance, a vapor, which loses in collective

intellectual energy in proportion
to the perfection of its expansion.[24]

In the absence of a sense of higher order,
liberalism has become what Leo Strauss terms "the
joyless quest for joy." Given the new society's lack
of a purposeful goal for the future and given its
definition of success and progress in material terms,
its only ideal is the accumulation of wealth.

In keeping with his understanding of the proper
functioning of democratic government, Adams would agree
with Madison that in a capitalist economy, government
should act as an arbitrator, above any class or group,
using its power to regulate the economic power of individuals, classes and groups for the common good. In
contrast to his ideal, the "polity" he describes is
dominated by selfish individualism and greed, and
governed by special interests. Gold tycoons, rail-
roads, trusts and corporation lobbyists manipulate
government in their own supposed interests, resulting
in policies designed to benefit the few. The "system"
is characterized by patronage, corruption and recur-
rent scandals. The result, Adams predicted, will be
bitterness, social strife and general unrest.[25]

Nowhere is Adams' view of the contrast between the
ideal and the reality of American democracy more clearly
stated than in his novel Democracy. Its heroine, a
young widow and social worker named Mrs. Lee, goes to
Washington to study the workings of democracy. There
she is wooed by a gentlemanly Virginian, John Carrington, and a loathesome senator, Silas Ratcliffe.

Ratcliffe, a ruthless industrial politician, is
patterned after Adams' contemporary, Senator James
Blaine. Motivated by greed and the desire for power,
Ratcliffe is ethically blind. Ratcliffe is at pains
to give the appearance of virtue. Clearly, for Ratcliffe's society appearance is "reality," and the ends
justify the means. Thus, Ratcliffe appeals to circumstances and principles like "preserving the union"
and "party survival" to justify his activities. The
irony is that Ratcliffe has no real end in mind. His
only real aim is to increase his own power, a goal
which he tends to assume will inevitably coincide with
the good of the community.

In the end, confronted with the political dis-

113

honesty of Ratcliffe, Mrs. Lee rejects his advances
and returns to social work. Her ideals of democracy
have been crushed by the realities of the American
"polity." No democratic idealism remains. "Democracy" consists merely of selfish cliques competing
for power. Those who, like Carrington, refuse to
engage in partisan activities of the lowest sort
remain politically powerless. Ratcliffe derides George
Washington for having been above partisan politics.
Today, he notes, Washington would be without influence.
Ratcliffe takes for granted that being powerless is
the worst evil that can befall a man.

For Adams, one final result of the eclipse of
democratic idealism involves a change in the function
of the American Constitution. The absence of a well-
defined end for government and the lack of a sense of
common purpose make the concept of an unchanging constitution based on eternal truths sterile. Thus, in
the eyes of many, like Wilson and Bickel, the Constitution becomes a malleable product of history.
"Truths" are seen as relative, limited in their applicability according to time, place and circumstances.

In the absence of a clear notion of the object
which constitutional principles were intended to promote, commitment is increasingly focused on the
principles themselves. In the absence of an overriding purpose, the means become the end. In their
fascination with the form of the Constitution and in
their concern for the mechanics of constitutionalism
and limited government, too many students of the
Constitution fail to consider its substance. The
question of the end of constitutional government--
"Liberty for what?"--is too little asked in an age
which tends to assume that the medium is itself the
message.

In any case, questions of purpose cannot be
effectively answered so long as it is assumed that
truth is relative and so long as the question of
natural law is effectively ignored. A society which
allows--indeed, encourages--men to choose different
notions of right can only be united in the search (or
means), not in the end sought.[26] The result is the
contemporary obsession with the mechanics of constitutionalism, and the lack of consideration of the end
which Hamilton, Madison and others assigned to constitutional government. The view of constitutional

114

government as a government system resting on the equilibrium of contending forces reflects the current concern with the means of constitutionalism at the expense of any substantive consideration of its ends.

For Adams it was no accident that respect for mechanical forms of constitutionalism remained deeply rooted in the American political culture. In his view, reverence for these forms was indicative of a residual belief in constitutionalism and limited government which had survived the destruction of their theoretical underpinnings. As Adams puts it, "That which formed a people, a block, ends by becoming an agglomeration of individuals without cohesion, still held together for a time by its traditions and institutions."[27] Adams makes it clear that devotion to traditions and institutions and to the forms of constitutionalism is not sufficient in itself to restore the constitutional polity.

In spite of the current concern with the forms of constitutionalism, then, ultimately no effective limits can exist to government activity in the absence of recognized natural law. Without some shared belief in transcendent truth, all "truth" is necessarily relative and society itself is competent to define such ideals as "right" and "justice." As Adams notes,

> In short, the social Organism, in
> the recent views of history, is the
> cause, creator, and the end of the
> Man, who exists only as a passing
> representative of it, without rights
> of functions except what it imposes.[28]

Constitutionalism has lost its meaning since democratic, limited government cannot ultimately be secure where right and justice can be defined only as society chooses to define them. The reader will recall that in Adams' view, an effective constitution cannot be based on reason alone. In this sense, it is important to recall that many of the truths of the founding fathers were regarded as self-evident. Adams ascribes many of the problems of his age to the supposed loss of emotion, feeling and instinct in modern times. "Self-evident truths" were based more on these qualities than on reason. This is why the notion of transcendent truth is essential to the constitutional polity.

115

Adams' view of the insufficiency of a concern
with the means of constitutionalism can be seen in
his calls for the abolition of the Senate in 1901.
What Adams perceived to be the structural defects of
the Constitution became important only when a higher
law or transcendent purpose was lacking. Without
these one can no longer trust the mechanical means of
constitutionalism to ensure the end, the creation and
maintenance of a constitutional polity.

IV

It remains to be seen how Adams defines the
individual's position in a democratic "polity" lacking
any transcendent purpose, characterized by disunity,
and dominated by special interests. In Democracy and
elsewhere, Adams acknowledges that in the America he
describes, a private individual is politically powerless unless he allies himself with a political party.
This act implies a denial of the common purpose which
was for Adams an essential part of the constitutional
polity. For Adams an individual's life, both public
and private, is meaningless if it is not spent in the
service of an ideal.

Adams often engaged in political affairs he felt
to be hopeless. As the reformist editor of the North
American Review and as a founder of the anti-Grantist
Liberal Republican Party, Adams fought for what he
considered to be constitutional principles over party
principles. As an author, Adams wrote numerous
articles[29] dealing with such topics as political corruption, federal financing, the manipulation of government by trusts and other special interests, the rise of
monopolies, and the dangers of imperialism and unbridled nationalism and "patriotism."

At other times, Adams seemed to be a detached
observer of America's decline. In his Education,
for instance, he reveals a sense of helplessness, a
sort of fatalistic acceptance of the inevitable.
Adams' revulsion for political power is reflected in
the Education, where he records how his friends changed
on taking office. In his biography of Randolph, he
notes how ideals are subverted in the interest of
power as an end in itself. In the absence of a common
end, Adams notes, power deadens the sympathies and
perception of those who hold it, making them egomaniacs.

Of course, nowhere is Adams' distrust of political power in the modern state more evident than in Democracy, in which Mrs. Lee leaves Washington and the political world and returns to her social work. In 1881, after Garfield's assassination and the revelation of the custom house frauds, Adams renounced politics completely. As things stood, he said, there were only two alternatives for a young man in politics. One could either stay honest, and therefore powerless, or one could betray his ideals for power, "succeeding" at the expense of his self-respect.[30] For Adams, the choice was clear.

Since Adams would agree with Plato that an ordered soul can exist only in an ordered society, in his view no individual can attain felicity in a society in which genuine constitutionalism has broken down. Thus for Adams, in such a society the "best"--those who seek some absolute or transcendent end[31]--are led to confusion, despair and alienation from society. The "worst"--those for whom political power is a sufficient inducement in itself--are left to dominate the political arena.

V

Adams saw the decline of the old sense of order, unity and transcendent purpose reflected in the scientific theories and intellectual climate of his time. In the scientific world, he notes, the "mechanical theory of the universe"[32] has given way to the "conclusion that physical science is more or less chaotic"[33] as the "evolutionists" have given ground to the "degradationists," and the now-aimless "progress" of technology is more rapid than the progress in man's ability to control it.

In the intellectual world, Adams notes, the notion of "degradation" has become commonplace among students of psychology and sociology. Likewise, philosophers assert the failure of society, while "By most artists modern life is assumed as decadence."[34] Adams observes that such notions have invaded the popular culture as well.

> . . . not only in Universities but also
> at every streetcorner of every European
> city, on every half-holiday, hundreds

117

of thousands of men are taught to
believe with delight, that society,
down to the present day, is an
unnatural abortion, sustained by
perverted illusions, and destined
to immediate suicide.[35]

In a world lacking all sense of the absolute,
Adams felt that the sense of unity, confidence and
stability could only continue to decline as such
symptoms became more apparent. Accordingly, he concludes,". . .nothing remains for the historian to
describe or develop except the history of a more or
less mechanical dissolution."[36]

In an age in which democracy was still widely
thought to be the way of the future, Adams foresaw
that the new synthesis most likely to arise in the
twentieth century would be what we call "totalitarianism." He writes of ". . . the phase when men, divided
by their interests and aspirations, but no longer
knowing how to govern themselves, ask to be directed
in their smallest acts, and when the State exercises
its absorbing influence."[37] In a politicized world,
Adams understood that totalitarian government can,
for a time at least, answer many of the human needs
which limited, constitutional government by definition
cannot satisfy. Adams saw clearly that, bolstered by
the inventions of modern technology, the modern and
totalitarian state can provide its citizens with a new
sense of purpose and even of transcendent truth, and
a new identity as part of a unified community. Yet
ultimately, for Adams, totalitarianism would fail to
halt the inevitable and irreversible movement from
"unity" or "people" to "a dust of isolated individuals, . . . a crowd."[38]

As an historian, Adams felt it unlikely that
society would, or even could, return to the vision of
the corporate society governed in accordance with
natural law. Yet for Adams, real constitutional
government is impossible in the absence of such a
vision. For Adams the democratic, constitutional
polity is in an advanced state of decay, without
redemption or virtue.

Adams saw the decline of the old sense of order,
unity and purpose reflected in the scientific theories
and intellectual climate of his time. In our own day,

118

he might point as well to much of contemporary
literature and even to the declining sense of the
transcendent in organized religion. In a society
which is characterized by extreme individualism and
"aggressiveness training," which is increasingly
incapable of distinguishing between means and ends,
and which remains fascinated with the forms of
constitutional government with no concern for its
substance, undoubtedly Adams would find little which
might lead him to reassess his position.

NOTES

[1] Significantly, Adams notes that since art, too, was seen as properly serving an ideal, the artistic creations of the early thirteenth century, unlike those of his own time, were impersonal.

[2] Elizabeth Stevenson, Henry Adams: A Biography (New York: Macmillan, 1956), p. 323.

[3] For a discussion of the connection between virtue and republican government in the context of American republicanism, see The Federalist (No. 55), last paragraph.

[4] Nevertheless, Adams was aware that for Aquinas "the work was still the labor of love which the mind took up from the simple piety of the mystics." J. C. Levenson, The Mind and Art of Henry Adams (Cambridge, Mass.: The Riverside Press, 1957), p. 285.

[5] See Henry Adams, "The Dynamo and the Virgin" (Chapter XXV), The Education of Henry Adams (New York: Modern Library, 1931), pp. 379-390.

[6] For Adams, the importance of this change is evident in the subtitles he chose for Mont-Saint Michel and Chartres ("A Study in Thirteenth Century Unity") and The Education of Henry Adams ("A Study in Twentieth Century Multiplicity"), which he intended to be read as companions.

[7] Indeed if one accepts de Tocqueville's conclusion that in a democracy there can be no private life, it follows that the realm of the transcendent, of the absolute, has disappeared completely in modern times.

[8] While Locke accepted the notion of the existence of a natural law in politics, he nonetheless reinforced the emerging "multiplicity" of his age in teaching that since the nature of the absolute which presumably lies behind the natural law cannot be proved, it follows that no one path to religious truth can be shown to be the correct one. Thus, Locke argued, freedom is essential in religious matters. In this conclusion, Locke unwittingly implies that "truth" is relative, depending on the seeker for its definition. In this sense, while Locke accepted the old idea of natural law,

he actively rejected the notion of an absolute transcendent truth. For Adams, the natural law was but a reflection of this more profound truth. Adams seems to have been unaware of this destruction of the theoretical underpinnings of the concept of natural law, and of its implications from the beginning for the American polity.

[9]Henry Adams, "The Heritage of Henry Adams," in The Degradation of the Democratic Dogma (New York: The Macmillan Co., 1920), p. 78.

[10]Ibid., p. 26.

[11]Ibid., p. 30.

[12]As, for example, the project of constructing the national turnpike, roads and canals, and a national university.

[13]Adams, Op. cit., p. 77.

[14]Ibid., p. 81.

[15]Ibid., p. 80.

[16]Ibid., p. 85.

[17]Ibid., p. 32.

[18]Ibid., pp. 78-79.

[19]Adams acknowledges in the Education that as a young man, as a result of his reading the works of such authors as John Stuart Mill, Herbert Spencer, and Henry Buckle, he became a determinist. Near the end of his career, in "The Tendency of History," part of The Degradation of Democracy, Adams asserted that there is a law of history and that therefore the historical process represents a fundamental unity.

[20]The tension between Adams' moralism and his scientism is evident in much of his writing.

[21]As such, they may be contrasted to the forces responsible for medieval unity, as exemplified by the Virgin of Chartres.

[22]Adams was aware that the failure might well

121

indicate the possibility that society is not grounded in moral law and that if such a law exists, its principles, like the "good constitution," may well be elusive.

[23]Henry Adams, Letter to H. C. Lodge in Worthington C. Ford, ed., Letters of Henry Adams, 1858-1891 (Boston, 1930).

[24]Adams, Op. cit., p. 109.

[25]Adams concluded that the financial crisis of 1891 and 1892 and the "bust" of 1893 signalled the failure of American capitalism, and of government and economics controlled by the trusts and big businesses. Against a background of the mass unemployment and the political, social and labor unrest of the 1890's, after 1893 Adams predicted the total breakdown of the American system.

[26]Despite his concern with the theme of natural law, Locke opened the gate to the "multiplicity" of modern times by his insistence that since no one truth is possible in religious matters, freedom of religion is necessary to the pursuit of truth. Ultimately, in such a system the searchers can only be united in their pursuit of truth (the means), not in their discovery of truth (the end) since, as Niebuhr notes, freedom allows men to choose different notions of right and truth. In this sense, in such a system there can be no underlying unity beyond that of the means, or form, employed.

[27]Henry Adams, "A Letter to American Teachers of History, 1910," in The Degradation. . . ., Op. cit., p. 252.

[28]Ibid., p. 260.

[29]Three of the best-known of these articles are "The New York Gold Conspiracy," detailing Gould and Fisk's attempt to corner the gold market; "The Legal Tender Act," dealing with the federal financing of 1862; and "The Session," an account of the scandal-ridden congressional session of 1869-70.

[30]Margaret J. Brown, Henry Adams and Robinson Jeffers: American Prophets of Decadence, unpub. M. A. thesis presented at Duke University in 1949, p. 24.

[31]Ironically, Adams had concluded that ultimately, such a search is probably futile. Like many modern men, Adams felt the need for some absolute without being able to affirm its existence. After a lifetime of searching for knowledge of the transcendent, Adams could only assert that in the thirteenth century, men believed that the universe represented a kosmos. In concluding that the medieval world-view was doomed to extinction, Adams implied that it was ultimately mistaken.

[32]"The mechanical theory of the universe governed physical science for three hundred years. Directly succeeding the theological scheme of a universe exising as a unity by the will of an infinite and eternal Creator, it affirmed or assumed the unity and indestructability of Force or Energy as a scientific dogma or law. . . " Adams, Op. cit., p. 140.

[33]Ibid., p. 239.

[34]Ibid., p. 246.

[35]Ibid., pp. 246-47.

[36]Ibid., p. 206.

[37]Ibid., p. 253.

[38]Ibid.

123

CHAPTER 6
"Robert Dahl: The Theory of Polyarchal Democracy"
Richard W. Krouse

Robert Dahl's A Preface to Democratic Theory[1]
ranks among the formidable and influential reinterpre-
tations of the theoretical foundations of American
constitutional democracy. This essay will present an
analysis and critique of Dahl's democratic theory,
with particular emphasis upon that work. It will
focus upon Dahl's interpretation of two major traditions of "classical" democratic theory, the
"Madisonian" and the populist," and his proposed
modernization and revision of these earlier approaches,
the theory of polyarchal democracy.

The argument will proceed in three steps. First,
Dahl's understanding of Madisonian and populist
democracy, which will be presented as the two major
theoretical traditions in the shaping of the American
democratic polity, will be considered and analyzed
critically. Here attention will be focused in particular upon Dahl's critique of Madisonian republicanism
and, more generally, upon his critique of American
constitutionalism. Second, Dahl's own theory of polyarchy, as developed in the Preface, will be considered
and criticized. Here particular attention will be paid
to the relationship between Dahl's own treatment of the
American polyarchy and earlier interpretations of
democracy in America, more particularly the Madisonian.
Specifically, it will be argued that, despite his own
claim to have broken radically with prior versions of
"classical" democratic theory, Dahl's own original
conception of polyarchy, with its severely diminished
emphasis upon political equality and popular sovereignty, is in important respects fundamentally
continuous with the Madisonian version of classical
democratic theory. Third, recent revisions in Dahl's
theory of polyarchal democracy, as outlined in his
After the Revolution? and elsewhere, will be considered
briefly. Here it will be argued that just as his
earlier concept of polyarchy bears a family resemblance
to the Madisonian understanding of republican rule, so
likewise can the leftward turn in Dahl's more recent
democratic theory--his commitment to a more communal
and participatory organization of politics and society,
and his increasingly explicit socialist aspirations--
be seen as a modernization and adaptation to the
realities of advanced industrial society of earlier,
more participatory understandings of American popular

democracy.

In the Preface, Dahl identifies two major ways of
theorizing about democracy, which he labels "the method
of maximization" and "the descriptive method" respec-
tively. The method of maximization is to specify a set
of goals to be maximized and then to conceive of
democracy in terms of the structures and processes
necessary and sufficient to maximize those goals. The
descriptive method, by contrast, is to consider as a
single class of phenomena all those political systems
and social organizations called democratic in everyday political language and then to discover, first,
the distinguishing characteristics that they share in
common and, second, the necessary and sufficient
conditions for politics and social organizations
possessing those characteristics "Madisonian" and
"populist" democracy are both seen by Dahl as instances
of his method of maximization. In Madisonian democracy, the goal to be maximized is a "non-tyrannical
republic." In populist democracy, the goals to be
maximized are political equality and popular sovereignty. The Preface begins with an effort to identify
the central deficiencies--logical, empirical, and
ethical--of these two maximizing approaches.

Dahl begins with an analytical reconstruction and
critique of "Madisonian democracy."[2] According to
Dahl, Madisonian theory can best be understood, in
summary form, as an effort to reconcile majority rule
with minority rights through the medium of constitutionalism and the separation of powers. The two
central hypotheses of the theory are as follows:
"Hypothesis 1: If unrestrained by external checks, any
given individual or individuals will tyrannize over
others" (P., p. 6).[3] And: "Hypothesis 2: The accumulation of all powers, legislative, executive, and
judiciary, in the same hands implies the elimination
of external checks" and therefore tyranny (P., p.6).

Hypothesis 1 is Dahl's version of the Madisonian
problem of faction (i.e. "a number of citizens, whether
amounting to a majority or minority of the whole, who
are united and actuated by some common impulse of
passion or of interest, adverse to the rights of other
citizens, or to the permanent and aggregate interests

of the community").[4] Because it is for Madison neither
desirable nor possible to remove the causes of faction,
which are sown in the nature of man, its mischiefs can
be cured only by controlling its effects, that is, by
imposing external checks upon man's ineliminable propensity to tyrannize. If unrestrained by such checks,
a minority of individuals will tryannize over a
majority of individuals (Hypothesis 3; P., p. 7); and
so, conversely will a majority of individuals tryannize
over a minority of individuals (Hypothesis 4; P., p. 7).

Popular government is Madison's cure for the
problem of minority faction. When a will in the
community independent of the majority rules, it will
invariably sacrifice either private rights or the
public interest, or both, to its own selfish, sectional interest. In a popular regime, by contrast,
minority factions can be controlled by the operation
of the "republican principle" of majority rule
(Hypothesis 8; P., p. 27). No equivalent protection
exists in such a regime, however, against the violation
of private rights or the public good, or both, by
selfish and sectional majority factions. Hence "To
secure the public good against the danger of such a
faction, and at the same time to preserve the spirit
and form of popular government, is . . . the great
object to which our inquiries are directed."[5] Popular
government, that is to say, is a necessary but not a
sufficient condition of nontyrannical (or nonfactional)
rule. Thus, for Dahl, "the Madisonian axiom": "The
goal that ought to be attained, at least in the United
States is a non tyrannical republic" (P., p. 10).

"Internal" (i.e. moral or religious) restraints
upon factions being, again, unavailable (or at least
insufficient), the effects of majority faction must be
controlled through external restraints. But these
external controls can in turn take at least two forms:
1) social checks and balances, and 2) prescribed constitutional checks and balances (P., p. 36). For
Madison, according to Dahl, both are necessary conditions of a non-tyrannical republic:

> Hypothesis 5: At least two conditions
> are necessary for the existence of a
> non-tyrannical republic:
> First Condition: The accumulation of
> all powers, legislative, executive,
> and judiciary, in the same hands,

126

whether of one, a few, or many, and
whether hereditary, self-appointed,
or elective, must be avoided.
Second Condition: Factions must be
so controlled that they do not succeed in acting adversely to the
rights of other citizens or to the
permanent and aggregate interests
of the community. (P., p. 11)

Dahl accurately argues that for Madison Condition
Two can be met only in a large republic. Direct
democracy, necessarily restricted in its geographical
scope, inevitably succumbs to the tyranny of homogeneous and cohesive majority factions. Non-tryannical
popular government must therefore, be a representative
republic rather than a direct democracy. For representation, in addition to increasing the likelihood of
wise and virtuous leadership, permits the creation of
an extended republic, in which majorities will be
heterogeneous rather than homogeneous. Or, as Dahl
paraphrases Madison's familiar argument, "To the extent
that the electorate is numerous, extended, and diverse
in interests, a majority faction is less likely to
exist and, if it does, it is less likely to act as a
unity" (Hypotheses 9 and 10: PP., pp. 16-17). A non-
tyrannical republic, of necessity an extended republic,
will thus institutionalize social checks and balances
within the majority.

Having to this degree accurately reconstructed
the logic of Madison's theory, Dahl's argument elsewhere in the Preface takes an entirely inexplicable
turn. He accuses Madison, in his alleged preoccupation
with constitutional checks and balances, of having
neglected if not altogether overlooked the vital importance of social checks and balances. Madison
"underestimates the importance of the inherent social
checks and balances existing in every pluralistic
society" (P., p. 22); "his primary concern was with
prescribed constitutional controls rather than with
the operating social controls, with constitutional
checks and balances rather than with social checks and
balances" (P., p. 82). But this is simply wrong, and
for precisely the reasons adduced elsewhere in Dahl's
own exposition. It is clear from both The Federalist
and from Madison's other writings upon the subject
that his primary solution to the problem of majority
faction lies, not in constitutional forms, but in the

social pluralism of an extended republic. Constitutional checks and balances are not discussed in
Federalist 10; and compared to the social checks and
balances secured through representative republicanism,
he writes elsewhere, the intrinsically desirable
effects of (trustee) representation are but a mere
"auxiliary desideratum."[6] Likewise in Federalist 51,
his discussion of constitutional checks and balances
is complemented, when he turns most explicitly to
the problem of majority tyranny, by a concise restatement of the theory of the extended republic. And no
other conclusion can be drawn from Madison's other
speeches, writings, and letters on the subject.[7] One
need not agree, as has been recently maintained, that
Madison himself sought to curb majority tyranny
exclusively through social checks and balances to
recognize that his cure for the ills of majority
faction relies primarily upon this device.[8] Here,
Dahl's argument is not merely wrong but, because he
himself recognizes as much elsewhere in the Preface,
plainly inconsistent.

Dahl's criticisms of Madison on this point form
part of a larger attack upon Madison's theory of the
constitutional separation of powers and, beyond this,
upon the doctrine of constitutionalism as such. In
criticizing Madisonian constitutionalism, Dahl seeks
to establish the thesis that "the first and crucial
variables to which political scientists must direct
their attention are social and not constitutional"
(P., p. 83); indeed, that compared to these social
variables the influence of the constitutional variable
is in fact "trivial" (P., p. 135). And by "constitutional" Dahl does not simply mean written constitutions strictly speaking but, much more broadly,
"determinants of governmental decisions. . .consisting
of prescribed rules influencing the legitimate,
distribution, types, and methods of control among
government officials. The rules may be prescribed by
a variety of authorities accepted as legitimate among
officials: the written constitution, if there is one;
decisions of a tribunal accepted as authoritative on
constitutional interpretation; respected commentaries
and the like" (P., p. 135). His claim is, therefore,
a strong one: constitutional factors, thus defined,
are trivial if not altogether irrelevant features of
political life.

Dahl's heaviest critical fire, in this context,

is directed against his Madisonian Hypothesis 2 ("The accumulation of all powers, legislative, executive and judiciary, in the same hands implies the elimination of external checks" and therefore tyranny). Such an accumulation of all power in the same hands must, for Madison, be avoided in any non-tyrannical republic (Hypothesis 5, First Condition); that is, a constitutional separation of powers (in some as yet unspecified sense) is a necessary condition of a non-tyrannical republic. But, argues Dahl, "if by 'power' we mean constitutionally prescribed authority," then the first condition is "demonstrably false:" the example of parliamentary systems such as Great Britain readily prove that a constitutional separation of powers is not a necessary condition of a non-tyrannical republic (P., pp. 12-13).[9] Madison (he continues) evidently had in mind something broader, namely, the concept of "reciprocal controls" among officials. However, the Madisonian argument "does not show, and I think cannot be used to show, that reciprocal control among leaders, sufficient to prevent tyranny, requires constitutionally prescribed separation of powers, as in the American Constitution" (P., pp. 21-22). Social checks and balances are clearly a necessary condition of a non-tyrannical republic; constitutional checks and balances, in the sense prescribed by Madison, clearly are not:

> Without these social checks and balances, it is doubtful that the intragovernmental checks on officials would in fact operate to prevent tyranny; with them, it is doubtful that all of the intragovernmental checks of the Madisonian system as it operates in the United States are necessary to prevent tyranny. (P., p. 22)

Now Madison, again, clearly agrees with Dahl that social checks and balances are necessary to non-tyrannical popular government: in a direct democracy, or even a small republic, constitutional forms alone would often not suffice to deter a tyrannical majority faction; hence the social pluralism of an extended republic is an indispensable requirement. But neither is this device alone (as Dahl sometimes comes close to implying) sufficient. Tyranny must, for Madison, be prevented on two fronts: not merely the tyranny of

129

majority factions, but also the independent tyranny
of governmental officials. Majority tyranny is
Madison's first and foremost, indeed exclusive,
concern in his theory of the extended republic. But
he is equally concerned with this second, independent
form of government tyranny--to which his first solution does not speak. Men not being angels, we must
enable the government to control the governed; angels
not governing men, we must oblige it to control itself.
Dependence upon the people is the primary control in a
republic, but (to quote Dahl's) "Hypothesis 6: Frequent
popular elections will not provide an external check
sufficient to prevent tyranny" (P., p. 13). Experience
has taught the necessity of "auxiliary precautions" in
the form of constitutional restraints upon power--
primarily to restrain the independent tyranny of
government officials, secondarily to bolster the
social checks and balances of an extended republic
in restraining majority tyranny.[10]

But what is the precise character of these constitutional restraints? Here Dahl wins an easy victory
by subtly, but significantly, altering the emphasis of
Madison's argument. He presents Madison as being
primarily concerned with maintaining an antiseptically
rigid constitutional separation of powers between
government departments. But here he is attacking
Madison for precisely the narrow, formal-legal constitutionalism that the latter himself rejected.[11] In
Federalist 47-51, Madison's primary purpose is to
contest the position that a pure and perfect constitutional separation of powers, secured through "parchment barriers" alone, would be sufficient to prevent
the undue concentration of all power in the same hands.
Against the view that a non-tyrannical republic requires a complete constitutional separation of powers,
Madison maintains that preventing the concentration of
all power in the same hands does not merely permit but
in fact positively requires a partial fusion of
constitutional functions. Only through such a partial
fusion of prescribed constitutional functions can we
securely guarantee intragovernmental checks and
balances and, therewith, the "reciprocal controls"
that flow from the countervailing ambitions of competing government officials; and only thus, Madison
contends, can we prevent tyrannical concentrations of
political power. Madison's primary concern--explicitly
formulated in Dahl's own statement of Madisonian
democracy (Hypothesis 2; Hypothesis 5, First Condition)

130

--is clearly not with preserving a pure and perfect
separation of constitutional powers but rather,
through the partial violation of that dictum, with
preventing a pure and perfect concentration of "all
powers, legislative, executive and judiciary, in the
same hands, whether of one, few, or many" (my
emphasis).

Nor is it fair to imply that Madison saw constitutional separation of powers or checks and balances
in their specifically American form--"as in the
American constitution"--as essential to secure this
objective. In fact, Madison himself (in Federalist
47) cites Montesquieu's apotheosis of the eighteenth
century English Constitution to support his stated
view that a partial fusion of constitutional functions,
insuring some intragovernmental checking and balancing,
is necessary to prevent still more complete, and thus
fully tyrannical, concentrations of political power.
The point is not, nor did Madison maintain it to be,
whether "all of the intragovernmental checks of the
Madisonian system as it operates in the United States
are necessary to prevent tyranny;" that is clearly a
straw man. It is rather whether some intragovernmental
separation of powers, insuring intragovernmental checks
and balances in some form--whether as in the American
or the English Constitutions, either in the eighteenth
or the twentieth centuries--must be seen as necessary
to prevent the tyrannical concentration of all political power in the same hands. The essential message
of Madisonian constitutionalism is that some such
restraints, in some form, are indeed necessary.

Although Dahl is critical of Madison, he has not
successfully refuted his constitutional argument.
Dahl's claim is that "constitutional" factors, taken
in the broader sense in which he himself defines the
term, are of "trivial" significance and therefore
inessential to the prevention of tyranny. He begins
by establishing, through his use of the British
example, that a strict separation of government powers,
formerly prescribed in a written constitution, is not
a necessary condition of a non-tyrannical republic.
However, when he uses the term "constitution" in his
own, somewhat broader and more functional sense,
focusing upon the presence or absence of rule prescribed intragovernmental restraints or reciprocal
controls, Dahl is forced to conclude that every polyarchal political system--including, therefore, the

British--is marked by both separation of powers and checks and balances (P., pp. 136-37). Dahl bravely concludes this to mean "that the range of the constitutional variable is even more limited than might be thought at first glance" (P., pp. 135-36), but surely his own evidence does not preclude exactly the opposite inference. For having deprived himself of the British counterexample, he is clearly no longer in any position to conclude definitively that constitutional separation of powers and checks and balances (in anything but their strictest sense) are not a necessary condition of a non-tyrannical republic.

Dahl's refutation of Madisonian constitutionalism rests upon a trick of definition. Dahl purports to establish the strong claim that constitutional forms, broadly conceived, are not necessary to the prevention of tyranny. He in fact succeeds in establishing only the weak, indeed fundamentally trivial, claim(s) that constitutional separation of powers and checks and balances in their strictest and most formal sense, or (alternatively) their specifically American sense, are not necessary to non-tyranny. Then, through a tacit conflation of "constitution" in its narrower and broader senses, he claims a major victory. But what Dahl manifestly does not establish--and must in order to refute Madison--is his own stronger claim: i.e. that in the broader sense in which he himself uses the term, no constitutionally (or rule-) prescribed separation of powers or checks and balances are necessary to prevent the tyrannical concentration of all power in the same hands. Since Dahl can point to no example of a non-tyrannical republic without some such prescribed intragovernmental restraints, insuring reciprocal controls upon leaders in some form, his claim that Madison's First Condition is demonstrably false, though it might still be true (depending, inter alia, upon Hypothesis 6), is at a minimum not demonstrated.

From Dahl's perspective, the cumulative effect of the various social, constitutional, and political checks and balances prescribed by the doctrine of "Madisonian democracy" has been to build severe constraints upon democracy into the American polity. Though he purports to view the influence of the constitutional variable as "trivial," Dahl sometimes sees these same constitutional factors as having been all-too-successful in a fundamentally antimajoritarian direction.[12] Likewise,

though he views the notion of majority rule (and therefore, a fortiori, majority tyranny) as "mostly a myth"
(P., p. 133), he is sometimes highly critical of specific American political institutions, such as the Supreme Court, for having frustrated the will of intense
legislative (but also, in some instances at least,
popular) majorities (P., pp. 105-112). In sum, Madisonian democracy for Dahl consistently sacrifices majority rule on the altar of minority rights--more con-
cretely, the property rights of privileged minorities.
In the interest of maximizing this substantive goal,
Madison "goes about as far as it is possible to go while
still remaining within the rubric of democracy" (P., p.32).

We may now turn, more briefly, to Dahl's version
of "populist democracy." The twin goals to be maximized by populist democracy are, again, popular
sovereignty and political equality. Dahl's Condition
of Popular Sovereignty requires that, whenever policy
choices are perceived to exist, "the alternative most
preferred by members" is chosen (P., p. 37). His
Condition of Political Equality requires that "the
preference of each member is assigned an equal value"
(P., p. 37). And the only decision-making rule
compatible with popular sovereignty and political
equality, Dahl argues, is the majority principle:
i.e. The Rule: . . .in choosing among alternatives,
the alternative preferred by the greater number is
selected" (P., pp. 37-38).

Dahl cites a number of technical, ethical, and
empirical objections to populistic democracy. The
technical and empirical objections need not detain us
further here.[13] Something further does, however,
need to be said about Dahl's ethical objections to
populist democracy. Dahl often chooses to rest his
arguments upon a thoroughgoing logical positivism in
philosophy and, likewise, a radical operationalism
in methodology.[14] In keeping with this emphasis, he
eschews any appeal to "transcendental" (or naturalis-
tic) proofs of the desirability of political equality
and popular sovereignty and turns instead to (ethically
subjective) proofs of an "instrumentalist" character.
Ultimately, for Dahl, the most compelling among such
"instrumental" justifications for democracy is the one
cast in terms of its consequences for goal-attainment--
goals being defined in terms of the antecedently-given
wants or subjective-determined preferences of
(abstract) individuals (P., pp. 46-51). One valid

ethical objection to the theory of populist democracy, in Dahl's view, is that it postulates only two such goals to be attained--political equality and popular sovereignty. Yet, clearly, only a "fanatic" (P., p. 50) would wish to maximize these goals at the expense of all others: "Political equality and popular sovereignty are not absolute goals; we must ask ourselves how much leisure, privacy, consensus, stability, income, security, progress, status, and probably many other goals we are prepared to forego for an additional increment of political equality" (P., p. 51). Political equality and popular sovereignty, will optimally be extended up to, but only up to, the point where they maximize overall or aggregate satisfaction of the antecedently-given goals, wants, or preferences of individuals.

The difficulty with this argument is that it offers us a thin and radically impoverished account of the ethical case for political equality and popular sovereignty. In contrast to "Madisonian democracy," which is grounded in a recognizable (albeit sometimes caricatured) theory, Dahl's image of "populist democracy" is a pure ideal-type or analytical construct. Yet if we look to actual theories of democracy more or less resembling this ideal type in their emphasis upon political equality and popular sovereignty, we find important justificatory dimensions lost in the process of translation. Perhaps the closest approximations to this image in the annals of American political thought can be found in the theory of Jeffersonian democracy, particularly as articulated in some of Jefferson's own later letters, and in the practice of American popular democracy as described, and in part prescribed, in Tocqueville's Democracy in America. In both instances we find, as in Dahl's account of populist democracy, a strong descriptive and prescriptive emphasis upon both political equality (as measured by historical circumstance) and popular sovereignty, or democratization of the institutions of government.[15] But whereas for Dahl popular sovereignty is implicitly conceived entirely in terms of the responsiveness of government to the predetermined preferences of individuals ("most preferred," "preferred by most"), which could in principle be enforced exclusively through the accountability mechanisms of representative government (or even, hypothetically, through benevolent despotism), in Jefferson and Tocqueville we find an account of popular sovereignty

134

cast heavily in terms of citizenship--democratic man
not as a passive consumer of the policy outputs of
government, but as an active "participator in the
government of affairs."[16] In both instances, that is,
popular sovereignty is conceived not merely or even
primarily in terms of indirect popular control over
representative institutions but also, and more
fundamentally, in terms of direct popular participation in democratic institutions--for Jefferson, in
the vision of a representative democracy built upon
the foundation of his participatory ward-republics;
for Tocqueville, in his account of the rich local and
associational democracy of America's vibrantly participatory political culture. And in both instances,
the end or purpose of these participatory institutions
is not simply to maximize the responsiveness of
government to the prepolitical preferences of private
individuals, but to educate the content of those
preferences: to shape and sustain the citizenship and
civic virtue (i.e. "internal restraints") essential,
both believed, to the spirit of republican government;
and--implicitly for Jefferson, explicitly for Tocque-
ville--to improve the moral and intellectual qualities
of citizens as social and political agents.

     This is clearly a dimension that disappears
entirely from Dahl's one-dimensional account. Con-
ceiving as he does in the Preface of political
institutions purely as want--satisfaction devices,
a truly "strong" theory of democracy--"populist"
democracy as participatory democracy--is altogether
outside his original field of theoretical vision.
We shall see this lacuna plague his own theory of
polyarchy in both its earlier and later versions.

                          II

     Having exposed the deficiencies of both Madi-
sonian and populist democracy, Dahl then seeks to
substitute for these older, classical alternatives a
more logically coherent and empirically realistic
theory of popular rule. He labels his revised, modern
version the theory of polyarchal democracy.

     Dahl begins his quest for a new democratic theory
by employing his method of maximization. He extracts
from populistic theory three possible characteristics
that might be made operationally useful: 1) popular

sovereignty, 2) political equality, and 3) majority rule. He then proceeds to specify eight observable conditions that would be necessary and sufficient to maximize attainment of The Rule and, therewith, political equality and popular sovereignty.

During the voting period:
1. Every member of the organization performs the acts we assume to constitute an expression of preference among the schedule alternatives, e.g., voting.
2. In tabulating these expressions (votes), the weight assigned to the choice of each individual is identical.
3. The alternative with the greatest number of votes is declared the winning choice.

During the prevoting period:
4. Any member who perceives a set of alternatives, at least one of which he regards as preferable to any of the alternatives presently scheduled, can insert his preferred alternative(s) among those scheduled for voting.
5. All individuals possess identical information about the alternatives.

During the postvoting period:
6. Alternatives (leaders or policies) with the greatest number of votes displace any alternatives (leaders or policies) with fewer votes.
7. The orders of elected officials are executed.

During the interelection stage:
8.1 Either all interelection decisions are subordinate or executory to those arrived at during the election stage, i.e. elections are in a sense controlling
8.2 or new decisions during the interelection period are governed by the preceding seven conditions, operating, however, under rather different institutional circumstances
8.3 or both. (P., p. 84)

136

Taken together, these eight conditions provide us with an operational definition of democracy.

Dahl is quick to add, however, that full or maximum realization of these eight conditions is a specifically utopian objective--"unattained" and "quite probably unattainable" (P., p. 75) in the real world.[17] But this is not, for Dahl, cause for following Mosca and others in denying the possibility of democratic rule. What is required instead is a shift from the maximizing to the descriptive mode. We must reinterpret these eight conditions as ends of eight scales or continua against which real-world achievement can be measured. Having done so, we may then establish some arbitrary but not meaningless threshold of minimum democratic achievement. Polities and social organizations which fall above this line, or in which the eight conditions exist to "a relatively high degree," can then be labeled "polyarchies." The question then becomes: "what are the necessary and sufficient conditions in the real world for the existence of these eight conditions, to at least the minimum degree we have agreed to call 'polyarchy'" (P., p. 75)?

The answer to this question can be found in Dahl's discussion of the "American hybrid" system of government. There we find the features that most saliently differentiate polyarchy from both dictatorship, on the one hand, and democracy (in the traditional understanding) on the other. Here Dahl argues that populist democrats who unlike Madison, stress the decisive importance of the electoral process to democracy are essentially correct, though for the wrong reasons. For while elections in fact tell us very little about a reified Majority Will, they are nevertheless critical techniques for maximizing political equality and popular sovereignty. Elections, combined with continuous political competition between individuals or parties or both, are "the two fundamental methods of social control which, operating together, make governmental leaders so responsive to non-leaders that the distinction between democracy (i.e. polyarchy) and dictatorship still makes sense" (P., pp. 131-32). Neither leads to majority government or rule by the people in anything like the literal sense, but taken together they do "increase the size, number, and variety of minorities whose preferences must be taken into account by leaders" (P., p. 132). And it is here that we find the key contrast between polyarchal

137

democracy and dictatorship. The difference "is not discoverable in the clear-cut distinction between government by a majority and government by a minority. The distinction comes much closer to being one between government by a majority and government by minorities" (P., p. 133). Polyarchy is neither pure majority rule, which is impossible, nor unified minority rule, which is undesirable; it is an open, competitive, and pluralistic system of "minorities rule" (P., p. 128).

Popular participation plays only a peripheral role in the theory of polyarchal democracy. Earlier populist theories, Dahl claims, were "demonstrably invalid" in their emphasis on maximum citizen participation. Polyarchy--"what we call democracy"--is a political process in which government responsiveness to the preferences of citizens is insured less by extensive mass participation than by ceaseless bargaining and negotiation between organized minorities "operating within the context of an apathetic majority."[18] It is, in other words, a variant--the competitive and electoral variant--of Mosca's elite principle.

And, as such, Dahl's theory of polyarchy has in recent years been sharply criticized as an "elite theory of democracy." Critics charge that Dahl has implicitly substituted polyarchy ("what we call democracy") for a stronger vision of broader and deeper democracy as his optimum political ideal. He has, that is, covertly transferred to existing "polyarchies," despite their patently oligarchical elements, the full commendatory force hitherto attaching to the phrase "democracy," thereby altogether supplanting the latter, taken in its stronger and deeper sense, as a constructive or reconstructive political ideal. The result, it is charged, is a deeply complacent and conservative political creed--a thinly veiled apology for the elite domination and mass apathy that suffuse the politics of Western liberal-democracies.[19]

Dahl has strenuously resisted these criticisms. He has since insisted that the Preface does distinguish clearly between a democracy--now polyarchy--as an actual class of real world political systems and social organizations and a democracy taken in a stronger and more literal sense, as a political ideal. The book, he claims, contains two separate and distinct theoretical modes: a normative theory of

138

democracy (following his method of maximization) and an empirical theory of polyarchy (following his descriptive method). And he has complained that his critics have ignored the explicitly normative component of the theory while treating the descriptive and explanatory component as if it were normative and prescriptive.[20]

Here, however, the critics are correct. A careful re-reading of the Preface suggests, against Dahl's more recent protestations, that the explicitly normative component to which he has referred, allegedly prescribing fuller approximation to the utopian standard of pure and perfect political equality and popular sovereignty, is in fact nugatory; and that the descriptive and explanatory component is normative and prescriptive in the sense that it contains a built-in value slope.[21] Quite simply, Dahl's empirical theory of polyarchy has become his normative theory of democracy. For the Preface presents the alternatives in such a way that we are virtually required to accept polyarchy as the optimum, and by default ideal, political system.

In an instructive and telling parallel, Dahl at one point in another essay likens his polyarchal regime to polity in the Aristotelian sense, both being mixtures of democracy and oligarchy. He then poses the following dilemma:

> For those who do not want to yield
> up the marvelous Utopian objective
> that animated the Declaration of In-
> dependence and the Gettysburg address,
> Aristotle's words will scarcely give
> complete comfort. Unless we abandon
> the ideal of political equality, and
> with it the American Dream, I do not
> see how we can live comfortably with
> the inequalities of power and political
> resources that we find around us. Can
> anyone who holds democratic beliefs
> remain satisfied with the American
> political system simply because it
> is not an oligarchy?[22]

Yet in the end, Dahl's Preface strongly implies that we should, indeed, refrain from calling for substantially fuller democratization of polyarchy because

it is already, not unlike Aristotle's polity, the best
available alternative.

The truly salient choice, we have already seen
Dahl imply, is between dictatorship and polyarchal
democracy, between monolithic and pluralistic forms of
elite rule, between minority and minorities rule.
Thus a third conceivable alternative, significantly
fuller democratization of existing polyarchies, is
thus by this presentation of the available alternatives
implicitly ruled out as impossible, or possible only
at unacceptable costs in terms of other values. The
question then becomes: why would it be necessary to
rule out fuller democracy as a viable and desirable
alternative in this way?

To answer this question, we must consider two of
the necessary social preconditions of polyarchal rule.
Among other things, polyarchy requies a) concensus on
the eight conditions, reforumlated as norms of rules
of the game, and b) political activity. Unfortunately,
above a certain threshold these two goals may be in
tension. A minimum level of political activity or
citizen participation is one necessary condition of
polyarchy. But we must, Dahl argues, face the dis-
concerting possibility that increases in mass participation above and beyond this level will have the effect
of eroding consensus on the norms, thereby counter-
productively undermining the stability of polyarchy
and threatening its replacement with totalitarian
oligarchy. If true, this effectively reduces the
available alternatives from three--oligarchy, polyarchy, and more complete democracy--to two, oligarchy
and polyarchy.

But why, in turn, would increased participation
destabilize polyarchy in this way? Because--and here
Dahl pursues a Madisonian intimation--of the illiberal
and anti-democratic attitudes of the ordinary citizen:

> Current evidence suggests that in
> the United States the lower one's
> socioeconomic class, the more author-
> itarian one's pre-dispositions and
> the less active one is likely to be.
> Thus if an increase in political
> activity brings the authoritarian-
> minded into the political arena,
> consensus on the basic norms among

the politically active certainly
must be declining. To the extent
that consensus declines, we would
expect. . . that, after some lag,
polyarchy would also decline.
(P., p. 89)

The implication is clear: we must somehow protect
polyarchy from the demos.

The solution, put forward most explicitly in
Dahl's Who Governs?, is to be found in the theory and
practice of elite consensus. Empirical evidence, he
argues there, suggests that support for the norms of
polyarchy is strongest among the minority of political
activists in society, just as it is weakest among the
ignorant and inactive majority. Democratic values
survive because their numerically outnumbered sup-
porters are actively united in intense opposition to
the authoritarian impulses, fortunately less intense,
of the inert and inarticulate many, who in turn
normally defer to this elite in the exercise of
political judgment. Because they are politically
apathetic, the authoritarian-minded accept rules and
procedures that they do not (except perhaps in the
abstract) support.[23] Thus, to put the matter bluntly,
consensus is best preserved by holding mass political
activity to a minimum. Polyarchy is a process of
elite competition within a framework of elite consensus
against a backdrop of mass apathy--enough competition
to insure system responsiveness, enough consensus to
insure system maintenance. A significant increase in
mass political activity could easily upset this finely-
tuned mechanism.

But why rely upon elite consensus combined with
mass passivity to preserve the stability of polyarchy?
Why not instead seek increased political activity
coupled with enhanced political education, flowing in
part from the experience of this activity? The
question becomes particularly germane when we recognize
that "social training in the norms" is already one of
the conditions of polyarchy. If the authoritarian
predispositions are genuine, the strategy is risky;
but if the commitment to fuller political equality
and popular sovereignty is also genuine, it must be
considered. Yet in his early work Dahl clearly rejects
this approach. He does so in part for the reason just
suggested, fear of its potentially authoritarian

141

consequences. However, there is another factor at
work as well. Dahl attaches little or no positive
value to participation above and beyond the minimum
level necessary to sustain polyarchy not merely
because he sees it as dangerous, but also because
his earlier work rests upon a moral psychology that
conceives of human beings as essentially apolitical
creatures.

Dahl is admirably explicit on this point. The
"ancient myth about the concern of citizens with the
life of the polis" (W. G., p. 281) notwithstanding,
most individuals most of the time find it natural
to seek their primary gratifications in the activities
of private life. Political activity occupies only a
peripheral status in the life of civic man (homo
civicus); it becomes salient only when the actions or
inactions of government impinge upon his primary, or
private, goals. "Homo civicus"--and it could not,
Dahl implies, possibly be otherwise--"is not by nature
a political animal" (W. G., p. 225).

This theory of human nature in politics, which we
have already seen surface in Dahl's discussion of
populist democracy, affects his statement of the
democratic ideal. Democracy and polyarchy both reside
on a one dimensional, want- regarding spectrum. Even
at its utopian outer reaches, pure and perfect political equality and popular sovereignty are seen
exclusively as instrumental means of insuring the
responsiveness of government to the policy preferences
of individuals.[24] Participation in popular sovereignty
is likewise purely an instrument for enforcing this
accountability. The ancient or classical vision of
participation in a common life as a civilizing process
of moral and rational education--implicit or explicit,
I have argued, in the earlier visions of Jefferson and
Tocqueville--is quite simply read off the theoretical
map.

The consequence of this is clear. Participation
is to be evaluated according to criteria of economic
rationality. In principle, the minimum participatory
input sufficient to secure maximum policy output is
optimum. In practice, polyarchy is already a
reasonably stable and efficient want-satisfaction
device. Therefore the marginal utility of increments
in participation above and beyond the minimum threshold
differentiating polyarchy from oligarchy drop rapidly,

for they must be traded-off against the privatistic values of homo civicus--i.e. "leisure, privacy, consensus, stability, income, security, status."

Dahl's Preface to Democratic Theory thus rests upon a political sociology and moral psychology that tacitly commends polyarchy as the best available alternative. Now, again, Dahl has since protested that he is not now, and has never been, an apologist for elite domination or mass apathy, arguing that his eight conditions can and should be read as a call for fuller democratization. But the Preface and his other earlier writings assign absolutely no urgency to this goal, and in fact strongly imply the opposite conclusion. Efforts to overcome the apathy and elite rule that pervade polyarchy are shown to be at worst dangerous and potentially counter-productive, and at best a pointless drain on time and energy better spent, for the vast majority of individuals, in the pursuit of other values. The pursuit of political equality and popular sovereignty above and beyond that necessary but also sufficient level already embodied in polyarchy would very quickly threaten the stability of the system and invade the sanctity of those private values that constitute the primary goals of human nature. Significantly, fuller actualization of these democratic objectives thus stands exposed as unattainable, or attainable only at the unacceptable cost of frustrating essential human wants, needs, and purposes. The normative theory of democracy thus merges with the empirical theory of polyarchy. And polyarchy, which is at least "not an oligarchy," is thereby indicated as the optimum, and by default ideal, political system.

Dahl insists strongly upon the magnitude of his revisionary break with earlier versions of "classical" democracy theory. But despite his severe strictures against "Madisonian democracy" for its anti-majoritarian emphasis, there is a clear sense in which Dahl's own original concept of polyarchy, with its tacit commendation of elite rule and mass apathy as conducive to the stability of liberal-democratic values, is in important respects fundamentally continuous with what Dahl sees as Madison's earlier attenuation, in the interests of those same values, of the twin goals of political equality and popular sovereignty. "Polyarchy" is to "democracy" for Dahl, we might say, as "republic" is to "democracy" for Madison.

Yet if there is a sense in which the early Dahl
is a Madisonian against himself, there is equally a
sense in which the later Dahl's efforts to revise his
own original concept of polyarchy can be seen as
a modernized version of earlier, more participatory
understandings of American popular democracy. We may
now turn, more briefly, to those revisions.

III

Dahl's After the Revolution?[25] in a sense takes up
where A Preface to Democratic Theory leaves off. Consistently distinguishing between democratic ideals and
polyarchal achievements in a way that the earlier
writings sometimes do not, Dahl emphasizes more
critically than before the gap between the two.
Existing polyarchies, he stresses, are incompletely
democratic; and most of their social institutions are
even less so. After the Revolution? seeks to examine
the possibility and desirability of reducing this
continuing gap between promise and performance in the
polyarchal regimes, especially the United States.

Dahl begins by postulating three basic criteria
for assessing the legitimacy or rightfulness of a
decision-making process. First, a process is valid to
the extent that its decisions correspond to my personal
choices (the Criterion of Personal Choice). Second,
it is valid to the extent that it insures decisions
informed by a special competence (the Criterion of
Competence). Third, it is valid to the extent that
it economizes upon the amount of time and effort that
must be expended upon it (the Criterion of Economy).
(A. R., pp. 3-58)

The Criterion of Personal Choice entails democratic conclusions by way of a Hobbesian principle of
rational self-interest. Rational egoists who wish to
gain their own ends must permit others to pursue theirs
on an equal basis. Hence with respect to key political
decisions, each must concede equal weight to the
choices of all via a process of popular sovereignty.
The Criterion of Personal Choice may therefore be
recast politically as the "Principle of Affected
Interests," which asserts that everyone who is affected
by the decisions of a government has a prima facie
right to equal participation in those decisions.
(A. R., pp. 64-67)

144

But the equal participation principle derived
from the Criterion of Personal Choice must be balanced
against the Criteria of Competence and Economy. The
Competence criterion permits us to accomodate a leadership principle. The Criterion of Competence is not
ipso facto undemocratic (since democracy is predicated
upon the assumption of roughly equal competence to
determine the basic ends of political life), but the
satisfaction of wants and the protection of interests
may themselves require that in specific instances we
sacrifice the participation of citizens to the need
for expert authority. Likewise, the principle of
participation must be weighed against the Criterion of
Economy. Since participation requires the expenditure
of two scarce resources, time and effort, it is not a
costless activity. A rational individual will participate only when the benefits outweigh the opportunity
costs. Hence a rational system of authority must
balance participation against the need to economize
upon time and effort. It will seek maximum policy
output (measured against the criteria of personal
choice and competence) at the expense of minimum
participatory input.

Employing these three basic criteria for authority, Dahl evaluates alternative forms of democracy.
There is, he argues, no One Best Form. Taking into
account costs and benefits, we will find that one
form (e.g. primary democracy) is optimum according to
the three criteria under some circumstances, whereas
another (e.g. representative democracy) is clearly
preferable under others. Nonetheless, in sharp contrast to his earlier work, Dahl evinces a consistent
prima facie preference for smaller, more participatory
democratic forms. He is now concerned with the loss
of human scale in modern political and social life:

. . . there is in Rousseau's vision
of the small democracy a conception
of human dimensions that we should not
lose sight of. As the dimensions of
our social universe have multiplied
over the last several centuries, man--
I use the vague collective noun thought
appropriate for statement of this kind--
has gained in power over his environment. Yet the mechanisms through which
man exerts that control are so complex
that man in the singular, the individual

man or woman, often has little sense
of control over the decisions that
flow from these mechanisms. Man has
grown vastly more powerful, but
individuals feel less powerful. Even
polyarchy is a democratic Leviathan--
like Kafka's Castle, vast, remote,
inaccessible (A. R., p. 98).

If Man is to regain control over an increasingly
leviathan-like social and political universe, Dahl
now argues, he must somehow reappropriate these
reified structures of power. To this end, Dahl offers
two particularly salient guidelines.

1. If a matter is best dealt with
by a democratic association, seek
always to have that matter dealt with
by the smallest association that can
deal with it satisfactorily.

2. In considering whether a larger
association would be more satisfactory,
do not fail to consider its extra costs,
including a possible increase in the
sense of individual powerlessness
(A. R., p. 102).

In keeping with these injunctions, Dahl himself
prescribes several specific forms of participatory
democracy designed to supplement the necessarily more
remote institutions of polyarchy. He focuses, first,
upon what he calls the Corporate Leviathan, now
explicitly conceding (in a way that his earlier work
implicitly did not) the applicability of his own
broad, behavioral definition of the political--"any
persistent pattern of human relationships that
involves, to a significant extent, power, rule or
authority"[26]--to the modern private corporation.
Thus exposed to the logic of accountability via his
Principle of Affected Interests, the Corporate
Leviathan must, Dahl now argues, be democratized--
not merely through external government controls, or
through polyarchy transposed to the government of the
firm ("interest--group management"), but internally
through direct worker's participation and control
("social self-management" on something like the Yugo-
slavian model). (A. R., pp. 130-140)

146

Second, Dahl applies much the same logic to
the democratization of public authority. Democratic
citizenship, he argues, would be thoroughly debased by
restricting it to purely industrial citizenship. But
the "Democratic Leviathan," as he now labels polyarchy,
is afflicted by an "irreparable flaw" (A. R., p.
142)--
the remoteness of the national government from the
everyday life of the citizen, limiting its ability to
engage his or her attention. Hence the need to construct units and forms of democratic citizenship that
mitigate this flaw. Dahl focuses his attention upon
three possibilities: participation by lot, neighbor-
hood government, and the city of intermediate size.
In each instance the purpose is to enhance the quantity
and quality of direct citizen participation in political
life by democratizing more fully the remote, representative forms of polyarchy. (A. R., pp. 140-166)27

After the Revolution? thus enunciates a program
for polyarchal democracy that in important respects
breaks sharply with the less than fully democratic
vision of the Preface and Dahl's other earlier writings.
There is a much stronger emphasis upon the twin goals
of political equality (including, more insistently than
before, its socio-economic foundations) and popular
sovereignty, understood as democratic control over the
institutions of representative government. More importantly, popular sovereignty is no longer conceived
purely in terms of the responsiveness or accountability
of government to the predetermined preferences of
private individuals; there is now in Dahl's account a
much stronger emphasis upon the value of direct citizen
participation in the processes of popular sovereignty.
Dahl now adheres to a much "stronger" theory of popular
government--polyarchal democracy as both representative
and participatory democracy.

Interestingly, however, although Dahl's more
recent work assigns a higher value to participation,
it appears to justify that participation largely in
terms of categories carried over from his earlier
work. Democratic participation, it would seem, is
still solely a device for the satisfaction of antecedently-given wants and the protection of subjectively-
determined interests. Dahl's principle of personal
choice omits the educative function of participation;
his theory is cast in a language which, taking preferences as given, appears to preclude their transformation
through the process of participation. And, likewise,

147

his principle of economy implies in exactly similar
fashion that participation is purely an economic
cost incurred for its extrinsic policy benefits, and
hence in no sense an educative process undertaken for
its intrinsic effects on the moral and intellectual
development of citizens as social and political agents.
In short, while Dahl may assign a greater rule to
participation in his recent work, his vision appears
to remain constricted by a theoretical perspective
that depicts human nature as essentially egoist and
privatistic and democratic politics as purely instrumental.[28]

This apparent continuity with the theoretical
perspective of his earlier writings poses problems
for Dahl, for it is anything but apparent that his
newly revised program for participatory democracy in
both economic and political life can be justified
exclusively in these terms. We have seen that Dahl's
criteria for authority suggest that participation
must defer to competence wherever the latter will
enhance the efficiency with which wants are satisfied;
and likewise that we should economize upon time and
effort wherever possible. But, first, Dahl's program
for industrial democracy seems to fly in the face of
these injunctions. He explicitly argues that in
trading off competence against participation, we
should be willing to accept a (modest) decline in
productivity as the price of increased participation
(A. R., p. 132). If, however, participation is an
instrument of personal choice (understood as efficient
and economical policy), then a trade-off of this nature
would be doubly irrational, since it would increase
time and effort in order to detract from the efficiency
with which wants could be satisfied. (It could, of
course, be argued that such a trade-off is necessary
to insure that policy, however technically competent
and economical, in fact conforms to the personal
choices of affected interests. But the point is that
Dahl seems willing to increase participation at the
expense of competence and economy even above this
want-satisfaction, interest-protection threshold--as,
for example, in his rejection of representative forms
of interest group management in favor of participatory
forms of social self-management.) Second, the same
can be said of Dahl's prima facie preference for
direct over representative forms in the politics of
the state. In both instances, competence and economy
would seem clearly to demand not the extension of

148

direct participation but rather its reduction through the use, wherever possible, of representative forms-- forms which, optimally at least, could protect personal choice while at the same time maximizing the efficiency and minimizing the effort with which affected interests are satisfied.

These theoretical tensions can be resolved if, and only if, Dahl now has a second justification for participation, having less to do with want-satisfaction and interest-protection than with its value as a process of political education and personal self-development. And, indeed, he does now speak occasionally of "the moral and psychological validity" (A. R., p. 81) of the participatory vision. He justifies sacrificing competence to participation, not in pure personal choice terms, but for the value we "attach to democratic participation and control, as good both intrinsically and in their consequences for human self-development and human satisfaction, quite independently of other outputs" (A. R., p. 132). In the end, it is difficult to see how Dahl's new program can be fully justified except in these terms--which are at odds with, or at least distinct from, the theoretical language that he himself more usually employs to justify his proposals.

Dahl has, therefore, travelled a considerable theoretical distance from his earlier to his later writings--the distance, we might say, from a neo-Madisonian vision of polyarchy as pure representative democracy to a richer, non-Jeffersonian-cum-Tocquevillian vision of polyarchy as participatory democracy as well. Just as there is a clear sense in which his own original theory of polyarchy bears at least a family resemblance to the "Madisonian democracy" that he criticizes so severely (and unfairly) in his Preface, so do the later versions of the theory unconsciously echo these classical, participatory visions of democracy in America. The "strong" theory of democracy enunciated in After the Revolution?-- political equality, popular sovereignty, citizen participation--can fruitfully be seen, in its explicit policy prescriptions, as a modernization and adaptation to the realities of advanced industrial society of earlier, Jeffersonian and Tocquevillian understandings of the structure of American democracy. And the largely implicit justification offered by Dahl for this enhanced popular participation--which collides

149

with his own earlier and still more explicitly-avowed
categories--can likewise be seen as an unacknowledged
return to a vision of citizenship and civic virtue,
of individuals as fully social and political beings,
seen by both Jefferson and Tocqueville as essential
to the spirit of American democracy.

IV

The theory of polyarchal democracy still remains
to be completed.29 In its present and hopefully
transitional state, there persist theoretically
important tensions, elements of incoherence, that require resolution. A full, final elaboration--informed
by an accurate appreciation of its own roots in earlier
visions of the American democratic polity--would, by
completing the trajectory of Dahl's changing political
science, further enhance our self-understanding of the
promise and performance of American polyarchal democracy.

NOTES

[1] Robert Dahl, _A Preface to Democratic Theory_ (hereinafter cited as _P._, with page references given in the text), (Chicago: University of Chicago Press, 1956).

[2] Dahl's model is derived from the writings of James Madison, but he does not hesitate to improve upon Madison wherever his original arguments can, in Dahl's view, be made "more logical, consistent, and explicit" (_P._, p. 5). In reconstructing Dahl's reconstruction of Madison, I have tried to preserve the logical structure of both arguments intact simultaneously; but where Dahl's critique seems to me to have made Madison's argument _less_ rather than more logical, consistent, and explicit, I have tried to assign priority to the latter.

[3] "Definition 2: 'Tyranny' is every severe deprivation of a natural right" (_P._, p. 6).

[4] _The Federalist_, ed. Jacob Cooke (Cleveland: World Publishing, 1961).

[5] _Fed._ 10, p. 61.

[6] _The Writings of James Madison_ (hereinafter Writings), ed. Gallimard Hunt (9 vols.; New York, 1900–1910). II 369 ("Vices of the Political System of the United States").

[7] See, e.g., _Ibid._, II, 366-68 ("Vices . . ."); V, 27-33 (to Thomas Jefferson, Oct. 24, 1787); and _The Records of the Federal Convention of 1787_ (4 vols.; New Haven: Yale University Press, 1966), I, esp. 134-36 (speech by Madison, June 6, 1787).

[8] Cf. George W. Carey "Separation of Powers and the Madisonian Model: A Reply to the Critics," _American Political Science Review_ 72 (March, 1978), 151-64.

[9] See also Robert Dahl and Charles Lindbloom, _Politics, Economics, and Welfare_ (New York: Harper and Row, 1953), pp. 308-309, where the critique of the constitutional separation of powers rests even more unequivocally upon the British example.

[10] Social checks and balances "ought not to be considered as superseding the use of auxiliary precautions" not merely against government tyranny but also against majority tyranny (Fed. 63, p. 425). Carey recognizes this point (161), but thereby contradicts his own earlier claim that Madison saw social checks and balances as a sufficient restraint upon majority tyranny.

[11] On this point, see also the helpful disucssion of M. J. C. Vile, Constitutionalism and the Separation of Powers (Oxford University Press, 1967), pp. 303-312.

[12] See, for example, his remarks (P., p. 81) on the role of constitutional checks and balances as one factor in a triple disenfranchisement of the unpropertied masses.

[13] See P., pp. 38-44, 51-60. It is worth noting that many of Dahl's technical and empirical objections to populistic democracy pose problems endemic to any theory of democracy, his own theory of polyarchy included.

[14] See, for example, Dahl's efforts to dismiss as meaningless the Madisonian concepts of tryanny and faction on the two-fold ground that rationally grounded consensus about natural rights or the public interest is impossible, and that the concept cannot in any case be given any precise operational meaning (P., pp. 22-27). As has been noted elsewhere, Dahl's argument amounts to an ostrich-like denial of the gross historical actualities of tyranny and faction because of our inability to operationalize the concepts precisely at margins (cf. Vile, p. 308).

[15] In citing Jefferson and Tocqueville in this context, I do not, of course, wish to imply that either himself embraced an unequivocally "populist" theory of democracy in Dahl's sense. Both partially embraced key Madisonian values; and Tocqueville, in particular, was severely critical of the excesses of "populist" democracy in Jacksonian America. I do, however, wish to suggest that both, without in any sense wishing indefinitely to maximize political equality or popular sovereignty at the expense of all other values, put forward "strong" theories of popular democracy embodying a dimension altogether lost from

Dahl's account of "populist" democracy.

[16]_The Life and Selected Writings of Thomas Jeffer-_
son, ed., Adrienne Koch and William Peden (New York:
Modern Library, 1944) p. 661 (to Joseph C. Cabell,
Feb. 2, 1816), also _Ibid_., pp. 604-605 (to Governor
John Tyler, May 26, 1810) 668-73 (to John Taylor,
May 28, 1816); and Jefferson, _Political Writings_
(Indianapolis: Bobbs-Merrill, 1955), pp. 95-101. For
an illuminating discussion of the Jeffersonian vision
of participatory ward-republics, see Hannah Arendt,
On Revolution (New York: Viking , 1971), pp. 234-42,
252-59.

[17]_"I think it may be laid down dogmatically that
no human organization--certainly none with more than
a handful of people--has ever met or is likely to meet
these eight conditions" (_P_., p. 71).

[18]Robert Dahl, "Hierarchy, Democracy, and Bargaining in Politics and Economics in H. Eulau et al.
(eds.) _Political Behavior_ (Glencoe, Ill.: The Free
Press, 1958), p. 87.

[19]For the most sohpisticated of the numerous
criticisms directed specificically at Dahl, see
Quentin Skinner. "The Empirical Theorists of Democracy
and Their Critics: A Plague on Both Their Houses,"
Political Theory 1 (August, 1973), 287-306.

[20]"Further Reflections on the Elitist Theory of
Democracy," _American Science Review_ 60 (June, 1966),
299-303.

[21]For a fuller explication of this notion, see
Charles Taylor, "Neutrality in Political Science" in
Peter Laslett and W. G. Runciman (eds.), _Philosophy,
Politics, and Society, 3rd Series_ (New York: Basil
Blackwell, 1967), pp. 25-27.

[22]Robert Dahl, "Equality and Power in American
Society," in William D'Antonio and Howard Ehrlich
(eds.), _Power and Democracy in America_ (South Bend,
Ind.: University of Notre Dame Press, 1965), p. 81.

[23]_Who Governs? Democracy and Power in an American
City_ (W. G.) (New Haven: Yale University Press, 1963),
esp. pp. 311-325.

[24]See also the definition of democracy offered in Dahl's later work. Polyarchy (New Haven: Yale University Press, 1967), pp. 1-3.

[25]Robert Dahl, After the Revolution? Authority in a Good Society (A. R.) (New Haven: Yale University Press, 1974).

[26]Robert Dahl, Modern Political Analysis (First edition; Englewood Cliffs, N.J.: Prentice Hall, 1963), p. 6.

[27]See also Polyarchy, pp. 226-27; Robert Dahl, "The City in the Future of Democracy," American Political Science Review 61 (Dec., 1967), 953-69; and Robert Dahl and Edward Tufte, Size and Democracy (Stanford: Stanford University Press, 1973).

[28]Cf. Peter Bachrach, "Interest, Participation, and Democratic Theory" in Roland A. Pennock and John W. Chapman (eds.), Nomos VI: Participation in Politics (New York: Lieber-Atherton, 1975), pp. 39-55.

[29]Dahl has promised two further volumes--one on democratic pluralism, the other on democracy and its critics.

CHAPTER 7
"A Responsible Electorate? Implications for Represen-
tative Interactions in a Democratic Republic"
William Hrezo

It is rare that any single work can reorient the
thinking of an entire discipline, but in many respects
V.O. Key's The Responsible Electorate has done just
that. Key laid the foundation for the reconstruction
of the image of the American voter with his radical
contention "that voters are not fools."[1] The Responsible Electorate has convinced a great number of
political theorists and practitioners that the vote
can be, and indeed often is, rationally involved in
the electoral processes of American government. And
even for those who have remained skeptical, two elements of Key's hypothesis--that the electorate votes
in a fashion which is consistent with its self-interest
and that this has an effect on the personnel and
policies of the governmental system--have served as the
focal point of extensive research.

The implications of Key's insights into American
voting behavior extend far beyond the important but
transitory impact of individual elections. With the
realization that "the voter may after all try to form
sensible judgments on those questions relevant to his
supposed duties as a citizen," many of the important
assumptions of the American constitutional system may
be thrown into a new light.[2] What becomes of the
necessity and complexion of delegated authority? Is
the reticence toward citizen involvement in the affairs
of government and the distrust of democracy often
voiced in constitutional debates appropriate and justifiable? Are politically oriented factions by their
very nature to be feared and combatted, or has their
role been altered?[3] The Responsible Electorate seems
to suggest answers to these questions that differ
significantly from the thinking of the authors of The
Federalist.

To explore the ramifications of Key's thought for
such constitutional concepts, it will be necessary to
examine The Responsible Electorate in some detail.
Two logically related questions arise from such an
investigation. How valid are Key's conclusions? And
how far can these conclusions, which center on presidential elections, be extended into the political
behavior of the American electorate? Discussion of
these questions will make it possible to discuss Key's

155

contribution to the interpretation of republican
government, democracy, and factions as they relate to
individual political activity.

I

While The Responsible Electorate is a relatively
brief and concise treatment of voting behavior in
presidential elections from 1936-1960, it is rich in
providing new perspectives and compelling reasoning.
From the diversity of insights and interpretations
offered the implications of four of Key's conclusions
seem to be particularly revelant. First, Key contends
that the American voter becomes involved in electoral
activity on an individual level, based on private
motivations. Second, he argues that the voter, whose
activity is based on such personal motives, behaves in
a rationally calculated fashion in making electoral
decisions. Third, the information on which the quality
of these decisions depends is often provided by, and
interpreted in the context of, the activity and interaction of political parties. Fourth, the elected
officials, and in turn the policies, of the American
government are influenced, albeit retroactively, by the
behavior of the electorate.

Central to Key's entire position is the ability
of the voter to make individual and independent judgments about candidates. Reflexive electoral choices
based on purely group related identification or sub-
conscious programming undermine the entire concept of a
responsible electorate. Key cautions against theories
of voting activity which use such categorizations as
age, occupation, religion or ethnic group. Such a
perspective "can be added up to a conception of voting
not as a civic decision but as an almost purely
deterministic act."[4] Obviously it is necessary to
counter such interpretations and establish individualism
as the basis of voting decisions.

Based on his data analysis, Key concludes that
different electoral situations and circumstances produce
entirely different patterns of voter response. "It
suggests that deliberate choices, appropriate to
differing circumstances, underlie the movements of
voters that our tables record rather than a special
disposition by members of particular sectors of the
population."[5] On the other hand Key is neither so

156

naive nor so insular as to ignore the relationships
between social variables and individual behavior.
Key's voters do not live in a vacuum. They are not
unaffected by factors which contribute to the formulation and definition of their respective personalities.
But it remains for the author to establish this
connection without individualism becoming submerged in
determinism. Key identifies the electorally related
intersection of influence and choice. It occurs
where an issue is both salient to the individual and
relevant to a group with which the individual
identifies:

> The fact that a person is, say, a Negro
> serves as an index to what he believes
> and to why he votes as he does only
> when an election concerns Negroes as
> Negroes and when the members of the
> group are aware of the issue and see
> it as basic among their concerns of the
> moment.[6]

In effect Key's overview can be summarized by the
following comment:

> Not every election generates group-
> related issues which drive a wedge
> through the electorate along lines
> easily identified by gross charac-
> teristics of the electorate. . .if
> one wishes to understand the election
> he should examine directly attitudes
> about issues and other questions of
> the campaign rather than attempt to
> deduce motivation from gross charac-
> teristics of voters.[7]

The thrust of an individualistic interpretation
often encounters another barrier. Many contemporary
theorists contend that a candidate's personality and
image appeal to a common, perhaps subliminal, psychological base which in turn stimulates an electoral
response. Key is aware of such a controversy and is
also ready with evidence to support individual
electoral decision-making. Two presidential examples
should illuminate Key's perspective on this argument.

Reviewing the electorate's response to Franklin
Roosevelt, Key is firm in his stance. Rhetorically

157

asking if Roosevelt's success was based solely on his personal image and appeal, the author responds strongly that "even the most cursory reflection destroys this type of explanation."[8] As he does throughout The Responsible Electorate, Key contends that image is the result of Presidential behavior and individual response. Roosevelt's position "derived not so much from the kind of man he was as from the kinds of things for which, and against which, he fought."[9] Thus, for Key, image is much more a cognitive than an emotive response on the part of the voter.

Turning to Eisenhower and his supposed "father image," Key comments that "one may doubt the necessity of resorting to such dubious hypotheses to explain the response of the electorate to the situation."[10] Again support for the president is part of a "complex pattern of gains and losses" based on voter reaction to issues as well as to personalities.[11] Indeed Eisenhower's public image may have restrained as much as supported him. "By 1956 he was the chieftan of a crusade that he could lead neither to the left nor to the right, even if he had been so disposed."[12] Once more voter cognition dictated and reinforced presidential image instead of image determining voter choice.

Given this capacity for individual judgment the foundation is set for Key's larger argument concerning voter rationality. At the core of the concept of responsible electoral behavior lies the ability to evaluate political activity in relation to perceptions of private benefit, and the motivation to vote according to such decisions. To establish the existence of such activities in the electorate, Key identifies three categories of voters--standpatters, switchers, and new voters. Analyzing data concerning each of these groups a pattern of self-aware and self-interested voting emerges.

Key defines the voter who stands-pat as a person who consistently votes for the candidates of a single party. Under such a definition it is easy to assume that such people are unreflective creatures of habit who vote for labels rather than on concerned and informed issue related preferences. But Key's study brings him to a far different conclusion. "The facts seem to be that, on the average, the standpatters do not have to behave as mugwumps to keep their consciences clear; they are already where they ought to be in the

158

light of their policy attitudes."[13]   To Key there is no
definitive evidence to support the idea that standpatters react automatically, and hence unthinkingly,
to political stimuli.

Similar misconceptions can easily arise about the
switchers, or voters who change their party votes from
one election to the next. Switchers are often perceived as rootless political drifters who make emotion-
al or irrational voting choices based on whim or
chance. Yet again Key perceives this group in a
different light. Using data from the 1936 presidential
election, he notes that "vote switches occured in
directions consistent with the assumption that voters
were moved by rational calculation of the instrumental
impact of their vote."[14] And the data from twenty
years later "suggests that deliberate choices, appro--
priate to differing circumstances, underlie the movements of voters."[15] Indeed Key bases his defense of
both standpatters and switchers on the relationship
between their issue sensitivity and their subsequent
voting behavior.

> The switchers. . . , are persons whose
> peculiarity is not lack of interest
> but agreement on broad political issues
> with the standpatters toward whom they
> shift. . .indubitably those who shift
> toward the winning side resemble (on
> major policy issues of wide concern in
> the population) the standpatters on
> that side."[16]

To Key, they are making conscious and intellectually
defensible decisions.

The final categorization utilized by Key is that
of new voters. These are individuals who either did
not or could not vote in the previous presidential
election, and thus are "new" in that they can neither
standpat nor switch from their previous choice. While
Key agrees that new voters often differ from the other
two major types of voters in such characteristics as
interest and political commitment, he focuses on a more
important feature. How do new voters act when they do
decide to participate in electoral activity? Here Key
argues that they behave in much the same way as do
standpatters and switchers. For example, concerning
the elections between 1940 and 1948, he observes that

"the nonvoters at the preceding election. . .have an
attitudinal resemblance to the standpatters with whom
they ally themselves."[17]   Thus they too may be display-
ing behavior consistent with their actual preferences.

Looking back over the body of his information,
Key offers the following conclusion concerning the
rationality of the voting activities of all three
groups:

> All these patterns of behavior are con-
> sistent with the supposition that
> voters, or at least a large number of
> them, are moved by their perceptions
> and appraisals of policy and perfor-
> mance.[18]

For Key, then, there is a match between preferences
and voting decisions.

From this it is clear that Key's entire analysis
takes place in relation to political parties. The
notions of standpatters and switchers imply two
critical points in respect to the function of political
parties. The activities of the American voter take
place predominantly in a party context. This includes
both the evaluation of policies and relevant electoral
behavior. "Those who agree with their party are most
inclined to stay with it. Policy preference reinforces
party loyalty. Those whose policy preference conflicts
with their party voting record are most likely to
deflect."[19] Parties appear as essential components of
any voting choice. The party activities observed by
Key--the recruitment of candidates, the formulation and
publicization of platforms, and the development and
execution of campaign strategies--all have a combined
impact on the behavior of the electorate which is
impossible to ignore and difficult to exaggerate.

For the purposes of this essay one final point
needs to be made concerning The Responsible Electorate.
There is a real impact on the policies and personnel of
government as a result of the individual, informed,
party related decision-making previously discussed.
According to Key voters judge the past performance of
presidents and parties.

> The patterns of flow of the major streams
> of shifting voters graphically reflect

the electorate in its great, and perhaps principal, role as appraiser of
past events, past performance, and
past actions. It judges retrospec-
tively.[20]

The electorate does examine and evaluate what the
representatives of both parties have done. Key
approaches this situation by asking rhetorically:

What if we should suppose that the
electorate looked at the public scene,
did not like what it saw, and per-
formed that act of goverance for
which an electorate is superbly equipped,
that is, it threw the ins out?[21]

Key concludes that this is precisely what voters
regularly do.

II

It is impossible to read The Responsible Electorate and to discuss the constitutional implications of
its conclusions without asking certain questions. Does
Key's methodology undermine the validity of his
analysis? Has other research confirmed Key's hypothesis? Even if Key is correct about policy-related
voter rationality in presidential elections, is there
evidence of similar behavior at other levels?

Many potential methodological problems are evident
in The Responsible Electorate, several of which are
admitted by Key himself. Perhaps most important is the
lack of any causal relationship between the data and
the conclusions. "Our correlations, . . .should not be
taken to mean that policy attitudes correlated with
changes and continuities in voting preference
necessarily cause those changes or continuities."[22]
While this certainly does not negate Key's interpretations, it would appear to restrict their scope.

Key also acknowledges some problems with his data
in terms of how it was accumulated and utilized. The
data is an amalgam of survey results from several
different sources. Therefore, he is using statistics
which represent similar, but not identical, formats and
questions. Even the questions of a single polling

organization have been altered over the years. The
danger of comparing responses to such diverse queries
is clear.[23] This process of combining and then
comparing the responses from different polls produces
at least one instance of using data from different
polls for entries in the same table.[24]

Another problem arises in the extensive use of
voter recall. As Key himself says,

> The skeptic may distrust a person's
> recall of his vote of four years ago.
> Commonly, even in surveys immediately
> after an election, a larger percentage
> claims to have voted for the winner
> than possibly could have, if the official
> election returns are assumed to be
> reasonably accurate measures of the
> vote.[25]

Indeed Key attempts to minimize or compensate for the
effects of recall error, but the fact remains that
such error exists and that many of Key's findings rest
on such compromised data.[26]

Despite such problems the ultimate question
remains the accuracy of Key's conclusions. And in this
respect the picture of the individual voter as a
rational, policy-oriented decision-maker seems to hold
up quite well. A number of studies using Key's
conceptualization of a responsible electorate as a
general research hypothesis have both supported and
extended the results of Key's original study.[27]

Two different examinations of the 1964 presidential
election came to conclusions similar to those of Key.
John E. Jackson essentially echoes Key when he writes
that

> This analysis argues quite strongly
> that voting and party identification
> decisions are political decisions
> motivated by individuals' desires to
> have public policy reflect their own
> judgements about what policies should
> be followed and by the policies which
> each party and its candidates advocate.[28]

And Martin Fishbein and Fred Coombs claim that their

162

"data clearly indicate that voters. . .do clearly discriminate between candidates vis-a-vis certain issues."[29] Clearly, then, Key's premise has found broad acceptance.

To provide some measure of analytic consistency Gerald Pomper and Mark Schulman attempted to question voter rationality over a period of time. Their interest was to approach several presidential elections from the same perspective. To further aid the explanatory capabilities of their findings the authors employed seven variables in their exploration of electoral behavior. In this way Pomper and Schulman hoped to avoid faulty generalizations based on single case studies and oversimplifications of policy influences on voting activity. This extended analysis produced the following statement:

> Our most general conclusion is that theory generated from any single election, must, necessarily, be incomplete and static. Voters must be studied comparatively, in a variety of empirical and temporal contexts. In doing so, we have found reason to support Key's view.[30]

Hence there is some evidence that the results of more detailed and extensive analysis conform to Key's hypothesis.

There are also grounds for projecting the image of voter rationality identified by Key in presidential elections to other levels as well. A study of presidential and congressional voting in one state in 1972 found differing tendencies at each level. But in total, even using criteria which may be overly strict, the data "indicate that although not all the voters met the standards of rationality a large percentage did conform quite well."[31] And another more extensive review of congressional elections produces seemingly definitive findings. Examining almost eighty years of House of Representatives' electoral results, Gerald Kramer finds pervasive individual rationality. His analysis yields results which are totally supportive of Key's hypothesis.

> One basic finding to emerge from this study is that election outcomes are in

substantial part responsive to objective
changes occuring under the incumbent
party; they are not 'irrational,' or
random, or solely the product of past
loyalities and habits, or of campaign
rhetoric and merchandising. In this
respect, our findings support those of
Key, based on quite different data.[32]

The bulk of the available evidence, thus, supports
Key's contention that voters display at least a modicum
of rationality.

III

The preceding discussion of The Responsible
Electorate provides a context in which the constitutional questions suggested in the introduction to this
essay can be examined and discussed. Implications
drawn from Key's arguments offer an interesting perspective on these complex issues and the often debated
ideas on which they are based. And such a study and
the insights which may arise from it are important,
since the meaning and interpretation of the Constitution
are questions as critical to the contemporary political
world as they were when Hamilton, Madison and Jay wrote
in support of the Constitution.

Of vital importance to the framers of the Constitution and the authors of The Federalist is the notion
of delegated political authority through representation.
Certainly Madison distrusted a purely democratic government. This concern, and an accompanying fear of unrestrained popular involvement in the activities of
government, is voiced in Federalist #1 and echoes
throughout the papers.[33] A republic, or representative
democracy, is suggested to overcome the weaknesses
inherent in a democracy, which often manifest themselves
in "the violence of faction."[34]

It is suggested that delegated authority in a
republican government can control the effects of
factions in two ways. First, it is supposed that the
people's representatives will be those "whose enlightened views and virtuous sentiments render them superior
to local prejudices, and to schemes of injustice."[35]
And second, a republic can be extended over a greater
territory than can a democracy. As a result of such a

164

flexible form of government, "you take in a greater variety of parties and interests" and factions are more likely to control themselves through increased competition.[36]

How is a republic founded with such an intent affected by The Responsible Electorate?[37] While the immediate impulse is to suppose that self-interested voters confirm the worst fears of The Federalist, the notions of a republic and of an informed, active electorate may be highly compatible. In reality, both of the means necessary to control factions suggested in Federalist #10 seem to benefit if Key is correct. Logic would suggest that the republic's chosen representatives are more likely to be virtuous and enlightened, and to act in that fashion, when the people that they represent are interested, informed, and involved in the personnel and policies of government. Similarly, citizens who make informed individual calculations of their interests in a changing political and social environment, would seem to represent less of a threat to join permanent factions based on "impulse of passion" and opposed to the "interests of the community."[38] Factions are to be controlled, since they cannot be eliminated, by having them check each other. Elected representatives will be aided in this both by coming from diverse constituencies and by having an intimate knowledge of local constituencies.[39] On the other hand, groups founded on the basis of knowledge and rational evaluation seem to be better equipped to provide the balance which Hamilton advocates.

However, the possible republican benefits which may accrue from a responsible electorate are difficult to realize. As Key notes

> In the large the electorate behaves about as rationally as we should expect, given the clarity of the alternatives presented to it and the character of the information available to it.[40]

It may well be that the government, founded on the principles of The Federalist, still distrusts the average voter. This in turn promotes an unwillingness on the part of representatives to interact with the electorate in a manner which may actually be in their best mutual interest.

165

Much of the case against democracy made in The
Federalist concentrates on conditions perceived to be
a part of the nature of man. From the perspective of
the authors of The Federalist, there are severe
inherent problems in human behavior. In Federalist #1
Hamilton writes that "ambition, avarice, personal
animosity, party opposition, and many other motives,
not more laudable than these, are apt to operate as
well upon those who support as those who oppose the
right side of the question."[41] And in Federalist #10
similar observations are made. "The latent causes of
faction are thus sown in the nature of man."[42] Thus
much of the anticipation surrounding the possible
development or implementation of a democratic government stems from concerns about human nature.

Yet one of the major strengths of both the
Constitution and of The Federalist is the ability to
combine theory and practice. Indeed the authors of
The Federalist steadfastly refuse to ignore either
theoretical or practical arguments. Historical pre-
cedents pervade The Federalist in order to demonstrate
the authors' conceptualization of the nature of man.
It is in this same vein that Key provides extremely
important contemporary information which could alter
the conclusions of The Federalist.

The crux of The Responsible Electorate is the
ability of voters to act in a rational and policy-
centered manner in political activities. Evidence of
this sort would not go unheeded by Hamilton, Madison,
and Jay. What Key demonstrates is the practical side
of the situation. There is no theoretical debate over
the nature of man. But Key points out the capacity
for political reason and action on the part of the
voter.

Viewing the complete picture from the unified
theoretical and practical perspective utilized in The
Federalist, Key demonstrates that factions based on
various self-interests do exist. But they need not
reflect only passion, irrationality, and greed.
Political activity can be, and following the premise
of The Responsible Electorate often is, thoughtful and
rational. Therefore, what Key implicitly suggests is
that the fear of democracy in The Federalist, stemming
largely from a view of the nature of man, can perhaps
be tempered by the demonstrated ability of the electorate to act responsibly.

These observations concerning the role of the
nature of man in understanding the tone and structure
of the Constitution do not stand alone. Since they are
closely related to the foundation of political factions, it becomes important to ask a final question.
Are factions intrinsically harmful to the causes of
liberty and republican government?

It would be difficult to confuse the position of
The Federalist on this issue. Hamilton clearly and
boldly says in regard to factions that "the regulation
of these various and interfering interests forms the
principal task of modern legislation."[43] While he
perceives the main source of factions to be economic,
they could develop from other differences as well. But
whatever the source, such factions are divisive and
serve as real and constant threats to the unity of the
republic.

However, Key's concept of a responsible electorate
suggests, although indirectly, that factions need not
necessarily undermine constitutional government. When
the diversity of both the source and goals of factions
is considered, then the potential for different forms
and behavior should be evident. In this context it
makes sense to ask if the concept of faction has not
evolved since the writing of The Federalist.

In contemporary American electoral politics it may
well be that parties have largely supplanted Hamilton's
factions. This is not to say that narrow factions no
longer exist, but interest group politics now often go
on below the electoral level and within the institutional framework which was designed in part to control
them.[44] Now political parties dominate the electoral
sphere and, while they represent factions, they are
fundamentally different from those envisioned in The
Federalist.

American political parties are not the feared
factions of Federalist #10. The major American parties
have members from all the social and economic strata
of the society. No particular or clearly enunciated
ideology either defines a precise, and therefore
limited membership, or severly constrains the nature of
party programs. To maintain the competitiveness which
is their political lifeblood, American parties cannot
afford to systematically exclude any group or interest.

Modern political parties still represent economic,
religious, ideological, and other interests. But they
do so in a much more inclusive fashion than that fore-
seen by the authors of The Federalist. As described
by Key, the major American political parties provide
the electorate with political information, aggregate
interests, aid in developing acceptable policies, and
help to keep elected officials attuned to their con-
tituencies. In this way the parties seem to aid the
stability of the constitutional system, a result that
the authors of The Federalist would certainly laud.
Factions of this sort unify rather than divide. In
fact parties may well bring the electorate as close to
the desired sense of polity described in The Federalist
as has ever been the case in the United States.[45]

IV

V.O. Key's The Responsible Electorate brings to
light several issues which are important to the understanding of the Constitution. Few works in political
science can match this brief book for the depth of its
implications concerning the American system of government. Indeed Key's argument has repurcussions for both
the underlying principles of the Constitution and for
the way the constitutional system operates.

The central theme of The Responsible Electorate is
the electorate's capacity to make individual, informed,
and consistent voting decisions. This would certainly
be important in and of itself; but two other factors
are implicit in this observation. First, Key has
revealed the potential and abilities of the American
voter. The apprehensions of The Federalist concerning
electoral behavior should be reduced if Key's conclusions are correct. Such capabilities should mitigate
fears of too much democracy.

The second factor arising from quality voter
participation involves the relationship between the
electorate and their representatives. Key talks predominantly about the retrospective evaluation of policy
and office holders. But this opens the door for more
extensive interaction between the voter and the government. Logic would suggest that if those in government
know that the electorate is going to rationally judge
policies and vote accordingly then it makes sense to
try to anticipate that evaluation and behave as the

electorate desires. Key makes reference to such
anticipatory behavior, observing that "governments must
worry, not about the meaning of past elections, but
about their fate at future elections."[46] If one is
future-oriented it would be foolish to sit back and
await its arrival. A politician concerned with future
electoral success will act in a way that will hopefully
be perceived as beneficial by the electorate.[47] Thus
there has been a real increase in constituency influence without disastrous results.[48]

The framers of the Constitution and the authors
of The Federalist were deeply concerned that an over-
emphasis on democracy and the behavior of factions
would thwart the goal of liberty and undermine the
chance of a unified federal government for the newly
formed United States. To establish this government
they felt it was necessary to give democracy a lesser
priority, in fact to restrict democracy so that the
more important goal of constitutional government could
be attained. The institutions and operations of this
new republic were designed to minimize the impact of
selfish democracy and factions.

The Responsible Electorate addresses these concerns in a new way. By demonstrating the electorate's
capability for voting in a rational, individual, and
policy-related manner, democratic participation looms
as less of a specter. And by clarifying the role of
political parties in contemporary elections the same is
true for this evolutionary type of faction. In fact,
by suggesting how voters and political parties influence both the reactive and anticipatory behavior of
elected officials, Key has shown the capacity of people
to provide some of the constraints and curbs that the
authors of The Federalist thought could only be maintained through institutional arrangements.[49]

The role of the electorate in the American
constitutional system is not fixed. The document
written in 1787 and so staunchly defended in The Federalist did not fix for eternity a limited role for the
individual voter. More realistically this relationship
is changing and evolving, as evidenced by the fifteenth,
seventeenth, and nineteenth amendments to the Constitution. The Responsible Electorate elucidates important
components of this evolution.

Key shows that increasing democracy does not

necessarily threaten the republic. Within the republican philosophical context of the Constitution, the
rational behavior of the individual voter can make
significant contributions to the operation of the
government. The constitutional system, rather than
suffering from the struggle between republican and
democratic extremes, may actually benefit from an
adaptive and evolving flexibility which results from
the dynamic tension arising from such differing
emphases.

Martin Diamond refers to the constitutional system
in terms of the acts of a play. His Act I focuses on
the Declaration of Independence and the promise of
democracy as the basis for equality. Act II centers on
the republican perspective of the Constitution and its
restrictions of democracy. In Act III American society
strives to re-establish democracy within the confines
of the Constitution. Act IV is in the wings, awaiting
the final triumph of democracy.[50] The insights of The
Responsible Electorate suggest another constitutional
alternative. Perhaps Act IV need not be written. It
is entirely possible that, by incorporating the unique
behavioral perspective of Key, democracy and the
American constitutional republic can complement each
other. A continuing Act III, with an expanding and
evolutionary understanding of both democracy and
republicanism, might be a prime source of the enduring
strength of the American constitutional system.

NOTES

[1]V. O. Key, Jr., The Responsible Electorate (New York: Vintage Books, 1968), p. 7. (Hereafter cited as Responsible).

[2]Ibid., p. 10.

[3]For background information concerning these questions see James Madison, Alexander Hamilton, and John Jay, The Federalist. Ed. Jacob E. Cooke (Middletown, Connecticut: Wesleyan University Press, 1961). Of particular interest here are essay Nos. 1, 9, and 10.

[4]Key, Responsible, p. 5. A more deterministically oriented interpretation can be found in both Bernard Berelsen, Paul Lazarsfeld and William McPhee, Voting (Chicago: University of Chicago Press, 1954) and Angus Campbell, Philip Converse, Warren Miller, and Donald Stokes, The American Voter (New York: Wiley, 1960).

[5]Ibid., p. 83.

[6]Ibid., p. 70.

[7]Ibid., p. 70. Key previews this idea in his introduction (p. 5).

[8]Ibid., p. 56.

[9]Ibid., p. 56.

[10]Ibid., p. 89.

[11]Ibid., p. 90.

[12]Ibid., p. 79.

[13]Ibid., p. 53.

[14]Ibid., p. 47.

[15]Ibid., p. 83.

[16]Ibid., p. 104.

[17]Ibid., p. 55-56.

[18]Ibid., p. 150.

[19]Ibid., p. 150.

[20]Ibid., p. 61.

[21]Ibid., p. 63.

[22]Ibid., p. 60.

[23]Key discusses the sources of his data and his analytical techniques on pages 12-13.

[24]For instance, the table on page 95 which compares the educational levels of switchers uses both National Opinion Research Center and American Institute of Public Opinon results.

[25]Ibid., p. 13.

[26]More extensive and detailed discussions of these and other methodological questions arising in regard to The Responsible Electorate can be found in Michael Margolis, "From Confusion to Confusion: Issues and the American Voter (1956-1972)." American Political Science Review 71 (1977), pp. 31-43; Blair T. Weir, "The Distortion of Voter Recall." American Journal of Political Science 19 (February 1975), pp. 53-62; Theodore F. Malcaluso, "Political Information, Party Identification and Voting Defection." Public Opinion Quarterly 41 (Summer 1977), pp. 255-260; and Gertrude Jaeger Selznick, American Sociological Review 35 (1970), p. 565.

[27]H. T. Reynolds cites and discusses research which supports the Key hypothesis (see especially footnote 8). H. T. Reynolds, "Rationality and Attitudes Toward Political Parties and Candidates." The Journal of Politics 37 (1974).

[28]John E. Jackson, "Issues, Party Choices, and Presidential Votes." American Journal of Political Science 19 (May 1975), pp. 183-84.

[29]Martin Fishbein and Fred Coombs, "Basis for Decision: An Attitudinal Analysis of Voting Behavior." Journal of Applied Social Psychology 4 (1974), p. 95.

[30]Mark A. Schulman and Gerald M. Pomper, "Variability in Electoral Behavior: Longitudinal Perspectives from Causal Modeling." *American Journal of Political Science* 19 (February 1975), p. 15.

[31]Kendall Baker and Oliver Walter, "Voter Rationality: A Comparison of Presidential and Congressional Voting in Wyoming." *The Western Political Quarterly* 28 (June 1975), p. 329.

[32]Gerald H. Kramer, "Short-Term Fluctuations in U.S. Voting Behavior, 1896-1964." *American Political Science Review* 65 (1971), p. 140.

[33]Similar sentiments are expressed in essay Nos. 9 and 10.

[34]Madison, *Federalist* No. 10, p. 56.

[35]Ibid., p. 64.

[36]Ibid., p. 64.

[37]There is an enduring argument concerning the motivation of those involved in the writing and defense of the Constitution. In "The Declaration and the Constitution: Liberty, Democracy and the Founders." Ed. Nathan Glazer and Irving Kristol, *The American Commonwealth: 1976* (New York: Basic Books, 1976). Diamond summarizes and discusses this question of self-interest versus sincere concern for liberty.

[38]Madison, *Federalist* No. 10, p. 57.

[39]Ibid., p. 63.

[40]Key, *Responsible*, p. 7.

[41]Hamilton, *Federalist* No. 1, p. 5.

[42]Madison, *Federalist* No. 10, p. 58.

[43]Ibid., p. 59.

[44]Support for this contention can be found in Theodore Lowi, *The End of Liberalism* (New York: W. W. Norton, 1969) and in Murray Edelman, *The Symbolic Uses of Politics* (Urbana, Illinois: University of Illinois Press, 1964).

[45]It is somewhat ironic that the agencies
(political parties) that potentially could be the
most effective in achieving the goals of stability
and unity within the polity are unable to do so largely
because The Federalist and the political theory under-
lying the Constitution assume that they will have the
opposite effect. C. B. MacPherson, "Social Conflict,
Political Parties and Democracy," Samuel Huntington,
"Political Parties and Social Stability" (both in
William Crotty, Donald Freeman, and Douglas Gatlin,
Political Parties and Political Behavior (Boston:
Allyn and Bacon, 1971) E. E. Schattschneider, The
Semi-Sovereign People (Hinsdale, Illinois: The Dryden
Press, 1975) and Party Government (New York: Holt,
Rinehart and Winston, 1942); and Walter Dean Burnham,
"The End of American Party Politics." Transaction 7
(December 1969), pp. 12-22, all detail the nature and
purpose of political parties in a democratic republic.
Burnham and Norman Nie, Sidney Verba and John Petrocik,
The Changing American Voter (Cambridge: Harvard
University Press, 1976), among others, also detail the
instability and cynicism on the part of the electorate,
and the electoral disaggregation that has resulted
because parties are prevented from aggregating interests and formulating policies.

[46]Key, Responsible, p. 77.

[47]Anticipatory behavior similar to that suggested
here is described by Lewis Anthony Dexter in "The
Representative and His District." Ed. Robert Peabody
and Nelson Polsby, New Perspectives on the House of
Representatives (Chicago: Rand McNally, 1977), pp. 3-
25.

[48]It can be argued that increasingly sophisticated
public opinion polling and the speed and influence of
the modern media make such relationships faster and
closer.

[49]Schattschneider, for one, argues that such
constraints are unnecessary because the very diversity
of interests within the polity will preclude a tyranny
of the majority and that, under a different set of
assumptions, parties can foster rather than undermine
a sense of unity in the polity.

[50]Diamond, "The Declaration and the Constitution,"
pp. 44-45.

PART III

The Principles Critiqued

CHAPTER 8

"John Taylor's An Inquiry Into the Principles and
Policy of the Government of the United States."
Gordon Lloyd

John Taylor of Caroline County, Virginia, was born
in 1753 and died in 1824. He wrote more profusely and
was engaged in more crucial arguments over a longer
period of time than most people who participated in the
critical politics of America's founding era. He wrote
five books and twelve pamphlets, delivered numerous important legislative speeches (at both the national and
state level), and left an extensive correspondence.[1]
The political thought of Taylor, however, has not been
given careful and thorough treatment.[2] He lived in an
era which produced many giants, particularly Virginia
giants. It is a difficult enough task to give the
political thought of John Adams, Alexander Hamilton,
Thomas Jefferson, and James Madison careful and thorough treatment. But Taylor was also in the Antifederalist tradition and scholarship on the American
founding has neglected Antifederalist political thought.
Even such prominent Virginia Antifederalists as Richard
Henry Lee and George Mason have not received their
proper due.[3] The scholarship which does exist on
Taylor represents his position as undemocratic and
reactionary. Taylor, however, considered his teaching
to be both democratic and progressive.

Taylor's concept of theory and practice in republican government are full of paradoxes. He vigorously
defended capitalism, yet he vehemently opposed capital-
ists; he warned that aristocracy was unnatural and
dangerous to liberty, yet he was the wealthiest and
most powerful figure in Caroline County; he argued that
political parties were antagonistic to republicanism,
yet he was instrumental in the formation of the Republican Party; he claimed that self-interest was natural
to man and that commerce was central to America, yet he
opposed the spirit of ambition and avarice; he played a
prominent and active part in the regular political
process, yet he frequently withdrew in disgust and
entertained ideas of nullification and secession; he
stoutly defended strict construction, yet he argued
strongly in favor of the Louisiana Purchase, he claimed
that equality and liberty were central to the American
experience, yet he defended the institution of slavery;
he argued that there was a united people of America, yet
he divided the people into several states; he claimed
that the will of the majority, not the minority, should

prevail, yet he erected a comprehensive system of
mutual vetoes which would have prevented even a decent
majority from governing. These paradoxes have been
either ignored or inadequately reconciled by the
secondary literature. It is the aim of this essay both
to reconcile these apparent contradictions and to
suggest the proper place of Taylor's thought in the
development of our understanding of constitutional
government in the republican tradition.

The person most responsible for our contemporary
understanding of Taylor's political thought is Charles
Beard.[4] He considered The Federalist and Taylor's
Inquiry Into the Principles and Policy of the United
States to be the two works in American political
thought most worthy of immortality.[5] Beard's understanding of The Federalist has been carefully examined
and generally refuted. But the process of rediscovering
the teaching of Publius has reinforced his judgment
concerning the immortality of that work.[6] Beard's
understanding of Taylor's Inquiry on the other hand has
been uncritically accepted with the consequence that
there has been little attempt to rediscover the teaching
of Taylor. The acceptance of Beard's interpretation
has secured a position of oblivion rather than immortality for Taylor's Inquiry.[7]

Beard considered Taylor "the philosopher and
statesman of agrarianism," and his Inquiry "the textbook
of agrarian political science, conceived in opposition
to capitalism and dedicated to a republic of small
farmers."[8] Beard relied on the Inquiry, as he relied
on The Federalist, to demonstrate his own thesis that
the divisions in early American politics were wholly
economic. Thus Taylor was the apologist and spokesman
for the agricultural class and the Inquiry was a statement of the agrarian doctrine designed to advance the
interests of the agricultural class.[9] Taylor, and his
Inquiry, epitomized for Beard the essential character
of "Jeffersonian Democracy."

> The possession of the federal government
> by the agrarian masses led by an aris-
> tocracy of slave-owning planters, and
> the theoretical repudiation of the right
> to use the Government for the benefit
> of any capitalistic group, fiscal,
> banking, or manufacturing.[10]

Beard's Taylor is an aristocratic agrarian who
leads the proletariat mass in its, ironically, reactionary class struggle against the capitalist class.
Those who followed Beard's mode of analysis easily
turned Taylor's work into a hastily contrived defensive
ideology on behalf of a dying aristocratic agrarian
order against the irresistible force of capitalism. On
the contrary, as we shall see, Taylor argued that the
essential political battle was between the people and
a class which had emerged unnaturally in classless
America. This new class was essentially foreign to
American soil and counterrevolutionary for it looked
to Britain and aristocracy as its models.

Other scholars have emphasized the federal features
of Taylor's thought in contrast to Beard who emphasized
the commercial aspects. Taylor's disagreement with the
McCulloch v. Maryland decision of 1819, as well as
the Missouri Compromise of 1820, have provided commentators with a counterpoint to John Marshall and an
introduction to the nullification and secessionist
controversies. The fact that three of his five books
were written in response to the decisions of the
Marshall Court and the emerging American system of
Henry Clay, as well as Thomas Jefferson's praise of
Taylor's later works, have helped establish Taylor as an
outspoken defender of states rights.[12] In these later
works, Taylor provides what has come to be called a
"systems approach" to the study of American government.
The essential features of this system are that each
department of each level of government is responsible
for a specific delegated function, and that each
department protects itself from invasion by another
department by means of a veto power. It is a short
theoretical step from Taylor's mutual veto system to the
doctrine of nullification and secession.

The wholly federal approach to Taylor, like the
wholly commercial approach, has effectively secured for
Taylor a position of anachronism and obscurity among
American political thinkers. The error of these two
approaches is that they fail to identify properly
Taylor's point of departure and overarching purpose.
To protect republican liberty from the threat of
minority tyranny is the central concern and unifying
theme in Taylor's reflective writing and his political
activity. He developed an alternative theory of democratic republicanism to the one normally associated
with the founding era and which subsequently came to

177

predominate American political discourse.

Taylor's views on federalism, as were his views
on agriculture, however, were informed by his views
concerning the fate of republicanism. During the
period 1787 to 1800, 1812 to 1824, Taylor perceived the
republican character of America to be in danger. Because he believed that such republican safeguards as
wise legislators, electoral accountability, commercial
freedom, citizen involvement, separation of powers, and
freedom of the press were inadquate, Taylor relied more
heavily on states rights, and agriculture, as a critical
support for republicanism. Taylor's disgust with the
principles and policies of the Federalist Pary in the
1790's, and his fear that the Republican Party after
1812 may have embraced these principles, encouraged him
to withdraw from active political life completely. He
immersed himself in regular party politics, developed
the agricultural interest into an effective political
lobby, and even suggested that Virginia secede from the
union. During the period 1800 to 1812, however, Taylor
considered the republic to be relatively secure, and he
urged that republican measures be taken to secure the
future of the republic. Taylor's reflective concerns
on the nature of republicanism find expression during
this more tranquil period in American politics. Most
of these years were devoted to the writing of The
Inquiry in which very little mention is made of agriculture, and even less of states rights.

I

John Taylor's point of departure is the republicanism of the Antifederalists.[13] Along with them, he
understood the basic choice facing mankind to be either
republicanism or despotism, and correspondingly argued
that the operating principle of the former was reason
and self-government while that of the latter was force
and fraud. Republicanism, they continued, relied on
the habits and customs of the people for its support
while despotism relied on the power of the one or the
few for its continued existence. The greatest challenge, according to the Antifederalists, was to protect
republicanism from degenerating into despotism. To
this end, they followed Montesquieu and argued that
small territory was a vital support for republican
liberty.[14] History had demonstrated that large territories to be governed successfully must be governed

despotically; free institutions are incapable of governing over an extended orbit. Yet the proponents of the new Constitution, especially the authors of The Federalist, presented the novel theory that the survival of republican liberty depended upon an extended territory.[15] The Antifederalist response was that smallness was necessary for republican liberty and that if the small territorial support was abandoned, then extensive precautions must be taken to make sure that only necessary and proper power was delegated to representatives. In addition, the representatives must be restrained by a Bill of Rights and be held accountable by means of recall and rotation. Only thus could the concept of smallness be secured. Because those who supported the Constitution were not prepared to include these institutional precautions when they abandoned small territorial size, the Antifederalists predicted that the government of the United States would degenerate into despotism.

The critical defect of the Constitution, the Antifederalists argued, lay in the proposed "scheme of representation." Representatives chosen from those who least sympathize with the well being of the people, armed with unlimited power of taxation, stationed at a great distance from popular view, free from accountability to the electorate will embark on policies which subvert the liberties of the people.[16] The decisive test of republicanism for the Antifederalists was the ease with which delegated power could be returned to the people.[16] On this point, the Antifederalists judged the Constitution to be defective. Furthermore, they disagreed strongly with The Federalist argument that the source of despotism was the majority rather than a minority of the population.

John Taylor fully inherited this Antifederalist understanding of republicanism. He joined Richard Henry Lee, George Mason, Patrick Henry, and James Monroe in an attempt to prevent Virginia from attending the Philadelphia Convention of 1787, and joined them in opposing Virginia's ratification of the Constitution in 1788.[17] Lee and Monroe were elected by the Virginia Legislature to be the first United States Senators, and when Lee resigned in 1792, the Legislature appointed Taylor as his replacement. During his brief stay in the Senate, he played a prominent part in the attack on Alexander Hamilton's political and economic system. From 1796 to 1800, he served in the Virginia Assembly

and in 1798 introduced the Virginia Resolutions
opposing the Alien and Sedition Acts. Taylor interpreted Federalist rule in the 1790's to be antagonistic
to the true principles of republicanism. He decided
that an accurate diagnosis and complete eradication of
the danger to republican liberty was vital if the American republic was to be more than a short-term abortive
experiment. The Inquiry was Taylor's reflective response to the crisis of the 1790's and his guide for
the future. Published in 1814, it covers the political
battles in American politics from 1787 to 1811. In
practical terms, Taylor's teaching is that the basic
choice facing Americans of every generation is between
the principles and policies of John Adams and those of
Thomas Jefferson. In theoretical terms, Taylor's
teaching is quite similar to John Adams' Defense of the
Constitution of Government of the United States of
America, as well as The Federalist, must be rejected as
the reflective foundation for republicanism in America.[18]
These works, argued Taylor, failed to develop a republican science of politics; they failed to preserve
political and social liberty from the dangers of faction, special privilege, consolidation, monopoly, and
tyranny.

"However disguised," said Taylor, "the true question is discernible." That the true question, "simply
is, whether the existing form of government of the
United States, or the English limited monarchy is
preferable. It is in this question that we are interested."[19] Taylor claimed that Adams' Defense, and
The Federalist, favored the "English system of balancing classes of power, and erecting the orders of
men," and because the authors were men of stature and
reputation, their work discouraged the American people
from seeing the nature of the difficulty and following
the only sure remedy for the disease, namely, a firm
attachment to sound moral principles.

II

In the Preface to his Inquiry, Taylor states that
the nine essays contained in the book are "a beacon
against an exchange of good and lasting moral principles for cobweb and fluctuating numerical balances."[20]
Adams' Defense and Publius' The Federalist are grounded
in the "numerical analysis of government," whereas the
Inquiry, Taylor asserts, is grounded in a "moral

analysis of government." The choice, according to Taylor, is between the ancient or old school of politics which uses Britain as its model and the modern or new school of politics which uses the American Revolution as its model. Adams and Publius assume that "there are only three generical forms of government: monarchy, aristocracy, and democracy, of which all other forms are mixtures."[21] This "ancient analysis of governments" pays attention to form rather than to substance and to numerical orders rather than to moral principles.

Taylor's discussion of morality is within the moral horizon of modernity. That is, he is not concerned with excellence, piety, or civic virtue in the ancient sense. His central concern is wholly modern, namely, to preserve individual liberty from the encroachments of tyrannical government. Like Locke, Taylor wanted a free, reasonable, and comfortable life for men in society. But the prerequisite for such support by Taylor was the moral behavior of men in society. Moral corruption would undermine the polity. The linkage between his moral and political concerns may conveniently be divided into three primary areas. First, the preservation of political liberty requires that certain critical rights be kept out of the hands of government and privileged groups, and placed securely in the hands of the people. Second, economic freedom, or the right to the fruit of one's own labor, requires the choice of a free distribution of income and wealth rather than aristocratic accumulation and concentration of private property. Third, philosophic and religious freedom requires the avoidance of sedition laws and established religion.

These issues constitute the substance of republicanism for Taylor. The Federalist, and Adams' Defense, in Taylor's judgment are concerned more with form than with substance. The republican polity needs a science of politics which can detect opinions and activities which are contrary to the substance of republicanism, and then provide remedies to preserve the purity of the republican enterprise. Taylor argued that the world needed a school of thought which emphasized substance rather than form. "The old school of monarchy, aristocracy and democracy is at issue with the new school of modifying governments with an aspect to moral qualities, and not to numerical orders .... The one found government in the elements of force and fraud, by always bestowing powers, so as to induce it to rest

181

on those elements; the other bestows power so as to
secure its dependence on national will, and compels
it to consult national reason."[22]

In contrast to a numerical classification of
governments, Taylor proposes an analysis which "divides
governments into two classes, distinguished by the
moral elements, good and evil. And the terms 'republic
and commonwealth,' have been used to convey an idea of
a government, which being founded in good moral principles, or principles both exciting good and restraining evil qualities, will produce public, common, or
national benefit."[23] The basic choice facing mankind,
therefore, is between republicanism and despotism, not
between government by the one, the few, or the many,
or a mixture of these three numerical classifications.
The unique feature of America, according to Taylor, is
that it destroyed democracy by introducing the principle of election, and destroyed monarchy and aristocracy
by adopting the principles of responsibility and a
division of power. America thus restrained the evil
qualities of force and fraud and encouraged the good
qualities of reason and self-government. The three
numerical forms of government produce bad moral effects
because they are based on the bad moral principle of
irresponsible and undivided power. The defect of the
old school of politics is due to the fact that "either
the use of division was unknown, or it was ineffectively
applied" prior to the American Revolution. In fact,
"Political Philosophy remained unimproved until the
American Revolution, because it assumed ancient
theories for settled facts."

Taylor, therefore, agrees with The Federalist that
improvements have been made in the science of politics
which "were either not known at all, or imperfectly
known to the ancients."[24] But The Federalist goes on
to claim that the separation of powers, legislative
balances and checks, an independent Judiciary, a scheme
of representation, and an extended territorial orbit
are improvements which will permit the first ever enlightened defense of popular government. The critical
modern improvement, continues Publius, is representation
in an extended territory. Since majority faction,
rather than minority faction, is the mortal disease of
popular government, and "faction is sown in the nature
of man," the wise and practical solution consistent
with popular government, is to control the impulse, and
the opportunity, of a majority to engage in activities

contrary to private rights and the public good. The
Publius solution is to extend the territory in order
to control the impulse and to exclude the people from
the ordinary operations of government in order to control the opportunity.

Publius devotes only one sentence to the problem
of minority faction; he argues that this species of
faction can be overcome by the regular operation of the
majority principle. It is unwise to eliminate the
cause of majority faction because that would require
the elimination of liberty; it is impractical to eliminate the cause because man will always discover something to be quarrelsome and contentious about. Moreover,

> Those who hold, and those who are with-
> out property, have ever formed distinct
> interests in society. Those who are
> creditors, and those who are debtors,
> fall under a like discrimination. A
> landed interest, a monied interest,
> with many lesser interests, grow up of
> necessity in civilized nations, and
> divide them into different classes,
> actuated by different sentiments and
> views. The regulation of these various
> and interfering interests forms the
> principal task of modern legislation,
> and involves the spirit of party and
> faction in the necessary and ordinary
> operations of Government.[25]

The Publius solution is two-fold; first, to divide the
society into a multiplicity of opposite and rival interests which collide and collude with each other in an
extended territorial orbit; second, by a "new and para-
doxical" scheme of representation totally exclude "the
people in their collective capacity from any share" in
the necessary and ordinary operations of government.[26]
These two solutions will break and control the "most
common and durable source of factions," namely "the
various and unequal distribution of property."[27]

Taylor, however, denies that representation in an
extended territory is the decisive modern improvement,
and claims that both Publius and Adams are part of the
old school of politics. The decisive modern improvement is the discovery of "ethereal moral principles"
which are "the only means for preserving a free and

moderate government." Publius and Adams follow the
British system by relying on ambition to counteract
ambition and power to control power. They also rely on
the British system of virtual representation rather
than real representation of the people. Everything in
their works can be found in the English writers of the
seventeenth century, rather than in the "strong home-
spun threads of plain principles" which characterize
the American experience. But "to moderate official
power by official power was something like weakening
alcohol with alcohol."[28] They fail to realize that
"Evil moral principles cannot be made to produce good
moral effects by the force or form of artificial
arrangement; it would be as possible that a less mechanical power should control a gerater."

Taylor's moral science of politics, in contrast to
that of Publius and Adams, is revealed most clearly in
the following critique of Adams Defense: "Our policy
divides power, and unites the nation into one interest;
Mr. Adams's divides a nation into several interests, and
unites power."[30] Taylor envisions a nation whose "moral
individuality" and "moral liberty" will be destroyed if
it is divided up into several "opposite and rival interests." Instead of a union of interests among equal
citizens who subject the government to the reason and
will of such a nation, a situation will develop where
a noble nation, a monied nation, a manufacturing nation,
and many lesser nations compete and balance each other.
This system of mutual jealousies disfigures the national
good, and a nation divided and distracted by separate
orders and distinct interests operates against reason
and on behalf of force and fraud. The great danger to
the American experiment in liberty, he wrote, "lies in
the legal depredations of the various parties actuated
by exclusive interests, natural to the British policy,
such as court interest, a military interest, a stock
interest, and various other separate interests, whose
business it is to get what they can from the rest of
the nation."[31]

Publius and Adams fail to understand that "a
government is good, when it is coupled to the general
interest and bad, when it is coupled to a particular
interest of any kind, whether military, hierarchical,
feudal, or stock." Publius and Adams fail to grasp the
importance of a nation retaining rights against the
government and special interests who will use the
governmental process for the promotion of their own

particular objectives.

The critical test of republicanism for Taylor, as it was for the Antifederalists, was whether or not there were clear provisions for the reversion of sovereignty from the representatives to the people short of revolution or secession. Taylor is critical of both Publius and Adams for their loose definition of republicanism. Publius defines a republic as a polity "derived from the great body of the society," administered by individuals who hold their appointments either for a limited period or during good behavior, and who are appointed either directly or indirectly by the people.[32] Taylor deemed this definition to be wholly inadequate. Furthermore, Adams' claim that republics are all forms of government except the despotism of one man is also totally inappropriate. Their definitions, according to Taylor, reflect their attachment to the ancient numerical science of politics and their ignorance of the division of power concept, the "most useful" of which is the "rights retained by nations, as unnecessary for governments." Both Publius and Adams, in effect, perceive sovereignty to rest in the government rather than in the people, and through their scheme of representation, the people delegate the whole force of governing. This is the anthesis of republican self-government as far as Taylor is concerned.

A republic, according to Taylor, is the only government "which would cautiously avoid to excite evil moral qualities, and carefully attempt to suppress them if they should appear."[33] But The Federalist and Defense encourage rather than discourage the evil qualities of jealousy, force, fraud, superstition, discord, avarice, ambition, and hatred. As a consequence, particular interests or orders will be advanced and balanced at the expense of popular sovereignty and the public good. Taylor warns repeatedly that "at this era of the world, avarice is man's predominant vice. It can only be gratified at the cost of man, and of the major number of men."[34] The true republican remedy is to defend the rights of individuals "against these very associations" animated by lesser motives.[35]

A republican government "produces public or national good" by relying on the sovereignty of the people and "a thorough system of responsible representation." To follow Adams and Publius is to encourage the demise of republican self-government and the return of despotism. The choice is clear:

> We must take our stand between govern-
> ments who leave to nations the right of
> self preservation, and those who wish to
> destroy it. No other government, ancient
> or modern, has fairly provided for the
> safety of this right. In all others, it
> is fettered by compounds of orders or
> separate interests, by force or fraud
> .... The national right of self-govern-
> ment and national orders, cannot associ-
> ate. Our policy is erected upon one
> principle; Mr. Adams's upon the other.[36]

Although this judgment refers specifically to Adams, it
also summarizes Taylor's judgment of the system explained by Publius. Taylor considers his approach to
be superior because, unlike the numerical system of
Publius and Adams, it defines a good form of government, detects infractions of its basic principles, and
shows a nation how to remove these infractions.

It is also important to note that Taylor also
differs with Adams and Publius in his understanding of
the nature of man. He does not believe that either
aristocracy or faction are natural and inevitable. In
his first, third, fourth, and eighth essays, Taylor
tries to show that Adams' idea of a mixed or balanced
government was derived from his understanding of the
nature of man which understanding was irrelevant for
modern democratic America. In his work, Taylor divides
the history of the world into three critical epochs,
two ancient and one modern. The first two epochs are
described as the aristocracy of the first and second
ages. Force and fraud were the dominant qualities of
these two earlier ages and consequently an aristocracy
prevailed. "For the sake of perspicuity, I shall call
the ancient aristocracy, chiefly created and supported
by superstition, 'the aristocracy of the first age;'
that produced by conquest, known by the title of the
feudal system, 'the aristocracy of the second age.'"[37]

But with the arrival of the Enlightenment, the
good moral principle of reason replaced these evil moral
principles. America, in particular, is part of the
modern democratic era where "clanship is melted down
into one mass of civilization."[38] Aristocracy is alien
to America because "talents and virtue are now so widely

distributed ... and the distribution of wealth produced by commerce and alienation, is equal to that of knowledge and virtue, produced by printing."[39] Adams' system of checks and balances, argues Taylor, assumes the existence of the aristocracy of the second age. But the social conditions for a mixed regime are absent in America. In particular, the landed interest in America is "irretrievably republican" rather than aristocratic. In short, the natural condition of man in America is freedom from aristoctracy and faction; there is a basic equality of social condition and unity of interests. To the extent that aristocracy and faction do exist in America, it is due to artificial rather than to natural causes.

III

Taylor accepts the premise of The Federalist that America is a civilized nation in the age of commerce. He also agrees with Publius that property should be distributed by talent and industry rather than by law. But whereas The Federalist diagnoses the greatest danger to be the "spirit of levillism," Taylor's Inquiry argues that the "spirit of monopoly" is the fatal disease to be avoided. The danger to republican liberty comes not from the majoritarian spirit of expropriation but from the aristocratic spirit of exploitation. Publius argued that the "most common and durable source of faction is the various and unequal distribution of property." The Founder's solution was to promote a system of opposite and rival commercial interests and regulate their activity, thus reducing the impulse of a majority to capture the government and redistribute the amount of property by law in their favor. Taylor, on the other hand, perceives the danger differently. The source of faction is the force and fraud of the few rather than the depravity of the many. The republican remedy is to eliminate the causes rather than to control its effects. The few can no longer monopolize virtue and talent, but in the age of commerce the few have the impulse to monopolize wealth. The danger of republicanism comes from the aristocracy of the modern or third age. The danger to civilization is civilized tyranny: "For the sake of perspicuity, I shall call that (aristocracy) erected by paper and patronage, 'the aristocracy of the third or present age.' It is the most dangerous enemy to the nation .... It enables a minor interest to guide and submit on a major interest."[40]

187

Taylor's _Inquiry_ argues that it is both wise and practical to eliminate this "new enemy to human liberty." Man is capable of self-improvement and reason can guide self-love. "Government is not simply a necessary evil but a moral agent whose object is to promote good and eliminate evil." "Our system does not attempt to restrain vice by provocative to vice." The error of both Publius and Adams, according to Taylor, is their failure to distinguish natural property from artificial property and natural interests from artificial interests. The true object of government is to protect those faculties by means of which natural property is acquired. Following Locke, the object of government is to protect the "industrious and rational" faculties. It is not the object of government to encourage "the fancy or covetousness of the quarrelsome and contentious." Most commercial interests do, as Publius claims, grow up by necessity and by the natural course of things in a modern capitalistic country. "Agriculture, manufacturers and commerce, are indigenous, as it were, to human comfort and happiness."[41] To be sure, these natural interests, "agriculture, commercial, mechanical, and scientific,"[42] do not have identical opinions, passions, and interests. But a basic harmony does exist between these interests, and their welfare is identical to the welfare of the nation.

Other interests, however, such as hierarchical interest, a patrician interest, a funding interest, a banking interest, and a stock interest are, Taylor argues, "factitious separate interests" of legal rather than of natural origin.[43] They do not grow up of necessity in civilized nations. These interests are incapable "of including a majority of the nation" and this minority subsists on the industry of the people by means of force and fraud. Among civilized people no species of tyranny can exist without the help of aristocracy and minority is the essential ingredient without which aristocracy cannot exist.[44]

These artificial interests attempt to seduce each of the natural interests into an alliance against the other natural interests. The agricultural interest is especially susceptible to temptation because many landowners perceive themselves to be aristocratic. But in America "the landed interest being incapable of becoming an aristocracy itself, must unite with the other natural interests of society in maintaining a republican government, or submit to an aristocratical monarchy of which it cannot constitute a part."[45] These sinister artificial interests enter the public councils through the election system and they influence public councils by temptation. They separate the representatives from the people, and divide the nation into artificial factions. The good moral principles of politics shows that "whatever destroys a unity of interest between a government and a nation, infallibly produces oppression and hatred."[46] They persuade the legislature to distribute property by law rather than leaving property to be regulated by natural talent and industry. According to Taylor "a transfer of property by law, is aristocracy, and ... aristocracy is a transfer of property by law."[47] The unnatural aristocratic faction thus acquires "power to take from a nation and give to itself." Such activity is the very definition of civilized tyranny. The principal task of modern legislation must not be the distribution of wealth by law, but the defense of the property of the people from the fraudulent and forceful activities of the ambitious and avaricious few. These few interests are artificial interests; they could not exist without legal support and these interests have opinions and passions adverse to the national good. "If separate legal orders or interest are the causes of social oppression, free government ensues of course, by avoiding them."[48] In other words, it is both wise and practical to eliminate the cause of faction.

IV

John Taylor's Inquiry offers an alternative teaching on republicanism from the teaching found in Adams' Defense and Publius' The Federalist. In the tradition of the original Antifederalists, Taylor warns that unless the scheme of representation is grounded in good moral principles and animated by good moral human qualities, then a form of tyranny far worse than ancient tyranny will emerge. Liberty has won the battle against superstition and feudalism. But now there is a new source of oppression which takes its bearings from the character of the new age. We are living in the age of commerce and, therefore, we must guard liberty from the danger of commercial tyranny. The problem with The Federalist, and Adams' Defense, from Taylor's perspective is that these works fail to design a science of politics which can diagnose the ills of the new age.

189

Whereas The Federalist wishes to prevent the existence
of the same opinion in a majority of citizens at the
same time, Taylor urges instead that the salutory
opinion of the people must be preserved. Whereas The
Federalist urges that the majority must find itself in
a difficult situation with respect to discovering and
acting on its strength, Taylor argues instead that the
purpose of republican constitutionalism is to make this
easy and safe. This purpose can be achieved because
the people of America are not wanton, disobedient, or
turbulent. Whereas Adams' Defense argues that classes
and orders must be balanced to preserve liberty,
Taylor warns instead that artificial and natural
interests are enemies. Taylor's Inquiry argues that
the preservation of liberty depends first on uniting
rather than dividing the society, and second on
dividing rather than uniting power.

    The crisis in confidence which has plagued
America's political and social institutions in recent
decades would come as no surprise to Taylor. He would,
and did, argue that to the extent that the American
system is guided by the principles of The Federalist
and the Defense, widespread citizen apathy and base
personal motives are to be expected. How could it be
otherwise when the people are deliberately excluded
from having an active role in politics and ambition
is supposed to counteract ambition? The two basic
principles of The Federalist and the Defense--of rival
and opposite interests, and the nature of representation respectively--received extensive comment by Taylor.
As we wrestle with our own problems of institutional
crisis, it will be helpful for us to keep Taylor's
original critique in mind. The American constitutional
system today is still guided by the principles of these
two seminal works.

NOTES

I wish to thank the Earhart Foundation for supporting
my work in American political thought.

[1]John Taylor's books are Arator: Being a Series
of Agricultural Essays, Practical and Political,
(Georgetown, Columbia: J. J. and J. B. Carter, 1813);
An Inquiry into the Principles and Policy of the
Government of the United States, (Indianapolis: The
Bobbs-Merrill Co., Inc., 1969), Construction Construed
and Constitutions Vindicated, (Richmond: Shepherd and
Pollard, 1820); Tyranny Unmasked, (Washington City:
Davis and Force,1822); New Views of the Constitution,
Washington City: Way and Gideon, 1923). All subse-
quent references to the second book mentioned above
will use the abbreviation Inquiry. Among the more
important of Taylor's pamphlets are An Enquiry into
the Principles and Tendencies of Certain Public
Measures (Philadelphia: Thomas Dobson, 1794; Definition
of Parties (Philadelphia: Francis Bailey, 1794); A
Defense of the Measures of the Administration of
Thomas Jefferson (Washington, D.C.: Samuel H. Smith,
1804). Taylor served in the Virginia House from 1779
to 1785 (with the exception of 1782) and again from
1796 to 1800 where he played a critical part in the
defense of the Virginia Resolutions of 1798. He
served in the United States Senate on three occasions:
1792 to 1784, 1804, and from 1822 until his death in
1824. His most noteworthy accomplishments include an
attack on Alexander Hamilton's funding system, and
later Henry Clay's American system, as well as a defense of the Louisiana Purchase.

[2]C. William Hill, Jr's., recent book on Taylor is
an attempt to rectify this defect. Hill has produced
the first comprehensive account of Taylor's political
thought, but he is more interested in testing Taylor
by the contemporary standards of political theory than
he is in taking the reader into Taylor's world and
being a critical guide. See C. William Hill, Jr., The
Political Theory of John Taylor of Caroline (Cranbury,
New Jersey: Associated University Presses, Inc., 1977).

[3]Scholarship on the Antifederalists has been
rejuvenated recently by the work of Cecilia M. Kenyon,
ed., The Antifederalists (Indianapolis: The Bobbs-
Merrill Co., Inc., 1966); Morton Borden, ed., The

191

Antifederalist Papers (Lansing: Michigan State University Press, 1965); Jackson Turner Main, The Anti-Federalists: Critics of the Constitution 1781-1788 (Chicago: Quadrangle Books, 1964).

[4]Charles Beard, Economic Origins of Jeffersonian Democracy (New York: The Free Press, 1965). See also Charles A. Beard, "Time, Technology, and the Creative Spirit in American Political Science," The American Political Science Review (Feb., 1927), especially p. 9.

[5]Beard, Economic Origins, p. 323.

[6]See, especially, Martin Diamond, "Democracy and The Federalist: A Reconsideration of the Framer's Intent," The American Political Science Review (March, 1959), pp. 52-68.

[7]Grant McConnell in an illuminating and sympathetic treatment of Taylor argues that Taylor's reputation "has suffered very nearly as much at the hands of his friends as at those of his detractors." McConnell makes the persuasive case that in presenting Taylor as an economist, Beard "opened the door to widespread misunderstanding of Taylor." See Grant McConnell, "John Taylor and the Democratic Tradition," The Western Political Quarterly (March, 1951), pp. 23-31.

[8]Beard, Op. cit., p. 322.

[9]Ibid. Beard pays almost exclusive attention to three of the nine essays in Taylor's Inquiry: "Aristocracy," "Funding," "Banking." The essential teaching of the Inquiry, therefore, is Taylor's attack on Hamilton's financial system.

[10]Ibid., p. 467. One year after Beard wrote his article in the American Political Science Review, Benjamin F. Wright, Jr. wrote a rebuttal. Wright agreed with Beard that Taylor was "the philosopher of Jeffersonian Democracy," but he denied that Taylor's essential teaching was economic. "The Philosopher of Jeffersonian Democracy," American Political Science Review (No., 1928), pp. 870-892.

[11]Avery Craven, "John Taylor and Southern Agriculture," Journal of Southern History (May, 1938), pp. 137-147; Bernard Drell, "John Taylor of Caroline

192

and the Preservation of an Old Social Order," The Virginia Magazine of History and Biography (Oct., 1938), pp. 285-298; Manning Dauer and Hans Hammond, "John Taylor: Democrat or Aristocrat?" The Journal of Politics (Nov., 1944), pp. 301-340.

[12]The most notable commentaries in this regard are Henry H. Simms, Life of John Taylor: The Story of a Brilliant Leader in the Early Virginia States Rights School (Richmond: The William Burd Press, Inc., 1932); William E. Dodd, "John Taylor of Caroline, Prophet of Secession," John P. Branch Historical Papers of Randolph-Macon College (June, 1908)., pp. 214-252.

[13]Op. cit., Kenyon and Borden readings. The following brief summary relies heavily on the pamphlets and letters of "Agrippa," "Brutus," "Cato," "Centinel," and "Federal Farmer" as well as on an unpublished manuscript by Gordon Lloyd and William B. Allen: "An Antifederalist Alternative to Federalist 10."

[14]Montesquieu, The Spirit of the Laws, trans. Thomas Nugent; rev. J. V. Prichard (London: George Bell and Sons, 1878), especially Book VII, chapters 16 and 19.

[15]Jacob E. Cooke, ed. The Federalist (Middletown: Wesleyan University Press, 1961). All references in this paper to The Federalist will be to this edition.

[16]For a response to these Antifederalist criticisms, see The Federalist numbers 55-58.

[17]According to William E. Dodd, Taylor followed Mason, his "beau-ideal in statecraft," and wrote several pamphlets, under an assumed name, against the ratification of the Constitution. Unfortunately, these pamphlets cannot be found in any known collection. Nevertheless, his opposition was considered important enough to prompt Madison to write a letter of warning to Edmund Pendleton. The latter was Taylor's Federalist uncle who along with James Taylor, John Taylor's Antifederalist cousin, represented Caroline county at the Virginia Ratifying Convention. For reasons more personal than political, John Taylor decided not to compete with Pendleton for admission to the Ratifying Convention.

[18]Several Antifederalists had argued that Adams'

<u>Defense</u> was influential in forming opinion at the
Philadelphia Convention, and represented a deviation
from republican principles. See, for example,
"Centinel I," <u>Independent Gazetter</u>, Oct. 5, 1787;
"Anon," <u>Conn. Journal</u>, Oct. 17, 1787; "John Humble,"
<u>Independent Gazetter</u>, Oct. 29, 1787; "Alfred," <u>New
York Journal</u>, Dec. 25, 1787. Taylor developed these
reservations into a comprehensive attack. The <u>Inquiry</u>,
in turn, generated a response from Adams who wrote
thirty-two letters objecting to Taylor's interpretation. The Adams-Taylor exchange, unfortunately, has
been overshadowed by the more famous Adams-Jefferson
exchange.

[19] <u>Inquiry</u>, <u>Op. cit</u>., p. 85.

[20] <u>Ibid</u>., p. 5. M. E. Bradford in his introduction
to a new edition of Taylor's <u>Arator</u> links Taylor's
teaching to the teachings of ancient historians and
social philosophers as well as to specific Greek and
Roman prototypes. Taylor, however, considers himself
to be wholly modern. Bradford's error is that he
assumes that a discussion of morality must be basically
ancient in scope and design because moderns are not
interested in morality. M. E. Bradford, ed., <u>Arator</u>
... by John Taylor (Indianapolis: Liberty Classics,
1977).

[21] <u>Ibid</u>., p. 14.

[22] <u>Ibid</u>., p. 141.

[23] <u>Ibid</u>., p. 97.

[24] <u>The Federalist</u>, <u>Op. cit</u>., number 9, p. 51. See
also Diamond, <u>Op. cit</u>. The following summary relies
heavily on the incisive interpretation given to <u>The
Federalist</u> by Martin Diamond. In addition to the above
mentioned article, particular attention should also be
given to his "Ethics and Politics: The American Way,"
in Robert H. Horowitz, ed. <u>The Moral Foundations of
the American Republic</u> (Charlottesville: University
Press of Virginia, 1977), and to his "<u>The Federalist</u>,"
in Leo Strauss and Joseph Cropsey, ed. <u>History of
Political Philosophy</u> (Chicago: Rand McNally and Co.,
1972).

[25] <u>The Federalist</u>, <u>Op. cit</u>., number 10, p. 59.

[26] _Ibid_., number 63, pp. 422-431. Emphasis in original.

[27] _Ibid_., number 10, p. 59.

[28] _Inquiry, Op. cit_., pp. 5-6.

[29] _Ibid_.

[30] _Ibid_., p. 368.

[31] _Ibid_., p. 6.

[32] _The Federalist, Op. cit_., number 39, p. 251.

[33] _Inquiry, Op. cit_., p. 74.

[34] _Ibid_., p. 454.

[35] _Ibid_., p. 335.

[36] _Ibid_., p. 375. See also p. 354.

[37] _Ibid_., p. 26.

[38] _Ibid_., p. 24.

[39] _Ibid_., pp. 32-33.

[40] _Ibid_., p. 6.

[41] _Ibid_., p. 234.

[42] _Ibid_., p. 479.

[43] _Ibid_., p. 228.

[44] _Ibid_., p. 472.

[45] _Ibid_., p. 475.

[46] _Ibid_., p. 41.

[47] _Ibid_., p. 342. Emphasis in original.

[48] _Ibid_., p. 552.

CHAPTER 9
"Legal Science Revisited and Reinterpreted: Roscoe
Pound's The Spirit of the Common Law"
Gary J. Jacobsohn

With few exceptions, the main figures in American
jurisprudence have been judges. Marshall, Wilson,
Holmes, Story, Kent and Cardozo were all renowned
jurists whose contributions to legal philosophy were
significantly, if not exclusively, influenced by their
experiences on the bench. This observation has its
parallel in American political thought where it is by
now a commonplace to observe that the field has been
dominated by politicians, generally those of the
first rank and importance. There is, however, a
difference. No non-politician has had the profound
impact on American political thought that Roscoe
Pound, a distinguished dean of the Harvard Law School,
but never a judge, has had on American jurisprudence.

Roscoe Pound's early career as a scientist--he
had a doctorate in botany--may be viewed, in hindsight,
as the formative stage of his legal training. As perhaps the central figure in the American school of
sociological jurisprudence, a school whose members
insist on applying a rigorous empiricism to the
analysis of law, Pound's scientific background was just
what the doctor ordered at a time when it was widely
felt that American law suffered from a growth-retarding
deductive abstractionism. Pound challenged the orthodoxy of his day and had the satisfaction of witnessing
the ascension of his own ideas to a place of prominence. Alexander Bickel, for example, depicted the
justices of the Warren Court as "children of the Progressive realists." Among this latter group none was
more important than Roscoe Pound.

This essay will examine Pound's science of law
and contrast it with the science of law of the founding
period. Both Pound and the Founders viewed their
respective philosophies as scientific, but that is
where the similarity ends. Pound's work constitutes
an explicit rejection of the prevailing jurisprudence
of the founding period, a point sometimes unappreciated
or overlooked by some operating within the Poundian
tradition so characteristic o f the modern era. This
rejection went to the very core of the Founders' constitutional philosophy--their definition of rights
and the relation of government thereto. His writings
enable us to distinguish between the principal juris-

prudential commitments of the two periods and to
consider what we have gained and lost in the movement
from one to the other. From among his numerous
writings this essay focuses upon The Spirit of the
Common Law, written originally as a series of lectures
delivered at Dartmouth College. It is an important
work that effectively summarizes the major ideas of
Pound's earlier writings and anticipates those that
followed. Moreover, it is Pound at his best in combining his considerable talents as legal historian and
legal philosopher.

I

    Pound's analysis of American law in the late
eighteenth century is clearer if viewed in the context
of his reaction to the legal condition of his own time,
the early twentieth century. "The present crisis" of
American law thus serves as the background for his
reflections on the past.[1] The crisis mentioned by
Pound was a result of the judiciary's inability or
unwillingness to adapt the techniques and sources of
their adjudication to the demands of a rapidly evolving
industrial society. The realities of the social situation require a new definition of justice, one more in
tune with "the world-wide movement for socialization of
law,"[2] one that recognizes the ineluctable trend toward
interdependence that characterizes the human situation.
But the sad fact, as Pound saw it, was that judges were,
on the whole, wedded to the ideas of the past, incapable
of transcending their commitment to abstract individualism in favor of a judicial empiricism responsive to
actual needs and wants. Thus, for example, the Supreme
Court could cavalierly assert and defend the primacy
of liberty of contract in the face of accumulating
evidence that the contractual parties to whom this
liberty applied were obligated to accept any agreement
dictated by the superior economic position of the
industrial elite.[3] Pound, it should be noted, was a
critic of the economic interpretation of legal history;
thus, the judiciary ought not to be viewed as a co-
conspirator in a cabal of the economic elite or as a
part of the superstructure of the society's mode of
production.[4] This had its positive and negative sides.
One did not have to wait for further evolution of the
economic order to alter the behavior of judges. On the
other hand, the extraordinary attraction of outmoded
ideas to jurists (and scholars as well) who should have

known better, testified to the formidable impediments standing in the way of any fundamental re-orientation in judicial attitudes and performance. "Tenacity of a taught legal tradition is much more significant in our legal history than the economic conditions of time and place."[5]

Pound's objectives were thus formidable. Challenging tenaciously held traditions is difficult enough; challenging one that had been sanctified by the founding fathers is even more so. The legal tradition that engaged Pound in intellectual combat was a legacy of the generation of Hamilton, Jefferson, Adams, and Wilson. It was not always faithful to the commitments of these men, but it never wavered from the basic assumption underlying their considerable achievement. For Pound, this assumption was individualism, or more to the point, "ultraindividualism."

As far as the law is concerned, this ultraindividualism may be defined as "an uncompromising insistence upon individual interests and individual property as the focal point of jurisprudence."[6] It is uncompromising in that it makes no concession to "social righteousness." "It is so zealous to secure fair play to the individual that often it secures very little fair play to the public."[7] This is not meant to deny the importance of protecting individuals in their personal rights, and for this Pound more than once expresses his gratitude and appreciation. But he does dichotomize private right and public welfare, seeing them in an age of interdependence in fundamental tension and contradiction. Inadequate, in Pound's view, is Blackstone's assertion that "the public good is in nothing more essentially interested than in the protection of every individual's private rights."[8] Indeed, Blackstone's "complacent nothing-needs-to-be-done attitude" is in large measure attributable to this narrow focus on the individual abstracted from his social context.[9] That the English legal authority was so influential in colonial America is, for Pound, as noteworthy as it is regrettable.[10]

Pound's analysis of early American law indicates the causes of our ultraindividualistic jurisprudence to have been plural not singular. They ranged from the environmental (the conditions of a pioneer society) to the historical (the contrast between the courts and the crown in the seventeenth century) to the religious

198

(the demands of Puritan doctrine) to the intellectual
(the attraction of the political and philosophical
ideas of the eighteenth century). His analysis, however, extends to the question of what might have been
as well as what was. It is here that Pound introduces
an historical model of legal interaction that, he
feels, has important contemporary significance. This
model is that of the common law, correctly perceived in
terms of its original spirit, feudalism. Now it may
appear strange for a social reformer like Pound to advocate a feudal model as appropriate for our circumstances. Moreover, it is initially jarring to confront
the observation that the Anglo-American common law of
the founding period, in grounding itself in notions of
contract and transaction, had departed from the true
spirit of the common law, one based upon the feudal idea
of relationships. But it is obviously not the feudal
social order to which Pound was attracted; rather "a
fundamental mode of thought, a mode dealing with legal
situations and with legal problems which. . .has always
tempered the individualism of our law. . . ."[11] Where
the individualism of our law in its beginning "insisted
that every man should stand upon his own feet and should
play the game as a man, without squealing," the "feudal
relation of lord and man regarded man in quite another
way."[12] Obligations between men existed not so much as
a matter of contract and rights but as incidents of a
relation. These relations bound not only individuals
but rulers and ruled. "In the feudal way of looking
at it, the relation of King and subject involved duties
of protection as well as rights to allegiance. The
King, then, was charged with the duty of protecting
public and social interests, and he wielded something
like our modern police power."[13] The feudal model
should thus be treasured in our present condition
where respect for the public interest is a matter of
survival and where such an interest must be distinguished from the totality of private interests.
Whereas we used to say by way of reproach that the
common law was feudal, we should today be grateful for
this heritage and the lessons to be learned from it.

Pound's history of the common law has a profound
bearing upon his jurisprudence. It enables him to
claim that "the natural rights of man deduced from a
social contract. . .is an alien conception in our
law."[14] This observation is ultimately critical in
understanding the difference between the Founders'
perspective on law and that of the sociological school

of jurisprudence. Unlike those who erroneously deny the Founders' jurisprudential commitment to eighteenth century natural rights philosophy, Pound correctly acknowledges their fundamental attachment to these principles.[15] His purpose, however, is to juxtapose these principles with alternative principles of justice in order to demonstrate the superiority of the latter in securing the social good, and with it the happiness of the many. We will see later that this involves the application of the feudal legal model to a new egalitarian social context.

Stated differently, Pound's objective was to replace an old legal science with a new one. He was careful to avoid a common misconstruction of the eighteenth century natural law school as pre-scientific, accepting instead the principles of law that were perceived as inherent in nature and derivable from nature as scientific within the Newtonian paradigm of the day. For Pound the key figure was Grotius, for it was he who "made reason the measure of all obligation."[16] Eventually, through the work of his philosophical successors --principally Coke--the common law of England was transformed into a closed system of legal rules and principles derivative from an immutable and eternal natural law. The Founders accepted this transformation and manifested their acceptance most clearly and emphatically in the various bills of rights that came to characterize their approach to law and obligation. In time there was constructed a "stone wall of natural rights" that served as a "clog upon social legislation."[17] Pound tends to view the later uses (or abuses) of natural law doctrine by the Supreme Court of the late nineteenth and early twentieth centuries as more or less faithful adherence to the tradition of the Founders. In this sense, for example, Justice Field's enlistment of the language of the Declaration of Independence for the purpose of thwarting governmental regulation represents an appropriate application of Jeffersonian principles.[18] In both cases the appeal to eternal verities forecloses inquiry into underlying social realities.

Thus, the legal science of the eighteenth century (witness again our bills of rights) conceived of law as something that the individual invoked against society.[19] For Pound, on the other hand, law was something created by society for the realization of social interests and the protection of social relations. The proper

criterion to be applied in evaluating law is social
utility, that is, the securing of as many interests as
possible without sacrificing other interests. More
will be said of this criterion later; for now it is
sufficient to note that this utility principle constitutes a major departure from the jurisprudence of the
formative era.

The commitment of the Founders to self-evident
truths concerning man and nature, a commitment that
extended to matters of law, precluded their adoption of
a utilitarian jurisprudence. As Morton White has
astutely observed, "The reason why the American revolutionaries were not utilitarians is that they thought
that men had certain duties and rights by nature in
the sense of 'essence'. . . ."[20] They did not accept
the utilitarian theory "according to which man's duties
and rights were expressed in contingent principles. . . ."[21] Pound's rejection of the Founders'
self-evident propositions was a reaction to the fact
that the rights deduced from these propositions were
necessarily impervious to the results of computations
about social felicity. Any law based upon presposi-
tions that are "self-evident" is evidently not scientific, at least not in the sense of the modern paradigm
accepted by Pound's sociological orientation. That
paradigm, in the words of Arnold Brecht, acknowledged
"the impotence of science to establish ultimate standards of justice."[22]

Alexander Hamilton, on the other hand, author of
The Federalist's essays on the judicial power, expressed
the prevailing sentiments of the Founders when he said
in #31: "In disquisitions of every kind there are
certain primary truths or first principles upon which
all subsequent reasonings must depend. These contain
an internal evidence, which antecedent to all reflection
or combination commends the ascent of the mind."[23] He
went on to argue that there are certain truths in ethics
and politics which are analogous to the maxims of
geometry in that they are agreeable to the dictates of
common sense. Hamilton referred to this as the
"sciences of morals and politics,"[24] a term chosen
for its literal meaning. When, in an earlier writing,
he quoted Blackstone's observation that "the first and
primary end of human laws is to maintain and regulate
(the) absolute rights of individuals,"[25] he was not
indulging in idealistic rhetoric, but scientific
analysis.

Stated thusly, the role of law and government
seems rather passive and narrow in scope. Indeed, for
Pound, much too passive and narrow. "Suppose," he
suggests, "we think of law not negatively as a system
of hands off while individuals assert themselves
freely, but positively as a social institution existing
for social ends."[26] Law, we might say, should seek
more than to guarantee the pursuit of happiness; it
should also secure some measure of happiness. It is
worth noting in this context that Jefferson's Rough
Draft of the Declaration of Independence read: "That
to secure these ends governments are instituted among
men, deriving their just powers from the governed,"
whereas in the final version the word "ends" was replaced by "rights." The change, as Morton White has
demonstrated, is significant. In the first case the
verb "secure" means "attain," whereas in the second
case it must mean "make secure" or "guard," since, when
speaking of rights, government need not "attain" what
people already have.[27] White's point is that the substitution represents a change in the intended purpose
of government from that of abettor of men in the attainment of specific ends to protector of their unalienable
rights.[28] If in fact the revision has these substantive
implications (rather than a mere stylistic significance), then we can say of Pound that his philosophy of
law is much more in the spirit of the Rough Draft than
of the actual Declaration. It suggests, as did Jefferson's original formulation, that those bearing the
responsibility of the public trust have an affirmative
duty to insure the well-being of the people, and that
this duty has both a moral and a legal significance.[29]

In saying this, however, one must raise a related
question. Does it necessarily follow from the distinction between happiness and its pursuit, and from the
distinction between social and individual interests,
that law must either be a progressive or conservative
force in society? Pound saw natural rights as the bane
of all social legislation, an observation that is historically accurate for the period during which he did
most of his important work. It is therefore under-
standable when he says: "When houses are scarce and land-
lords are grasping, Blackstone's proposition that the
public good is in nothing more essentially interested
than in the protection of every individual's private
rights is not the popular view. A crowded, urban,
industrial community looks to society for protection
against predatory individuals, natural or artificial,

202

and resents doctrines that protect these individuals against society for fear society will oppress them."[30] Thus, in the early years of the republic, when things were much simpler, and society was much less a problem, the natural rights doctrine, in Pound's view, did not stand in the way of social happiness. Implicit in his analysis is the notion that even before the law had reached its "state of maturity" in the nineteenth century, its underlying natural rights doctrine naturally inclined it against organized societal efforts at social improvement through law.

There is reason, at this point, to question Pound's analysis. For example, he writes: "Under the influence of the theory of natural rights and of the actual equality in pioneer society, American common law assumed that there were no classes and that normally men dealt with one another on equal terms. . . ."[31] A classless society, however, was never an assumption of Lockean natural rights philosophy, as critics and defenders of Locke have long agreed. As Madison put it in Federalist 10, the first object of government is the protection of the "different and unequal faculties of acquiring property."[32] This acquisition would surely not eventuate in equality, but it would, so the theory went, lead to general well-being (i.e. the public interest). Moreover, it is easy to see how the protection of this right of acquisition might partake of positive as well as negative governmental action. If private factors are themselves responsible for the infringement upon the right of acquisition (e.g. through the accumulation of monopoly power), then it becomes the obligation of government to intervene in behalf of those individuals whose exercise of a natural right is being effectively denied. This is in part the theory behind the "police power" of the state, a term first appearing in Chief Justice Marshall's opinion in Brown v. Maryland.[33] The unlimited acquisition of the few may have to be regulated in order to secure the basic right of acquisition of the many. Pound appeals to the feudal conception of law in order to legitimate the police power. But the defense of the police power, and also the case against the old "property Court," may be made in Lockean terms.

A second problem in Pound's consideration of natural rights is his failure to acknowledge the reasonable limits to the exercise of any absolute right that the exponents of the theory themselves insisted

203

upon. In civil society the regulation of rights is necessary for the maintenance of rights. Thus, Pound's depiction of a radical separation between private rights and public good in the theories of Blackstone and his American followers is exaggerated. To be sure, Blackstone did say that the "first and primary end of human laws is to maintain and regulate (the) absolute rights of individuals." But on the next page he defined civil liberty (the end of civil society) as "natural liberty so far restrained by human laws (and no further) as is necessary and expedient for the general advantage of the public."[34] This, of course, falls considerably short of Pound's own expectations for law, but it does indicate an important omission in his assertion that "eighteenth century justice meant the securing of absolute, eternal, universal natural rights of individuals. . . ."[35] This should be qualified in a way that would indicate that while the goal of justice in the abstract was absolute natural rights of individuals, the practical goal in civil society allowed for something less grandiose in scale. The use of natural rights became the abuse of natural rights when judges and others failed to appreciate the significance of this distinction. Jefferson, for example, defined justice in terms of natural rights ("Nothing is unchangeable but the inherent and unalienable rights of man."[36]), but he was a social and institutional reformer all the same. He was indeed an individualist, but he was not (and this applies to someone like Hamilton as well) an ultraindividualist.

Pound's criticism of eighteenth century natural rights philosophy has implications for the structure of law as well as its foundations. In particular, it has an important bearing upon the role of judges in a constitutional democracy. We hear a great deal today of judicial policy-making, not simply the kind that is an inevitable part of all judging, but the determined, active, discretionary exercises of judicial power to effect desirable social change. A debate ranges between those seeking to justify the expanded judicial role and others raising questions about the capacity and legitimacy of the courts acting in this manner. It is a new debate about an old issue--the status of adjudication in a regime of separated powers.

Pound goes to the core of this issue. "We have to combat the political theory and the dogma of the separation of powers."[37] Of course, at the time of

Pound's writing it was not unusual to see attacks directed at the separation of powers; Progressives such as Herbert Croly, Woodrow Wilson, and Arthur Bentley were well known for their critiques. Like these thinkers, Pound was distressed by the seeming inability of government to act effectively in dealing with social and economic problems, and like them he felt that the doctrine of the separation of powers, with its unrealistic division of authority in terms of function, prevented concerted, purposeful government action. Unlike these others, however, Pound's attention was focused upon the courts. The separation of powers stood in the way of judicial empiricism.

As in the discussion of natural rights, Pound seeks to make clear that our political theory of the nature of the judicial function, in which judges interpret and apply law but do not make it, constitutes a departure from the true common law tradition. Rather, "in its origin it is a fiction, born in periods of absolute and unchangeable law."[38] The notion that there are certain immutable laws that are merely discovered and then applied by judges (one of Blackstone's more familiar doctrines) means that whenever judges in effect make law, as they must and have always done, they stand open to the charge of having exercised a usurped authority. "Today, when all recognize, nay insist, that legal systems do and must grow, that legal principles are not absolute, but are relative to time and place, and that juridicial idealism may go no further than the ideals of an epoch, the fiction should be discarded."[39] Later legal realists developed this point and carried its logic to an extreme from which Pound felt compelled to withhold his assent. Nevertheless, it illustrates, even in this moderate version of the argument, a decisive difference in the two approaches to jurisprudence under consideration. Compare, for example, John Adams, who declared in 1786, in reference to the separation of powers, that "It was not so much from attachment by habit to such a plan of power, as from conviction that it was founded in nature and reason, that it was continued."[40] Hamilton echoed these sentiments, describing the doctrine in The Federalist as a "celebrated maxim," and affirming that "there is no liberty if the power of judging be not separated from the legislative and executive powers."[41]

The latter's famous statement that the judiciary "may truly be said to have neither FORCE nor WILL, but

merely judgment"[42] has been generally taken to mean
that the power of judicial review does not confer upon
judges discretion in matters of policy-making. The
opponents of the Constitution had attacked the document
in part for what they perceived to be potential abuses
in the grant of judicial authority. Hamilton was defending against these charges by asserting that the
rule of law, the very essence of constitutional government, precluded judicial discretion. As Marshall said
some years later, the "Courts are mere instruments of
the law and can will nothing."[43] In large measure the
rule of law meant that government officials must stay
within the prescribed limits established by the Constitution for the institutions of which they are a part.
Applied to the courts this implied that judges trans-
gress the rule of law whenever they determine policy
instead of adhering strictly to their assigned task,
the policing of constitutional boundaries and the
application of statutory law.

    Pound was correct in linking this separation of
powers argument to natural law commitments. If we
turn to common law adjudication, Pound's principal
concern, we note that the idea that judges could make
law as an instrument of social change was alien to the
thinking of the constitutional period. The reason for
this is discussed in an important essay by Morton J.
Horwitz. Judges were not to exercise discretion in the
application of common law rules because those rules
were perceived as derivative from natural law principles of justice.[44] They were, therefore, to be discovered, not made, in contrast to statutes, which were
acts of will and hence suitable instruments of innova-
tion. Horwitz argues that the eventual change that
saw common law judges assuming some importance in
directing the course of social change came about only
because the prevailing attitude of the common law as
embodiment of permanent and immutable principles lost
its hold upon the legal and popular imagination.

    It is thus clear why Pound, believing that "legal
principles are not absolute, but are relative to time
and place," should find disagreeable a doctrine that
constrains judges in adapting these principles to
changing values and conditions. A story told to Pound
by William James expresses very nicely what is involved.
"A small boy asked his mother if it were really true
that God had made the whole world in six days. 'Oh
yes,' she answered, 'it was quite true.' 'Did he make

206

it all in six days,' asked the boy? 'Oh yes,' she said, 'it's all done.' 'Well then,' said he, 'mamma, what is God doing now?'"[45] From Pound's perspective, the Hamiltonian view of the judicial power left the judges with nothing to do. It sapped them of their creative potential, making of them automatons engaged in a sterile mechanical jurisprudence. But in doing nothing they were, of course, doing something. They were, Pound felt, playing into the hands of those whose interests lay in the perpetuation of an unjust status quo.

What, then, is the Poundian solution? Not surprisingly, it emerges out of the true "spirit of the common law." "It assumes that experience will afford the most satisfactory foundation for standards of action and principles of decision."[46] It is, in short, a pragmatic solution, in which principled judgments are not derived from a fixed code of ethics, but from an objective, problematic situation that indicates an objective need to the observer. The desire for change stimulated by deficiencies in the environment defines for that observer (for example, a judge) the particular "good" that is to be the goal of his actions.[47] Pound presents his alternative in terms of a novel jurisprudential example. "Let us put the new point of view in terms of engineering; let us speak of a change from a political or ethical idealistic interpretation to an engineering interpretation. Let us think of the problem of the end of law in terms of a great task or great series of tasks of social engineering."[48]

Social engineering is now a familiar term, although in some circles it has acquired a pejorative connotation over the years. When used today it is frequently intended to convey a sense of disenchantment with governmental efforts to restructure a social situation in conformity with some theoretician's vision of the good life. Judges are accused of being "social engineers" by those dissatisfied with judicial policy-making efforts. Indeed, the frequency of the allegation has varied in proportion with the increasing boldness of the courts in attempting to resolve social policy questions. The Warren Court has, rightly or wrongly, come to symbolize the engineer in judicial garb.[49]

If we examine Pound's concept of social engineering we may discern the jurisprudential foundation for much of the work of the modern Court. Pound was himself

rather prophetic on this point. In speaking of the
need for working over the jural materials of the past,
he said: "We shall be warranted in prophesying that
this working over will be effected by means of a
philosophical theory of right and justice and conscious
attempt to make the law conform to ideals. Such a
period will be a period of scientific law, made, if
not by judges, then by lawyers trained in the univer-
sitites. . . ."[50] In this he was influenced by Justice
Holmes, who had said: "I have in mind an ultimate
dependence (of law) upon science because it is finally
for science to determine, so far as it can, the relative worth of our different social ends."[51] That
judges and legal philosophers committed to keeping the
law up to date should be attracted to modern science
is not surprising. A discipline that thinks it should
keep up to date could do worse than to become dependent
upon a discipline that must keep up to date. Once
again, it is important to note that the normative implications of the old science do not apply to this new
dependency. The modern scientific approach provides
the engineer with his methodology, not his ends.

     Social engineering does not require a new vocabu-
lary; only new meanings. Thus, it is not even necessary
to discard the term "natural rights" as long as we
abandon its eighteenth century definition. Instead we
shall take it to mean "interests which we think ought
to be secured; demands which human beings may make
which we think ought to be satisfied."[52] Our focus
should henceforth be on the demands, claims, desires,
and wants involved in social life rather than upon the
rights of abstract man. Pound acknowledges, in this
context, a considerable debt to William James' ethical
philosophy, a cardinal principle of which was "that
the essence of good is simply to satisfy demand."
"Since everything which is demanded is by that fact a
good, must not the guiding principle for ethical
philosophy (since all demands conjointly cannot be
satisfied in this poor world) be simply to satisfy at
all times as many demands as we can?"[53] Pound applies
this Jamesian formulation to the law in a statement
repeated in a number of his writings. "For the purpose
of understanding the law of today I am content with a
picture of satisfying as much of the whole body of human
wants as we may with the least sacrifice."[54] The task
of the legal order is one of precluding friction and
eliminating waste," of "seeking to secure as much of
human claims and desires," as possible.[55] This Pound

208

calls the "engineering interpretation."

Throughout his writings Pound, like James, insisted that the law is not equipped to make distinctions between competing demands according to their intrinsic worth. Skepticism best describes his attitude toward the possibility of developing any absolute standard by which the law can determine the relative weight of the various claims that cry out for recognition. At one point he suggests that while lawyers as a rule still believe in absolute, eternal legal principles of universal validity, the people know better.[56] They understand that law is the reflection of their desires. The appeal of this orientation in a populistic era is unmistakable, as is its attraction to a Supreme Court whose judges, as Alexander Bickel put it, marched to the tune of egalitarianism.[57]

Pound, to be sure, was determined to limit the satisfaction of wants to those that would not disrupt the pattern of civilized society, but his formula for addressing this problem, "the theory of social interests," does not, in the end, serve as a significant limiting factor over demand.[58] Now it must be acknowledged that there is a sense in which his Jamesian ideal is consistent with the intentions of the Founders, although they would have vigorously dissented from this ideal's formulation of the political good. The Founders, particularly Madison, also viewed the political community in terms of "various and interfering interests," each of which would be asserting want-regarding claims in the public arena. And since, as Martin Diamond has argued, their new political science "gave a primacy to the efficacy of means rather than to the nobility of ends,"[59] the new regime did not seek to elevate these wants in the direction of virtue and the good life. Their ethical aims were much less lofty than the ancients, and their politics, the unspectacular goals of which were comfort and security, reflected these lowered expectations. With this much Pound's pluralism was in essential agreement.

But ultimately, the purpose of the Founders' reliance upon a multiplicity of competing interests was the advancement of the public good defined in terms of rights. Maximum aggregate want satisfaction, the hallmark of Pound's social utilitarianism, was not the purpose of the political order. In fact, given their overriding concern with majority faction, a system of

209

this kind was part of the problem, not the solution. They sought the satisfaction of wants only within the framework of a just distribution of rights. Madison's famous definition of faction is suggestive of the difference: "a number of citizens, whether amounting to a majority or minority of the whole, who are united and actuated by some common impulse of passion, or of interest, adverse to the rights of other citizens, or to the permanent and aggregate interests of the community."[60] Unlike the ethical philosophy of James, relied upon by Pound, Madison does not view "anything which is demanded (as) by that fact a good." To the contrary, he assumes that the claims of groups and interests are adverse to the rights of others and the interests of the whole. Moreover, the community is said to have permanent interests separate from the totality of group interests. In the end it is the commitment to this idea of permanence (as opposed to Pound's "ideals of the epoch") that serves to limit demand and circumscribe the satisfaction of wants.

The contrast between these two want-regarding approaches sharpens further if we turn once again from the subject of Madison's essay to the subject of Hamilton's. Whereas in #10 the permanent interest is to be protected by indirection, as it were, through the multiple interactions occurring within the political economy; in #78 it is the role of spokesmen for a body of permanent political principles that legitimizes the judiciary's power in a constitutional democracy. It is in the judicial context, in the treatment of individual cases, that the critical evaluation of claims and desires can be accomplished with special regard given to the primacy of fundamental rights. In a certain sense, then, Pound was correct in saying that "a body of law which will satisfy the demands of the society of today cannot be made of the ultra-individualist materials of eighteenth-century jurisprudence. . . ."[61]

It is, finally, Pound's image of the social engineer that perhaps best suggests the distance we have travelled in American jurisprudence. An engineer, be he of the social or electrical variety, has an obligation to the present. His is an applied science, the task of which is to make useful to man the multiple sources of the physical (or legal) world. He is to accomplish this, in Pound's words, with a minimum of friction and waste; that is, the satisfaction of the desires of those to whom he is responding, must seek to maximize efficiency. While the Founders surely did not countenance inefficiency, their view of the judicial role insured some sacrifice in that direction. Thus, in #78, Hamilton views as "indispensable in the courts of justice" the "inflexible and uniform adherance to the rights of the constitution and of individuals."[62] This necessarily invites a certain measure of friction and waste, for uniformity and inflexibility are rarely the basis of engineering efficiency. The system, however, will tolerate the judiciary's sacrifice inasmuch as its overriding commitment is not to the gratification of immediate desire. Rather, it is to the timeless principles of morals and politics which, according to Hamilton in #31, only the "passions and prejudices" of men can subvert. Thus it is that in #78 he sees as the unique function of the judges, the guarding of the constitution and the rights of individuals "from the effects of those ill humors" associated with "the arts of designing men."[63] The judge as guardian is to be replaced by Pound's engineer. Guardianship and engineering are, of course, not mutually exclusive activities, but the terms do convey a sense of the difference between the old and the new legal science. Guardians can be innovative and creative--indeed they may have to be in order to fulfill their raison d'etre resistance to threats against a set of permanent legal-political principles. Engineers, in turn, cannot ignore the essential judicial function of protecting rights, but their abandonment of the natural law perspective that informed the work of the Founders means that the rights to be guarded vary with the adaptation of law to changing mores and values--vary, in other words, with what is perceived by the new legal science as the central task of adjudication.

NOTES

[1]Roscoe Pound, The Spirit of the Common Law (hereinafter cited as SCL) (Marshall James Co., 1921), p. 7.

[2]Ibid., p. 7.

[3]Most notably in Lochner v. New York, 198 U.S. 45 (1905).

[4]Because they shared much in common it is easy to overlook the fundamental differences between Pound and Charles Beard, the period's foremost proponent of the economic interpretation of constitutional origins and development.

[5]Roscoe Pound, The Formative Era of American Law (Peter Smith, 1960), p. 82. "The outstanding phenomenon is the extent to which a taught tradition, in the hands of judges drawn from any class one will, and chosen as one will, so they have been trained in the tradition has stood out against all manner of economically or politically powerful interests." p. 83.

[6]SCL, p. 37.

[7]Ibid., p. 13.

[8]Quoted in Ibid., p. 53.

[9]Ibid., p. XII.

[10]Blackstone's influence in America is an interesting and oft-told story. See, in particular, Dennis R. Nolan, "Sir William Blackstone and the New American Republic: A Study of Intellectual Impact," 51 New York University Law Review 731 (1976). One should note that Blackstone's ideas were not met with universal acclaim in America. James Wilson and Thomas Jefferson, for example, expressed major disagreement on a number of key issues.

[11]SCL, p. 15.

[12]Ibid., p. 20.

[13]Ibid., p. 68.

[14] _Ibid._, p. 26.

[15] The most notable denial may be found in Raoul Berger's book, _Government by Judiciary_ (Harvard University Press, 1977).

[16] _SCL_, p. 89.

[17] Roscoe Pound, _An Introduction to the Philosophy of Law_ (New Haven, 1922), p. 1.

[18] See, especially, Field's opinion in _Butcher's Union Slaughter-House and Live-Stock Landing Company_ v. _Crescent City Live-Stock and Slaughter-House Company_, 111 U.S. 746, 756-757 (1884). As an earlier example of the judicial practice of "laying out philosophical and political and legal charts by which men were to be guided for all time," Pound cites Chief Justice Marshall's opinion in _Fletcher_ v. _Peck_. _SCL_, p. 97.

[19] _SCL_, p. 204.

[20] Morton White, _The Philosophy of the American Revolution_ (New York, 1978), p. 238.

[21] _Ibid._, p. 239.

[22] Arnold Brecht, _Political Theory: The Foundations of Twentieth-Century Political Thought_ (Princeton, 1959), p. 159.

[23] _The Federalist_, Jacob E. Cooke, ed. (Middletown, Conn., 1961), No. 31, p. 193. It should be noted here that modern scholarship lacks a consensus regarding the epistemology of the self-evident propositions referred to by the Founders. One school of thought, best represented in the work of Carl Becker (e.g. _The Declaration of Independence_), maintains that Locke's rational intuitionism is the key to this epistemology; another, reflected in the recent work of Garry Wills (_Inventing America: Jefferson's Declaration of Independence_), argues for the decisive influence of the "moral sense" understanding of the Scottish Enlightenment. Of course, it is quite possible that disagreement also characterized the Founders' thinking on these matters.

[24] _The Federalist_, No. 31, p. 195.

[25]"The Farmer Refuted," in Harold C. Syrett, ed., The Papers of Alexander Hamilton (New York, 1961), I, p. 88.

[26]SCL, p. 197.

[27]White, The Philosophy of the American Revolution, p. 249.

[28]Ibid., p. 251.

[29]In recent years the notion of affirmative constitutional obligations has received growing attention. See, in particular, Arthur Selwyn Miller, "Toward a Concept of Constitutional Duty," The Supreme Court Review, 1968.

[30]SCL, p. 102.

[31]Ibid., p. 135.

[32]The Federalist, No. 10, p. 58.

[33]12 Wheat. 419 (1827).

[34]Sir William Blackstone, Commentaries on the Laws of England (New York, 1859), I, p. 125.

[35]SCL, p. 151.

[36]Letter to John Cartwright, June 5, 1824, in The Political Writings of Thomas Jefferson, ed. Edward Dumbauld (Indianapolis, 1955), p. 126. Consider in this context the sentiments of James Wilson: "The law of nature, though immutable in its principles, will be progressive in its operations and effects. Indeed, the same immutable principles will direct this progression." Quoted in Benjamin F. Wright, American Interpretations of Natural Law: A Study in the History of Political Thought (Cambridge, 1931), p. 284.

[37]SCL, p. 181.

[38]Ibid., p. 171.

[39]Ibid., p. 172.

[40]Quoted in Wright, American Interpretations of Natural Law., p. 123.

[41]The Federalist, No. 81, p. 543 and No. 78, p. 523. This should be contrasted with Pound's declaration that "We should abandon to some extent the hard and fast line between the judicial and the administrative involved in our legal tradition." SCL, p. 215.

[42]The Federalist, No. 78, p. 523.

[43]Osborn v. Bank of the United States, 22 U.S. 738, 866 (1824).

[44]Morton J. Horwitz, "The Emergence of an Instrumental Conception of American Law, 1780-1820," 5 Perspectives in Legal History 287 (1971), p. 295.

[45]SCL, p. 193.

[46]Ibid., p. 183. This is a view that was shared by Benjamin N. Cardozo, with whom Pound had much in common. See, for example, The Nature of the Judicial Process (New Haven, 1921), p. 116.

[47]For an extended discussion of Pound's relationship to the pragmatic movement in American philosophy, see Gary J. Jacobsohn, Pragmatism, Statesmanship, and the Supreme Court (Ithaca, 1977).

[48]SCL, p. 195.

[49]See, for example, Alexander M. Bickel, The Supreme Court and the Idea of Progress (New York, 1970).

[50]Ibid., p. 84.

[51]Oliver Wendell Holmes, Jr., "Law in Science and Science in Law," 12 Harvard Law Review 443 (1899), p. 462.

[52]SCL, p. 93. See also his discussion of a new natural law ("with a changing or a growing content") in his Interpretations of Legal History (New York, 1923), p. 149.

[53]William James, "The Moral Philosopher and the Moral Life," in The Will to Believe and Other Essays in Popular Philosophy (New York, 1908), pp. 201, 205. This essay had a profound impact upon Pound, who remarked that "this seems to me a statement of the problem of the legal order." Interpretations of Legal

History, p. 157.

[54]Pound, An Introduction to the Philosophy of Law, p. 47.

[55]SCL, p. 196.

[56]Ibid., p. 99.

[57]Alexander M. Bickel, The Supreme Court and the Idea of Progress (New York, 1970), p. 103.

[58]I have discussed the limitations of this theory elsewhere. See Jacobsohn, Pragmatism, Statesmanship, and the Supreme Court, pp. 76-78.

[59]Martin Diamond, "Ethics and Politics: The American Way," in Robert A. Horwitz, ed., The Moral Foundations of the American Republic (Charlottesville, 1977), p. 47.

[60]The Federalist, No. 10, p. 57.

[61]SCL, p. 190.

[62]The Federalist, No. 78, p. 529.

[63]Ibid., p. 527.

CHAPTER 10
"Interpreting the Constitution for a New Era: Woodrow
Wilson's Constitutional Government in the United
States."
Sidney A. Pearson, Jr.

Woodrow Wilson's Constitutional Government in the
United States (1908) is one of the genuine classics of
American government. As with so many "classics," however, it is more often cited than read. The neglect of
this work is unfortunate, because even if Wilson had
not been elected President it would still stand as one
of the major interpretations of the American polity.
The fact that Wilson was elected President within four
years of its publication only serves to make it doubly
interesting. It is the one work that represents Wilson's fullest academic maturity; his final statement on
the nature of the American system of government before
he entered active politics. As such, the argument of
Constitutional Government must be read as a significant
part of the intellectual furniture that filled the
Wilson White House. In addition, Constitutional Government is among the most subtle and influential critiques
of the Constitution produced by the Progressive Movement. It is important to keep in mind both the academic
and political influence of Wilson's work as we explore
its meaning and its argument. Wilson's thesis remains
one of the most influential interpretations of the
American constitutional system, even as the specific
origin of the argument in Wilson's writing have been
largely forgotten.

                           I

    We must begin our study of Constitutional Govern-
ment by pointing out that it is of a very different
genre of political writing than The Federalist. This
difference is crucial for any complete understanding
of Wilson's constitutional interpretation. Wilson was
sensitive to the fact that The Federalist was a work
by practicing politicans whereas his own work was as an
outsider to practical politics. In his own words,
Wilson was a "literary politician." He knew that by
both logic and tradition the Founders were the most
authoritative interpreters of their own intentions and
that The Federalist must therefore be regarded as the
greatest treatise on American government. The Founders'
status was unique and derived from their dual standing
as practicing politicians and as philosophers of their

own political acts; men for whom there was no overwhelming rift between the theory and practice of
politics. The Federalist fit perfectly Spinoza's
dictum on the higher value of this genre of writing;
"...there can be no doubt, that statesmen have written
about politics far more happily than philosophers.
For, as they have had experience for their mistress,
they taught nothing that was inconsistent with practice."[1] Wilson was fully cognizant of this difference
between the Founders and himself and the difference
dictated his approach to constitutional interpretation.

The broad conceptual outline of Wilson's academic
work is readily discernible. Beginning with Congressional Government (1885), he had sought to explain and
describe what he perceived to be discrepancies between
constitutional theory and practice. In Constitutional
Government he presented his arguments in a comprehensive vision that seemed to heal the rift between theory
and practice. In the process of making his final
argument he disputed the fundamental understanding of
constitutional government embodied in The Federalist.
In it he continued to see the central problem of
American politics as one of closing the gap between
what the polity is and what it ought to be. But he
had also come to realize that closing the gap involved
more than the work of practicing politicians. What if
the practice of American politics was already consistent with the intentions of the Founders? If this were
the case, no critique of the practice alone would be
sufficient. The critique of the practice of politics
ultimately involved a critique of the Founders' philosophy as well. In Constitutional Government Wilson was
prepared to make explicit the grounds for his break
with The Federalist; especially the doctrine of the
separation of powers. The price of the separation of
powers, he argued, was a fragmented government incom-
petent to its modern tasks. In practice, the doctrine
worked to frustrate majority rule and democratic government. What he implicitly denied was the Founders'
science of politics; that a free and democratic form of
government was dependent on the proper ordering of
political offices. For Wilson, democracy meant something "organic" very much in the Hegelian sense of
fusing together will and spirit into a single, albeit
popularly elected, leader. In the true form of democracy, which was to be taught by philosophy and not
statesmanship, freedom and democracy would not be
separate principles requiring a separation of powers

in order to hold them in balance.

Wilson's authority as the interpreter of constitutional government depended on two main points.
First, the superiority of philosophy over statesmanship,
even the philosophic statesmanship of the Founders.
Second, Wilson's own unique self-understanding of the
relationship of his writing to the American polity:
that he was engaged in a feat of intellectual endeavor
that would make his work an American "philosophy of
right."

Wilson argued the superiority of his version of
philosophy in a defense of what he called "literary
politicians." In an early essay entitled "Mere
Literature," he sought to counter the notion that
academic scribblers had nothing useful or substantive
to say about politics. Wilson replied to this charge
by arguing that working politicians tended to be little
more than worker bees, caring for the political hive
efficiently enough perhaps, but at best lacking any
comprehensive vision of exactly what they were doing.
The superiority of the academic, such as himself, lay
not in his mastery of insignificant details, but in his
"conviction and vision" of a higher purpose to politics.
Significantly, the status of the literary politician
did not derive primarily from reasoning about the political order, but from poetic insight. The literary
politician, he wrote, "is a very fine, a very superior
species of the man thoughtful...It is necessary to stand
with the poets as well as with the lawgivers."[2]

Wilson's work on the Constitution was basically a
projection of his own philosophy as both subject and
analysis; the Constitution was only the starting point
of his philosophical reflection. He wrote more to teach
his own conviction and vision of what the polity ought
to be than to describe the existent practice of American
government. Constitutional Government is a work of
prophecy; a description of what the United States is
becoming, or will become under the guidance of a new
understanding of political principles. It is intended
to replace The Federalist as a blueprint for a second
founding.[3] The new political system will be characterized by strong presidential leadership that will
replace the separation of powers doctrine as the organizing principle of American constitutionalism. There
is no doubt that Wilson viewed his work as having resolved the tensions and dilemmas of the original

219

Constitution. The problem of practical politics, therefore, was one of translating his political philosophy into political statesmanship; the very opposite of the intention of The Federalist. He consciously adopted a model of political statesmanship that would both conform to his academic status and place his work on a superior footing with The Federalist. The scope and meaning of his work was revealed in his private journal where he wrote, "Why may not the present age write, through me, its political Autobiography?"[4]

II

Wilson's political thought is by no means easy to understand despite its stylistic clarity and the seemingly obvious character of his comments. It is a complex and subtle body of work that has spawned a multitude of strikingly different interpretations. In part this may be traced to the underlying dichotomy between statesmanship and philosophy that pervades his work. His first study, Congressional Government, concentrated on working politicians as a way to dramatize the gap between constitutional theory as taught by The Federalist and the actual practice of American politics. His last work, Constitutional Government, is more philosophical in tone and is presented as a treatise that has bridged the gulf between theory and practice. Scholars who have focused on Wilson's practical teaching about politics have tended to see in his writing a series of disconnected and often antithetical views about American politics.[5] Students of his philosophical framework have been more impressed with its theoretical consistency but have been just as sharply divided over whether it is a liberal or conservative consistency.[6] Some of these divergent interpretations may be reconciled if we keep in mind the fundamental teaching o f Constitutional Government; a new founding of the American polity based on a new set of political principles. Political philosophy at this level of argument is not easily classified as either liberal or conservative, nor is the philosophical side of the argument disposed of by references to inconsistencies in its practical application. Wilson's work can only be critiqued by the standards he set for himself; that is, by contrasting it with The Federalist.

Wilson did not begin his study of American government with a clear and articulated thesis on the nature

of the American Constitutional government. In Congressional Government it was sufficient to point out that
"We are the first Americans to hear our own countrymen
ask whether the Constitution is still adapted to serve
the purposes for which it was intended; the first to
entertain any serious doubts about the superiority of
our own institutions as compared with the systems of
Europe; the first to think of remodeling the administrative machinery of the federal government, and of
forcing new forms of responsibility upon Congress."[7]

Wilson's early reluctance to define the term
"constitutional government" in Congressional Government
resulted in an ambiguous discussion of the relation of
theory to practice in American politics. Congressional
Government contains three overlapping and somewhat
contradictory views of the Constitution: first, that
it is an inadequate basis for a modern democratic
government; second, that it has ceased in fact to be
the organizing basis for American politics; third, that
it is, by the very nature of constitutional development,
shaped by certain external historical forces that continually change the Constitution itself.[8] Wilson
himself was at least partly aware of these conflicting
theoretical views. In a letter to his future wife he
confided that he could not bring himself to use the
word "constitution" in the title of his book because
he could not reconcile his understanding of the term
with the actual practice of American government.[9] His
reading of Walter Baghot on the British Constitution
had convinced him that the United States could not be
studied as a true form of constitutional government.
Until theory and practice could be joined there could
be no true constitutionalism. The unresolved problem
of Congressional Government was the reconciliation of
constitutional theory and practice. What was needed
was a working definition of constitutional government
that would combine with a new statesmanship to replace
the outmoded work of the Founders.

The significance of Constitutional Government in
the development of Wilson's political thought is two-
fold. First, it combines constitutional philosophy
with a form of academic statesmanship appropriate to
Wilson's self-image. Second, the way he combined
philosophy with statesmanship established the pattern
for subsequent arguments supporting presidential
government. Later generations of scholars soon lost
interest in the first point; they nevertheless tended

implicitly to develop the principles inherent in the
second. Although Wilson never used the phrase, the
heart of his argument is essentially that of the
"living Constitution" school of American government.[10]
The major difference between Wilson's work and that of
other proponents of the living Constitution school
concerns the question of whether the President or the
Supreme Court is to be the proper interpreter of the
Constitution. The notion of a living Constitution is
best summarized in the remark attributed to Charles
Evans Hughes, "We are under a Constitution, but the
Constitution is what the Supreme Court says it means;"
that is, the Supreme Court amounts to a permanent
constitutional convention, continually changing the
substance of the Constitution in order to meet changing
circumstances. Wilson would have strongly disagreed
with Hughes. He would have changed the phrase to say,
"We are under a Constitution, but the Constitution is
embodied in the President's conviction and vision of
what the polity ought to be;" that is, only the President can combine constitutional philosophy with the
democratic ethos that is the genius and destiny of the
American people. Wilson's conception of the living
Constitution is neither that of the Founders nor that
of judicial supremacists; rather it is a highly per-
sonalized vision of the "best" constitution as it
exists in the mind of the philosopher and as it will
be realized in practice by the philosopher who becomes
a statesman.

Constitutional Government is carefully organized
around three separate but mutually supporting arguments. First, constitutional government evolves
historically from primitive beginnings of the state
toward a universal and ideal form. It is this his-
toricist element in Wilson's work that most strongly
suggests the influence of the German historical tradition. Second, his historical thesis contains an
analysis of where and how the United States Constitution fits into this evolution. This analysis provides
the basis of his criticism of the Founders' understanding of constitutional government. Third, the
historical thesis itself suggests a prescription for
bringing American government into accord with this
ideal form of the best constitution. It is this last
aspect of his work that contains his new model presidency that breaks dramatically from the Hamiltonian
model in The Federalist.[11] It is a formidable under-
taking by any measure, but one which Wilson effectively

222

made for subsequent generations of scholars who have
followed the constitutional trail he helped to blaze.

Constitutional Government begins with a definition
of the term "constitutional government" that is altogether missing from his earlier works. "A constitutional government is one whose powers have been adapted
to the interests of the people and to the maintenance
of individual liberty."12 This definition, however,
raises certain questions of its own; questions Wilson
sought to answer through his paradigm of constitutional
development. What are the interests of the people?
What are the proper criteria for deciding whether the
constitution has been adapted to the interests of the
people? What tension, if any, exists between the
interests of the people and individual liberty? It is
at this point of defining constitutional government
that it becomes clear that Wilson is not talking about
a legalistic definition of the United States Constitution; that is, the same document defended in The
Federalist as a limited government with enumerated
powers. What Wilson gives us is a verbal picture of
historical progress that culminates in what is essentially a poetic vision of a democratic community. Until
that vision can be made real there can be no true constitutional government.

Wilson's history of constitutional development
begins with the Magna Carta. His omission of the Greek
experience as the starting point for his discussion is
both deliberate and significant. In his earlier work
on comparative government, The State (1890), Wilson
had devoted considerable attention to ancient constitutions and was well aware of how Aristotle had defined
them. His rejection of ancient political philosophy
as the basis for constitutional philosophy involved a
conscious acceptance of modern historicism as superior
to ancient philosophy. The Founders had also rejected
much of ancient political philosophy; specifically,
they had rejected the notion of the best regime based
on virtue for the best possible regime based on a new
understanding of republican virtue. Wilson's argument
reintroduced the notion of the "best" regime as the
basis for political philosophy, but based it not on
virtue, however that ambiguous term might be defined,
but on a notion of historical evolution toward perfection. The Magna Carta and the English historical
experience then became the universal model for constitutionalism.

223

Although Wilson carefully begins his discussion of
constitutionalism with the Magna Carta, he is also careful to point out that constitutionalism has no necessary
connection with a written document.[13] The only true
form of constitutional government is that found in
modern democracies that are a "harmonious community";
not a community of diverse factions as is to be found
in The Federalist. Indeed, the very existence of
factions may be taken as proof that a democracy does
not exist in political reality. He wrote, "A people
not conscious of any unity, inorganic, unthoughtful,
without concert of action, can manifestly neither form
nor sustain a constitutional system... Nothing but a
community can have a constitutional form of government,
and if a nation has not become a community, it cannot
have that sort of polity."[14] The question of whether
the United States is a constitutional polity in Wilson's
meaning of the term thus comes to depend on the nature
of the American community. Is the American community
characterized by a harmony of interests? Wilson's
answer is "no" and the reason for it is rooted in his
historical thesis of constitutional development.

According to Wilson, constitutional government
develops through four distinct stages along a historical
continuum that is universal in its descriptive features;
each step being progressively more harmonious than the
preceding one. In the first stage, government is described as the "master" and the people are ruled by
sheer force. In the second stage, government continues
to rule by force but force is combined with the superior
virtues of an aristocratic ruling class; the great majority of the people are not yet ready to rule themselves. The third stage is really more of a transitional process than a clearly defined stage but it is
the most critical point in the evolutionary process.
It is a revolutionary stage that witnesses a breakdown
of traditional, aristocratic authority, the overthrow
of the ruling elites, and the first tentative signs
that the people are ready to rule themselves. Once the
right of the people to self-rule is established, the
pathway is open to the fourth and final stage of constitutional development in which "the leaders of the
people themselves become the government, and the
development is complete."[15]

The first two stages are relatively unimportant
because they deal with historical development before
actual constitutions make their appearance. Wilson

wastes little time discussing politics in these types of regimes. It is the third and fourth stages that are most important in Wilson's argument. In the third stage communities stand on the threshold of harmony and constitutions begin to take shape. But only in the fourth stage can a polity experience true constitutional government. It is this framework of historical development that provides the key to an understanding of Wilson's final criticism of the Founders and the existent Constitution.

In Wilson's definition of constitutional government the United States has not yet become a constitutional polity because the people have not yet entered into the fourth and final stage of development. Properly understood, the Constitution defended in the pages of The Federalist ought to be nothing more than a historical footnote in the third stage; interesting in an antiquarian sense, but not especially useful in understanding either the theory of constitutionalism or the actual practice of American government. Furthermore, because the United States Constitution is a written document it has had the effect of permanently freezing the development of the American polity in the third stage. By contrast, Wilson described the British constitution as superior because it is an unwritten constitution that permits the unimpeded movement of the community through each of the successive stages of development. Wilson did not believe that the United States had become a "single, homogeneous community" in his own day, but he did believe that the nation stood at the threshold of the final stage and that the Constitution was an impediment to reaching true constitutionalism; "we have come within sight of the merely nationalizing process. Contrasts between region and region become every year less obvious, conflicts of interest less disturbing."[16]

In Wilson's scheme of constitutional development, factional diversity is only found in the first three stages. The Federalist mistook factional diversity that was real enough in at the time for a permanent frature of the human condition. When that assumption was written into the organization of the Constitution the result was that the government remained static while the community continued to develop.[17] As the American community moves further and further away from the time of the founding, the rupture between the theory and practice of constitutionalism becomes more

225

and more pronounced. The continued existence of factions in American politics then came to be explained as due to an improperly designed government rather than to any intrinsic qualities of human nature. The sin of the Founders lay in their institutionalization of a transitory diversity within the community.

Wilson's argument that the Constitution was fundamentally undemocratic was characteristic of the Progressive Movement. Charles Beard made essentially the same point in his An Economic Interpretation of the Constitution of the United States (1913). Progressives saw the Constitution as a problem to be overcome for the realization of democracy rather than as a promise to be fulfilled.18 Their proposals for political reform reflected this basic understanding of the Constitution. What did set Wilson apart from many of his contemporaries was the absence of economic determinism in his work. His writing reflected an intensely pure theory of politics in which economic considerations were of secondary importance. When the Constitution was drafted it was during the third stage of political development and the community did not have the prerequisites for true constitutional government. Madison's conception of factions was pragmatically correct but theoretically false; he was too much the statesman and hence lacked the philosopher's vision of constitutional government. This eighteenth century Constitution, whatever its original merits, was simply an anachronism in the twentieth century. The Federalist theory of constitutional government could never achieve what Wilson called "a vital synthesis" between the will of the community and its government.19 There could be no doubt that the ultimate interest of the people was self-government, but likewise there was no doubt that self-government was impossible under the present Constitution.

The practical problem for Wilson was one of finding the political means to achieve the vital synthesis between the community and the government. Furthermore, since the existing Constitution was not going to be rewritten or significantly amended, any solution would have to be within the basic framework of the separation of powers. Wilson's answer to the problem was a new conception of the presidency and party government that would become the dominant force in American government.

226

III

The importance of the presidency in Constitutional
Government has caught the attention of every reader of
Wilson. In part this is due to the scant attention
paid to the office in his earlier works. How do we
account for this dramatic change of emphasis? Much of
it is surely due to Wilson's careful reading of
Theodore Roosevelt's use of the powers of the Chief
Executive. But Wilson was too much the philosopher
to merely rationalize pragmatic use of political power.
Any exercise of power would have to be philosophically
justified and integrated into a general theory of constitutional government. The example of Roosevelt was
no exception; his presidency confirmed Wilson's belief
that the United States was on the verge of becoming a
harmonious community ready for genuine constitutionalism.

When a community has reached the threshold of self-
government, Wilson wrote, only two forms of government
are theoretically possible; a parliamentary form, such
as Great Britain, or a presidential form, such as the
United States.[20] While Wilson expressed his preference
for the parliamentary form as "simpler and still more
advanced" than the presidential form, he also knew that
the Constitution was not going to be changed in order
to make it conform to his theoretical model of constitutional evolution.[21] His intention was to leave the
outward form of the American Constitution untouched
while its substance was changed beyond the Founders
recognition. This, for Wilson, was how a Constitution
was a living thing, changing or mutating to adapt to
the organic evolution of the community.

Wilson's discussion of the President in Constitutional Government is not a conventional historical
account of past presidents. Nor is it a legal analysis
of the powers of the office as interpreted by the
Supreme Court, debated in Congressional legislation, or
drawn from presidential reflections such as William
Howard Taft's Our Chief Magistrate and His Powers
(1916). Rather, it is a guide for presidental behavior
in office, more akin to Machiavelli's Prince than to
his own earlier, descriptive political science. It is,
however, a logical outgrowth of his conception of the
duty of the literary politician to bridge the gap
between the theory and practice of politics.

Wilson envisoned the President as the instrument
which would attune the practice of American government
with enlightened theory.[22] In order for the President
to fulfill this function to usher in the fourth stage
he would have to find political powers outside of the
formal Constitution. This appropriation of extra-
constitutional powers was justified by his "living
constitution" interpretation of political evolution.
And because the community was on the brink of this
organic unity, the new model presidency was now possible. This development of a harmonic democratic ethos
is intensified by a heightened popular instinct for
unified action that can only find expression in "a
single leader."[23] The public senses the rupture between
the Founders' theory and practice which calls attention
to the distinction between the formal powers of the
presidency and the political powers that originate
outside the written Constitution. Strictly constitutional powers are held by the President as one would
hold a "commission", whereas his "political powers
more and more center and accumulate within him and are
of their very nature personable and inalienable."[24]
Constitutional sources of power have become relatively
insignificant and in any case are to be subordinated to
new sources of political power built on a unified and
homogeneous public opinion. This new democratic reality
means that "The President is at liberty both in law and
conscience to be as big a man as he can. His capacity
will set the limit."[25] The office of the President "is
anything he has the sagacity and force to make it."[26]
From this perspective the Constitution is viewed as
less of a document inhibiting the exercise of power and
more of a means of extending power. As long as the
President acts on behalf of the harmonious will of the
community, there can be no constitutional restrictions
on his behavior.

    Wilson's understanding of presidential power seems
to have been borrowed from Baghot. As Wilson understood
the English Constitution through Baghot, the Constitution was whatever Parliament said it was; there was no
check by another branch of government and no judicial
review in the American sense. Further, because the
Prime Minister did not represent a constituency separate
from the majority party in the legislature, the will of
the community and the will of the Prime Minister seemed
to be one. Under the American system the President
could not make his will identical with that of Congress,
but he could represent the nation as a whole in a way

that Congress could not. Wilson's President was more of a Prime Minister than a President as Hamilton had defined the office. To make the conception even larger, Wilson's President exercised what the Founders might have viewed as a judicial function in his ability to define the Constitution itself. When all these powers and prerogatives are added up, we have an office and a Constitution that is squarely at odds with the founding philosophy of American government.

Wilson's critique of the separation of powers doctrine raises important questions; can the new model presidency abuse his powers?; Is there a tension between the interests of the people as expressed in a democratic majority and individual liberty that may involve the problem of minority rights? The problem was a central concern of the Founders. The reason for stressing the separation of powers was to prevent tyranny, and any argument against the doctrine must deal with the issue of the abuse of power by the government.

Wilson did not directly deal with this problem, but it is possible to reconstruct the logic of his argument in order to see how he conceived the problem. Since the President's real power comes from the community and not the Constitution, abuse of power is linked to the congruence between the will of the community and the will of the President. The misuse of power results whenever the President does not adequately represent the harmonious interests of the people. The perversion of power is more of a philosophical than a legal concept. It is reminiscent of Rousseau's General Will that is violated whenever an individual acts contrary to it. In a similar manner, Wilson linked the individual morality of the leader to his ability to embody the true public opinion. In such a scheme, the distinction between individual liberty and the will of the community would be blurred. Minorities by their very nature could not represent the nation, even should these minorities unite in some sort of coalition to form a temporary majority. It was the duty of the President to transcend political parties in this sense and become, if necessary, a majority of one in his representation of the true community.[27] Wilson was quite explicit on this point; "the personal force of the President is perfectly constitutional to any extent he chooses to exercise it, and it is clear by the logic of our constitutional practice that he has become alike the leader of his party and the leader of the nation."[28]

In this final stage of constitutional development, the President acts according to the will of the community as it is expressed directly through himself. The separation of powers is not so much formally abolished as it is superseded by a new founding of the polity by the President. That is, a President whose vision of the true form of the community commands him to found anew the true form of constitutional government. It is not absolutely clear from Wilson's work whether this is a one-time act of presidential founding or something each president will have to do in turn. It is clear, however, that this view of the presidency corresponds to his view of England as having reached the highest stage of constitutional development.[29] In an earlier essay praising the British Prime Minister, William Gladstone, Wilson set forth his views on what he believed to be the most advanced form of constitutional leadership in the truest form of democarcy: "The great men of the future must be of the composite type of greatness: sound hearted, hopeful, confident of the validity of liberty...They must be wise with an adult and not with an adolescent wisdom. Some day we shall be of one mind, our ideals fixed, our purposes harmonized, our nationality complete and consentaneous."[30]

The role of the President in forming a democratic polity is closely tied to Wilson's advocacy of party government. Wilson's views and influence on the scholarship of party government have been definitively discussed by James Caeser in his study on presidential selection.[31] A full discussion need not be repeated here but a few observations are necessary to complete our picture of Wilson's argument on constitutional government.

Wilson saw the emergence of political parties in the post-Civil War era as a perfect reflection of the tendency of the polity to move toward a more homogeneous community. The imperfections and fragmented nature of the parties were less significant than what they could become. Because parties operated outside of the formal constitutional arrangements of the government they could adapt more readily to changes within the community than could the government. Further, the method of presidential selection and election makes the President both party and national

230

leader.[32] In the past these two roles had not always
been compatible, but as the parties come to reflect the
homogeneity of the community and cease to be coalitions
of diverse factions these two roles of the President
would merge. The proper function of party conventions
is to nominate a candidate who will appeal to the new
community of the fourth stage and not to the diverse
and often conflicting factions of the past. In this
dual role of party and national leader, the President
is a "man who will be and who will seem to the country
as some sort of embodiment of the character and purpose
it wishes its government to have--a man who understands
his own day and the needs of the country, and who has
the personality and the initiative to enforce his views
both upon the people and upon Congress."[33] Whether new
presidents would fully recognize these new facts of
political life depended more on their conviction and
vision than on the appearance of reality around them.
The higher reality was the future and not the past or
present. "We can safely predict," he wrote, "that as
the multitude of the President's duties increase, as
it must with the growth and widening activities of the
nation itself, the incumbents of the great office will
more and more come to feel that they are administering
it in its truest purpose and with greatest effect by
regarding themselves as less and less executive officers and more and more directors of affairs and leaders
of the nation--men of counsel and of the sort of action
that makes for enlightenment."[34]

IV

     The picture of constitutional government that
emerges from Wilson's Constitutional Government in the
United States is one that is characterized by evolutionary change rather than the continuity of fundamental principles. Wilson saw the difference between
his work and that of the Founders as one rooted in a
radically altered view of the basis of "science" in
political science: "The government of the United States
was constructed upon the Whig theory of political
dynamics, which was a sort of unconscious copy of the
Newtonian theory of the universe. In our own day,
whenever we discuss the structure or development of
anything, whether in nature or in society, we consciously or unconsciously follow Mr. Darwin; but before
Mr. Darwin, they followed Newton."[35] The driving force
of constitutional evolution is democracy, understood as

the striving toward harmony and political unity.
Democracy then became an end in itself in Wilson's
thought; this is why there is no apparent tension
between individual freedom and majority rule in Constitutional Government. At the point where the community becomes harmonious, the individual will and the
will of the community are identical. But in the United
States the picture is not yet complete; the community
is not yet harmonious and constitutional government
cannot be consummated. The consummation of constitutional government for the American polity must await
a presidential leadership that recognizes both the
theoretical and practical side of American politics.

Because of the permanence of the nature of the
human condition, the authors of The Federalist argued
for permanent political principles in their constitutionalism. In this sense Wilson is, of course
correct; the Founders did see the world in terms
analogous to Newton's universe of "symmetry and perfect
adjustment." Any science of politics that aspired to
practical application must be built on the "givens" in
the life of political man. The argument for the separation of powers was based on precisely the assumption
that it was applicable for any regime built on the
reconciliation of freedom with justice. In Madison's
words, "As long as the reason of man continues fallible,
and he is at liberty to exercise it, different opinions
will be formed."[36] Diversity and factions were a
permanent part of a free government and the separation
of powers was intended to control the effects that
would inevitably follow in a polity built on such
freedom.

Wilson's understanding of constitutional government was very much in keeping with the nineteenth
century idea of Progress. It was obvious to an observer
as acute as Wilson that the republican principles of
the Founders had given way in popular consciousness by
a new, dynamic commitment to democracy. This new
democracy was placing severe strains on certain Constitutional institutions, most especially the office of
the President.[37] The growing incongruity between the
Founders' and the Progressives' understanding of constitutional government was rooted in different understandings about the nature of democracy. The Founders
were not opposed to popular government, but they did
see democracy, as they saw all forms of government, as
problematical. To them, any form of government could

degenerate into a tyranny unless the ordering of
political offices involved a system of checks and
balances. In contrast, Wilson could not imagine a
democratic tyranny. He saw in the Constitution a complexity that violated his understanding of democracy.
One need not agree with all of Wilson's arguments concerning the nature of true constitutionalism in order
to concur that there may be problems in a democratic
polity that would not necessarily be found in a republican regime. And one of those problems associated
with the rising democratic spirit of the nineteenth
century is the problem of the presidency.

Leadership may be more than simply a problem in
the American Constitution; it may well be the Achilles
Heel of any democratic polity. Democracy tends by its
very nature toward an egalitarianism that undermines
leadership based on received authority, such as an
aristocratic or monarchial form of government. In the
Republic of the Founders the crisis of received authority
was still on the nineteenth century horizon. Paradoxically, however, as American democracy developed
according to the complex principles of the founding,
the Constitution itself came to function in a quasi-
aristocratic manner, as it became the revered source
of received authority. To an extraordinary degree for
a democratic polity, the Constitution enables leadership to be based on a fixed authority. Ordinarily
democracy confers power upon persons who must lead not
by authority but by persuasion through rhetoric. This
is why democracies always tend toward demagoguery.
When the President is persuasive and possesses a nobility of character, the problem of authority is masked
by the charismatic qualities of his leadership. When
he is not persuasive, he may retain the residue to
constitutional powers but authority tends to dissipate
as public opinion becomes an inchoate mass.

The modern President described by Wilson is called
upon to build a political community and give the
government a direction that neither Congress nor the
Courts can provide. But as Wilson viewed American
society, there was no community that could provide the
basis for leadership as he perceived it. The fault
seemed to lay not in any permanent features of human
nature, but in the Constitution; change the Constitution and changes in the nature of the human condition
would follow. From this perspective the existent
Constitution and the philosophy behind it that supported

it came to be seen as an impediment to democracy. This
realization led to Wilson's subtle redefinition of constitutional government. By noting this reorientation,
the careful reader can understand that the constitutionalism described in Constitutional Government is
substantially at odds with that of The Federalist.
Wilson did not describe the Constitution as it is, but
rather what it would become in its ideal form.

There remains a final irony in the legacy of Wilson's political science that is especially noticeable
today. Presidential leadership occupied the most
exhaulted position in Wilson's hierarchy of political
virtues. This Wilsonian idealism was nowhere better
illustrated than in his conception of the personal
qualities required for that high office. Yet some
three quarters of a century later we see in the modern
presidency a Machiavellian cynicism that is unprecedented in American politics. It is a cynicism all the
more perplexing to deal with because it is built on the
twin notions of a living constitution and the President
as the most democratic branch of government, two principles of constitutional interpretation Wilson helped to
make a part of our national political consciousness.
How did such a change come about? Wilson as President
was no demagogue in the ordinary sense of the word. He
was a truly great President, personifying the highest
order of statesmanship. But his science of politics
emptied the Constitution of any substantive meaning,
leaving it open to the widest possible interpretations.
Wilson sought to avoid the demagoguery to which democracies are prone by emphasizing the nobility of
character required of a democratic leader. In contrast
with the Founders, the living constitution school of
jurisprudence, of which Wilson was very much a part,
could not imagine the problematic nature of a liberal
democracy and hence it could provide no institutional
checks and balances to demagoguery in democratic
leadership. The result has been a debased idealism
that threatens to open a far wider rift between the
theory and practice of a liberal polity than anything
Wilson thought possible. Without a system of restraints
on the exercise of political power we are left with few
defenses against the erosion of the founding principles
of the nation. No doubt a reliance on the good sense
of the people must remain the primary check on abuses
of power in a democratic regime, but, as Madison observed, "experience has taught mankind the necessity of
auxiliary precautions."

NOTES

[1] Benedict de Spinoza, A Theologico - Political Treatise, and A Political Treatise. Tr. by R. H. M. Elwes. New York: Dover Publications, Inc., 1951. p. 288.

[2] Woodrow Wilson, Mere Literature and Other Essays. Boston: Houghton Mifflin Co., 1896. pp. 21, 101-102.

[3] This point is made by Paul Eidelberg in his A Discourse on Statesmanship. The Design and Transformation of the American Polity. Chicago: University of Illinois Press, 1974. esp. pp. 279-311.

[4] Woodrow Wilson, in his "Confidential Journal," December 28, 1889, in Authur S. Link (ed.), The Papers of Woodrow Wilson, Princeton: Princeton University Press, 1966 - present. Vol. VI, p. 463. (Hereafter cited as Link, Papers.)

[5] See for example, James MacGreger Burns, Presidential Government: The Crucible of Leadership. Boston: Houghton Mifflin Co., 1965; and, Wilfred E. Binkley, American Political Parties. Their National History. Fourth Edition. New York: Alfred A. Knopf, 1962.

[6] The best treatment of Wilson's academic years, and the one that sees a fundamental Liberalism in Wilson's philosophy, is Henry Wilkinson Bragdon, Woodrow Wilson. The Academic Years. Cambridge, Massachusetts: Harvard University Press, 1967. New Left scholars have emphasized the conservative nature of Wilson's thought; see Gabriel Kolko, The Triumph of Conservatism. A Reinterpretation of American History. New York: The Free Press, 1963.

[7] Woodrow Wilson, Congressional Government. Baltimore: The Johns Hopkins University Press, 1981. p. 27.

[8] Christopher Wolfe, "Woodrow Wilson: Interpreting the Constitution," The Review of Politics, Vol. 41, No. 1, January, 1979. pp. 121-124.

[9] Wilson to Ellen Louise Axson, March 11, 1884, in Link, Papers, III, p. 80.

[10]For a discussion of the "Living Constitution" school, see Richard G. Stevens, "Felix Frankfurter," in Morton J. Fisch and Richard G. Stevens (eds.), American Political Thought. The Philosophic Dimension of American Statesmanship. New York: Charles Scribner's Sons, 1971.

[11]Wolfe has correctly noticed that the implications of Wilson's constitutionalism extends logically to the Supreme Court as well as the presidency. It is all a part of the living Constitution school. Yet it must also be pointed out that the thrust of Wilson's argument is in support of presidential government and not judicial supremacy. See Wolfe, Op. cit.

[12]Woodrow Wilson, Constitutional Government in the United States. New York: Columbia University Press, 1908, p. 2.

[13]Ibid., p. 1.

[14]Ibid., pp. 25-26. It should be noted that Wilson's definition of "Community" is almost identical with that of Alexis de Tocqueville. But whereas Tocqueville went on to argue that the United States was such a community and therefore a constitutional government was possible, Wilson thought otherwise. See Alexis de Tocqueville, Democracy in America. Edited by J. P. Mayer. New York: Doubleday and Co., 1966, p. 373. Compare this also with Wilson's definition in The State. Elements of Historical and Practical Politics. Second Edition. Boston: D. C. Heth, 1897. p. 476.

[15]Ibid., p. 28.

[16]Ibid., p. 220. For other examples of Wilson's views on the "harmonious" or "organic" community, see his review of James Bryce's American Commonwealth, in Ray Stannard Baker and William E. Dodd (eds.), The Public Papers of Woodrow Wilson, Vol. I. New York: Harper and Brothers, 1925. pp. 159-178. (Hereafter cited as Public Papers.).

[17]For a more complete treatment of this theme than the one found in Constitutional Government, see Wilson's essay "Character of Democracy in the United States," in Public Papers, pp. 104, 135-136.

[18] For an excellent discussion of this problem, see Robert A. Goldwin and William A. Schambra (eds.), _How Democratic For the Constitution?_ Washington, D.C.: American Enterprise Institute for Public Policy Research, 1980.

[19] Wilson, _Constitutional Government_, pp. 25-26, 46, 169-170.

[20] _Ibid._, p. 40.

[21] _Ibid._, pp. 44, 86-87.

[22] On the theoretical as opposed to the practical origins of Wilson's conception of the presidency, see Arthur S. Link, _Woodrow Wilson and the Progressive Era, 1910-1917._ New York: Harper & Row, 1954. pp. 34-35. See also the observations by Edward S. Corwin in William Starr Myers (ed.), _Woodrow Wilson. Some Princeton Memories._ Princeton University Press, 1946. pp. 27-28. The theoretical basis of Wilson's argument is insightfully explored in James W. Caeser, _Presidential Selection: Theory and Development._ Princeton University Press, 1979. pp. 170-212.

[23] Wilson, _Constitutional Government_, p. 68. Wilson was well aware that his conception of presidential leadership was at odds with _The Federalist_. But it did accord with the notion of sovereignty he developed in one of his most important essays, "Political Sovereignty" (1891), which also contains the first outlines of his historical thesis on the stages of constitutional evolution. This essay appears in two, slightly different versions; the first draft is in Link, _Papers_, VI, pp. 325-341; the final, published version can be found in a collection of Wilson's essays, _An Old Master and Other Political Essays._ New York: Charles Scribner's Sons, 1893.

[24] _Ibid._, p. 67.

[25] _Ibid._, p. 70.

[26] _Ibid._, p. 69.

[27] On Wilson's views of party government, see Caeser, _Op. cit._

[28] Wilson, _Constitutional Government_, pp. 71-72.

[29]See Eidelberg, Op. cit., on Wilson's idea of the new founding.

[30]Wilson, Public Papers, I, p. 65.

[31]Caeser, Op. cit.

[32]Wilson, Constitutional Government, pp. 60-66.

[33]Ibid., p. 65. The extra-constitutional basis of Wilson's theory of the presidency was noted with some alarm by Edward S. Corwin in his essay, "Woodrow Wilson and the Presidency," in Richard Loss (ed.), Presidential Power and the Constitution. Essays by Edward S. Corwin. Ithica: Cornell University Press, 1976. pp. 52-53.

[34]Ibid., pp. 54-55.

[35]Ibid., pp. 54-55.

[36]James Madison, "Federalist No. 10," in Jacob E. Cooke (ed.), The Federalist. Middletown, Connecticut: Wesleyan University Press, 1961. p. 58.

[37]The best discussion of this phenomena is in M. J. C. Vile, Constitutionalism and the Separation of Powers. Oxford: The Clarendon Press, 1976, esp. pp. 263-293.

CHAPTER 11
"William Edward Burghardt Du Bois 1868-1963"
Margaret Hrezo

> There are many causes of the crises
> (in American justice) but none I
> believe as basic as our neglect in
> reaching the ideal we fashioned for
> ourselves in the Declaration of
> Independence that 'all men are
> created equal'. . .(Earl Warren)[1]

For William E. B. Du Bois, the problem of constitutional government in America was primarily one of
reconciling the stated values and principles of the
founding period with the actual development of government under the Constitution. Central to his writing
on the nature of constitutional government was his
awareness of a profound gap between the ideals of the
Declaration of Independence and the operation of a
government under the Constitution that he viewed as a
denial of those first principles. This disparity between
the real and the ideal led him to examine the very idea
of the Constitution from the perspective of a Black man
in America. He saw the Constitution in its original
and evolved form as a statement of national principles
and ultimate purpose; it represented the ideals of the
polity as a whole. It was on this level of national
ideals, as he understood them, that Du Bois sought to
understand, critique, and ultimately to reform the
American polity .

     Institutions and structures for Du Bois as for the
Founders, were means of attaining goals not ends in
themselves. The weakness of his thought is his failure
to perceive how much institutional means have to do
with the attainment or frustration of national ideals
and ends. While he well understood the nature and
substance of the eighteenth century version of democracy
he faulted, Du Bois may not have comprehended fully the
idea that the expanded version of democracy he sought
was not completely compatible with structures designed
to implement the Founders conception.

     Du Bois focused on the ideals which he believed
underlay the American Constitution--liberty, equality,
government based on the consent of the governed, the
development of a political community in which each
could fulfill his or her potential and be judged on
their merits as individuals. He found these ideals

239

worthy, often lauded, and very little practiced. In
the America which spanned the seventy years of his
career as a spokesman for the American Negro Du Bois
saw the profound contradiction between American ideals
and American practice engendered by race and made this
contradiction his paradigm for all the problems and
possibilities of the American polity. Race hatred and
the political, social, economic, and psychic scars
accompanying it became the symbol of the forces seeking
to curb the development of individuals and of the human
race both in America and in the world. With Chief
Justice Warren, he argued that no problem within the
American republic has caused greater tension, bitterness or damage than that of race. The Negro problem,
as he called it,* was "the concrete test of the underlying principles of the great republic" and America
had failed the test.[2] He wrote repeatedly that

> the problem of the twentieth century
> is the problem of the color line, the
> question as to how far differences of
> race. . .will hereafter be made the
> basis of denying to over half the
> world the right of sharing to their
> utmost ability the opportunities and
> privileges of modern civilization.[3]

If there was ever going to be true democracy in the
world--liberty, equality, the acceptance of universal
suffrage, majority rule and respect for minorities--it
would be because of the strivings of all the colored
peoples of the world and especially because of the
strivings of the American Negro. The elimination of
racial barriers to individual development and opportunity meant the discarding of all such artificial
barriers. Only then could the individual triumph and
humanity progress.[4] Until that time the Negro must
"never cease to protest and assail the ears of America,"

---

*The word "Negro" is the most commonly used appellation
by Du Bois. When he used the term "colored races" it
was to refer to a wider group than American blacks.
Patterns of usage in America have variously included
"Colored," "Negro," and "Black," each with different
connotations at different times. The word "Negro"
will be used throughout this paper in order to remain
consistent with Du Bois' own terminology.

for America must change:

> The battle we wage is not for our-
> selves alone but for all true
> Americans. It is a fight for ideals,
> lest this, our common fatherland,
> false to its founding, become in
> truth the land of the thief and the
> home of the slave--a byword and a
> hissing among the nations for its
> sounding pretensions and pitiful
> accomplishment.[5]

The fight for ideals formed the basis of Du Bois' life
and of his battle against one of the most destructive
of tensions in this republican polity--racial confict.

Du Bois' most explicit statement of the guiding
principles of political organization are found in his
"Credo."[6] This "Credo" articulates his belief in the
brotherhood of all humanity; the goodness and salva-
tional message of the Negro race; the pride of "race,
lineage, and self"; the necessity of service to others
instead of selfishly seeking only personal gain and
pleasure; and in the tragedy of the narrowing of opportunity and the hatred among men which Du Bois called
the work of the devil.[7] Further the "Credo" stresses
his notion that "war is murder"; the necessity of
liberty for all to think and dream and work and vote
in equality; in patience; and in the training of children "the leading out of little souls. . .for life lit
by some large vision of beauty and goodness and truth."[8]
Finally, very late in his life, Dr. Du Bois added
another ideal

> I believe in communism. I mean by
> communism, a planned way of life in
> the production of wealth and work
> designed for building a state whose
> object is the highest welfare of its
> people and not merely the profit of
> a part. I believe that all men should
> be employed according to their ability
> and that wealth and services should
> be distributed according to need.[9]

These ideals of his "Credo" relate to one overriding concept which shaped his thought and works--a
modern "humanism." It was characterized by a deep and

reverential belief in life itself and in the infinite
possibilities of the human soul. His view of the tensions in the American polity and the solutions he proposed were informed by the necessity of increasing the
sphere of human perfectibility so that life would be
better for all and each individual would have the
opportunity to develop the full potential of his or
her capacities. Du Bois' ideals envisioned shaping the
human environment in order to promote an ever larger
realm of human potential. Humanity's shaping environment would include education, critical thinking and
analysis, liberty, the absence of war, sacrifice, the
inclusion of and equal opportunity for each individual.

> The vast and wonderful knowledge of
> this marvelous universe is locked in
> the bosoms of its individual souls.
> To tap this mighty reservoir of
> experience, knowledge, beauty, love
> and deed we must appeal not to the
> few, not to some souls, but to all.
> The narrower the appeal, the poorer
> the culture; the wider the appeal
> the more magnificent the possibili-
> ties. Infinite is human nature. We
> make it finite by choking back the
> mass of men, by attempting to speak
> for others. . .and we end by acting
> for ourselves and using the world as
> our personal property. If this were
> all, it were crime enough--but it is
> not all; by our ignorance we make
> the creation of a greater world im-
> possible.[10]

This world view does not mean that Du Bois was a philosophical determinist in the development of either
individuals or nations. Rather, environmental factors
could help or hinder that development. Adherence to
such principles as liberty, equality, consent of the
governed and education should aid in the advancement
of individuals and, indirectly, of nations. Their
absence (as in an environment dominated by economic
or racial barriers) would produce the racism that he
saw permeating the American polity. By widening or
narrowing individual opportunity humanity assigns
itself to either progress or retrogression.

It was through these ideals and their relation to

242

human development that Du Bois developed his criticisms
of what he believed were tensions and hypocrisies in
the American political, social and economic system.
His fundamental disappointment in America was tied to
the vast potential for the realization of his ideals
that he perceived in her founding principles that was
lacking in the subsequent development of the polity.
Du Bois believed that the principles of The Federalist
should have led to the kind of society he envisioned.
For him, "the meaning of America is the beginning of[11]
the discovery of the Crowd"--the masses of citizens.
He viewed America as a potential refutation of "that
widespread assumption that the real makers of the world
must always be a small group of exceptional men, while
most men are incapable of assisting civilization or of
achieving culture."[12] America showed, or could show,
that most men could effectively participate in civilization, and that as human opportunity widened so too
would human progress. And, as with the founding principles, it is this potential for the development of
mankind's capacity to self-rule on which the argument
for democracy must rest.[13] Paradoxically it was for
this reason that he came to admire Soviet Russia. The
Russia of 1917, he felt, made the same assumption he
did, "that out of the downtrodden mass of people,
ability and character sufficient to do this task (rule)
effectively could or would be found."[14]

The founding principles of the American constitutional system had not led to what Du Bois felt was a
truly democratic society and the reason they had not
was racism. The effect racial conflict had created
was what Du Bois called the "Veil." The "Veil" was
the color line that provided the Negro with "second
sight in his American world--a world which yields him
no true self-consciousness, but only lets him see
himself through the revelation of the other world."[15]
And that other world looked on with contempt. Without
the Veil Du Bois readily admitted that he would have
embraced what he saw as the aristocratic and elitist
individualism of The Federalist:

> Had it not been for the race problem
> early thrust upon me and enveloping
> me, I should have probably been an
> unquestioning worshipper at the
> shrine of the social order and
> economic development into which I
> was born. But just that part of

243

> that order which seemed to most
> of my fellows nearest perfection,
> seemed to me most inequitable and
> wrong; and starting from that
> critique, I gradually. . .found
> other things to question in my
> environment.[16]

By intelligence, taste and capacity Du Bois would have
preferred to be an aristocratic individual of a
Hamiltonian mold. But the Veil ruled his life through
economic discrimination, social humiliation, civil
disfranchisement and lynchings. The Veil came to reveal to him all the tensions and contradictions of
American republican democracy and an economic organization which exacerbated them. Du Bois viewed his task
as that of helping to lead the Negro and, through the
Negro the United States, to genuine emancipation and a
return to the principles of the founding.

In 1888 when he entered Harvard to prepare for
this task he was "blithely European and imperialist in
outlook; democratic as democracy was conceived in
America."[17] The problem was, he thought, a relatively
simple one. Democracy was the logical and inevitable
course of the world. He merely had to find the means
of ensuring that "black folk in America" were "openly
and freely admitted."[18]

Du Bois' view of democracy accepted a republic--
provided it was based on universal suffrage, majority
rule and concern for minority rights. He apparently
never fully realized the tension between majority rule
and minority rights. He followed Madison's definition
of a republic as a "government which derives all of its
powers directly or indirectly from the great body of
the people. . ."[19]

He agreed that no other form of government rested
so much on the capacity of mankind for self-government.[20] Originally Du Bois even agreed with classical
liberal economists that

> Wealth was the result of work and
> saving and the rich rightly inherited
> the earth. The poor, on the whole,
> were themselves to be blamed. They
> were unfortunate and if so their
> fortunes could easily be mended with

244

care. But chiefly they were 'shift-
less' and 'shiftlessness' was unfor-
giveable.[21]

Further he saw no problem initially with the protection
of private property by the government, particularly as
reflected in The Federalist #10. As an individualist
he believed that without the artificial barrier of race
individuals would rise and fall according to their
merits.

Du Bois understood and partially agreed with
Madison's views on faction, the dangers of unbridled
majoritarianism and the greed and selfishness of man.
He would not have disagreed in principle with Madison's
contention that individuals were more likely "to vex
and oppress each other than to cooperate for their
common good."[22] He realized that human beings were
fallible and often did not choose the right.[23] He knew
first hand how much men could fear and resent the idea
of equality.[24] Du Bois believed, as shown in his own
elitist notion of the "Talented Tenth," that the best
elements should govern and that the best elements would
rise to the top. He was not opposed to the idea that
it was "sometimes best, that a partially undeveloped
people should be ruled by the best of their stronger
and better neighbors for their own good, until such
time as they can start and fight the world's battles
alone."[25] These best elements would, through their
wisdom, courage, and altruistic sacrifice, lead the
masses of benighted humanity to higher levels of
development and civilization. But no system of law,
caste, class or privilege could ever define those best
elements. Above all, he argued, society could not base
that definition on race. Only the most thoroughgoing
democracy and respect for individual differences could
allow those elements to define themselves.

The divergence between Du Bois and the Founders
turned on the question of government as a contract vs.
government as a community. Influenced by the rationalism of the Enlightenment, the founding of the American republic was a contractual attempt to establish
"good government through reflection and choice."[26] The
basic questions asked in The Federalist suggests the
Founders roots in eighteenth century rationalism. What
set of institutions will best control human malevolence
and greed?[27] How best can one structurally balance
the rights and privileges of property against the

strivings of the masses?[28] What organization will
allow the government to run without popular intervention but with popular consent?[29] How best can one
delicately balance all the contending factions and
opinions so that one can answer the principle purposes
of union--"the common defense of the members; the
preservation of the public peace; as well against
internal convulsions as external attacks; the regulation of commerce with foreign countries?"[30] How can
politics and economics be separated so that the
economic sphere can be guaranteed against intervention
on the part of the masses? How can the protection of
differences in faculties, and therefore property, be
made "the first object of government?"[31]

     As set forth in The Federalist, the Constitution
is an exercise in Newtonian equilibrium. The problem
was conceived in terms of how mankind can found a
republic so as to guarantee commerce, industry, privilege and popular consent and achieve a state of static
equilibrium so that, for the most part, it need not be
tampered with again.[32] The essential problem confronted in The Federalist is that of political control.[33]
How can a governmental system control its citizens and
still maintain a viable level of consent? The answer
given in The Federalist is that this can be accomplished through the structural components of the Constitution.[34] The authors of The Federalist saw human
nature as a constant. In fact "so strong is this
propensity of mankind to fall into mutual animosities,
that where no substantial occasion presents itself,
the most frivolous and fanciful distinctions have been
sufficient to kindle their unfriendly passions and
excite their most violent conflicts."[35] Because of
differences in interests, faculties, and property
there will always be factions. These factions will be
inherently unfriendly to one another and often adverse
to the public good. Especially is a majority faction
to be feared for it is more often ruled by passion than
by intelligence and may easily succumb to "a rage for
paper money, for an abolition of debts, for an equal
division of property, or for any other improper or
wicked project."[36] Further the majority may cause
confusion and instability if allowed to rule without
structural hindrance. Thus the principle task of
modern legislation is "the regulation of these various
and interfering interests."[37] The whole of Madison's
Federalist #10 is an exercise to demonstrate how
representation and a large territory will control the

effects of faction and especially of a majority
faction. Because human nature cannot change it must
be controlled.

For Du Bois, on the other hand, the question is
one of human development and education.[38] Human nature
was neither fixed or permanent. He viewed democracy
as an educational experience for both the individual
and the polity. For Du Bois governing is a human
problem not a mechanical one of Newtonian physics; a
question never finally decided but constantly evolving
with the whole process of human development and involving an intricate interweaving of politics and
economics. From this he derived a remedy aimed at the
organic growth of the individual and society. Democracy was universal suffrage and majority rule. It
was a means of achieving a community where each
individual would benefit from the thoughts and experience of other individuals and from the combined wisdom
of all. In the process Democracy became almost an end
in itself. Each individual has some thought or experience or criticism of worth to add to this pool and "it
is possible through this pooled knowledge and experience to come to decisions much more fundamental and
much more far reaching than can be had in any other
way."[39] If the ideals of liberty, peace, brotherhood,
and education are practiced, then the field of human
opportunity will ever widen and so too will human
progress. Republican democracy should be the method
of guaranteeing this process. Ignorance or inexperience can never be a reason for withholding the fullest
possible participation from any individual or group
because

> in the people we have the source of
> that endless life and unbounded
> wisdom which the rulers of men must
> have. A given people today may not
> be intelligent but through democratic
> government that recognizes, not only
> the worth of the individual to him-
> self, but the worth of his feelings
> and experiences to all, they can
> educate, not only the individual unit
> but generation after generation,
> until they accumulate vast stores of
> wisdom.[40]

All may not be equal in ability, wealth, wisdom and

experience, but all have something to offer and all must receive equal opportunity to offer what they have. Only democracy allows for this form of growth.

Du Bois agreed with Madison on the dangers in unbridled majoritarianism. He saw a distinct potential for a tyranny of the majority to dominate political and social life and to stifle free, critical thought and analysis. The many may tyrannize the few. It certainly did with regard to racial minorities during Du Bois' lifetime. But the tyranny of the majority is neither inevitable nor eternal. It is not a constant quality of human nature. As human opportunity widens and ever increasing numbers of individuals receive education and begin to learn and think there will come also an increasing respect for the gift each brings. Humanity will come to listen to, respect and synthesize different viewpoints. It will come to venerate not destroy individual and group differences. So

> in future democracies the toleration and encouragement of minorities and the willingness to consider as 'men' the crankiest, humblest and poorest blackest people, must be the key to the consent of the governed. Peoples and governments will not in the future assume that because they have the brute power to enforce momentarily dominant ideas, it is best to do so without conference with the ideas of smaller groups and individuals.[41]

Minority rights for Du Bois would include all points of view in the decision-making process of the polity. In this way society will seek to increase its wisdom and strength. Indeed Du Bois foresaw a time (similar to contemporary pluralism) when factions (interest groups) be actively encouraged as a means of including minority viewpoints.[42]

Du Bois was aware that the continuing expansion of democracy could cause confusion and instability. At some point government could not accommodate every point of view. But unlike Madison he did not fear that confusion because it was part of the process of education of both citizens and government. He considered the expansion of democracy a necessity for individual spiritual growth since "no one knows himself but that

self's own soul."[43] No one else can explain for an
individual what he or she thinks or where they hurt.
Therefore each individual citizen must take on this
task for themselves. This

> addition of the new wisdom, the new
> points of view, and the new interests
> must, of course, be from time to time
> bewildering and confusing. . .The
> appearance of new interests and com-
> plaints means disarrangement and con-
> fusion to the older equilibrium. It
> is, of course, the inevitable pre-
> liminary step to that larger equili-
> brium in which the interests of no
> human soul will be neglected.[44]

As Du Bois read the Founders intentions, Madison had
missed the point. Humanity does not need to be controlled structurally. Instead it must be developed,
respected and educated to the essential meaning of
constitutional ideals. It will make mistakes but will
learn from them and use them as steps toward increased
human progress. Ultimately humanity will attain the
constitutional ideals but not through the institutions
and arrangements of any specific constitution.

It was the emphasis in The Federalist on political
control that led to the betrayal of the possibility of
America's founding principles--the possibility of the
crowd. The extension and fulfillment of these principles became Du Bois' goal. However, in order to fulfill these principles the tensions of race and economic
oligarchy had to be faced and resolved. Until about
1920, Du Bois believed that race was the fundamental
tension eroding the republic. It was costing America
"certain fundamental principles of democratic government, peace and development in the labor world, and
enhanced difficulty of getting a world market for our
goods."[45] The abolition of racism could help fulfill
the promise of the founding for

> Democracy was not planted full grown
> in America. It was a slow growth be-
> ginning in Europe and developing
> further and more quickly in America.
> It did not envisage at first the man
> farther down as a participant in
> democratic privilege. . .democracy

in the world first meant simply the
transfer of privilege and opportunity
from waning to waxing power. . .Divine
Right of birth yielded to Divine Right
of wealth. Growing industry, business
and commerce were putting economic
and social power into the hands of what
we call the middle class. Political
opportunity to correspond with this
power was the demand of the eighteenth
century and this was what the eighteenth
century called democracy.[46]

W.E.B. Du Bois agreed that the Constitution was a
democratic document. And he would have agreed with
Martin Diamond that "as votaries of freedom, individual
liberty was to the Founders the comprehensive, unprob-
lematic good; and they were determined to secure that
good by an experiment in democracy."[47] However for
Du Bois there was an inherent difficulty with this
experiment. That difficulty was the Founder's
exclusive rather than inclusive definition of the
American political community. Again, the Constitution
to Du Bois was democratic according to the eighteenth
century version of democracy. It included more people
than any European society had ever done. It was,
however, fundamentally restrictive and "was not
designed to be a democracy of the masses of men."[48]
Both Merritt and Higgenbotham have documented the
difficulties encountered by the colonists in developing
a sense of community and consensus.[49] Further liberal
political philosophy seemed to automatically define out
certain groups or individuals from full citizenship in
the polity.[50] But most obvious to Du Bois was the fact
that "the very legal process that had been devised to
protect the rights of individuals against the will of
the government and the whim of the majority" had been
"often employed so malevolently against blacks."[51]

Disenfranchisement of the Negro vote made a
mockery of the suffrage and of both northern and
southern political principles. Du Bois' analysis
suggested to him that "according to the political
power which each actual voter exercised in 1946, the
southern South rated as 6.6, the Border states as 2.3,
and the rest of the country as about 1."[52] While
democracy is not solely a question of mathematics, the
ballot is the primary method the constitutional system
accords individuals to express their needs to the

government. Such a great disparity in the power of
the ballot and its near complete denial to blacks made
the assessment of popular consent difficult. The
inferior status of the Negro in the polity showed
Du Bois that republican principles had failed. Democracy had failed because "so many fear it. They believe
that wealth and happiness are so limited that a world
full of healthy, intelligent and free people is impossible if not undesirable."[53] The wealth of some must
therefore depend on the poverty, ignorance, and degradation of others and what others were more suited to
the task than the supposedly non-human darker races.
Thus, the original political community of the United
States was an artificial one that depended on the
exclusion of certain groups for its survival. It was
not a truly democratic community. But as Becker observed, liberal philosophy had some utopian leanings
and tended to be ahistoric. Once the fundamentals are
settled "we feel safe. . .we feel we have a foolproof
and enduring government."[54] The place accorded blacks
and other excluded groups also tended to become ahistoric or permanent. Unfortunately their place was
founded on the "untenable position that the Constitution (and the community it set up) might never be any
larger than the restrictive vision of eighteenth
century America."[55] The liberty of the Constitution,
based on a highly individualist philosophy, was liberty
for the middle-class to establish its political power.
It was a liberty that required certain limitations on
the most feared aspects of human nature--aspects
identified with those outside the middle-class and
consequently outside the political community.

The universality of the terms in which the principles of the Constitution and Declaration of Independence were stated, coupled with the union movement and
especially the fight of the Negro for freedom, allowed
a strengthening and broadening of the ideal of democracy. Without the struggles of the American Negro,
democracy would "have continued to mean in America what
it means so widely still in Europe, the admission of
the powerful to participation in government and privilege in so far and only in so far as their power
becomes irresistible."[56] The battle of the Negro for
recognition and respect "meant a recognition of humanity as such and the giving of economic and social power
to the powerless."[57] This was the extension of the
founding principles which Du Bois sought. The Negro
would force and continue to force Americans to realize

251

that as long as there were those who lay outside the
pale of society, government, and industry "our democracy has failed of its greatest mission."[58]

From his return from Europe in 1894 until about
1910, the method Du Bois turned to for this democratizing mission was that of the burgeoning social
sciences:

> My vision was in the beginning clear.
> The Negro problem called for systematic
> investigation and intelligence. The
> World was thinking wrong about races
> because it did not know. The ultimate
> veil was ignorance and its child
> stupidity. The cure for it was knowl-
> edge based on study.[59]

Once Americans were faced with scientific truth they
would be bound to accept it. When the world acknowledged Negroes as fully human it would acknowledge that
all were fully human. Only then would the dreams of
the founding fathers be realized. Besides the gifts
of song, spirit, and labor this would be the great
gift of the Negro to America.

Over time, however, it became apparent to Du Bois
that science alone could not accomplish this task. By
1910 he had reached the conclusion that reason can only
prevail through publicity.[60] He still believed, and
never ceased to believe, in the importance of scientific research and fact finding for the solution of
the world's problems. As his ideas matured, however,
he began to emphasize other solutions as well. It
was at this point that Du Bois turned his skills to
agitation for black rights through the National Association for the Advancement of Colored People and its
monthly periodical The Crisis. It was during the
period in which he moved from study to agitation he
began to rethink his formulation of the tensions
within the polity. As his personal disappointments
mounted and he was increasingly unable to explain them
in traditional categories of analysis, Du Bois began
to discover a relationship between politics and
economics. It led him to openly advocate the formation
of industrial democracy in the United States.

As early as 1910 Du Bois began to argue that
American free market economics fostered and exacer-

bated racial prejudice.[61] He found, as had Madison, that "the most common and durable source of factions has been the various and unequal distribution of property."[62] Caste and segregation turned a handsome profit. Thus if, overnight, the majority of Americans accepted Negroes the color line would still exist. It would continue because it increased the purely economic welfare of many individuals. For, "so far as they (whites) were ignorant of the results of race prejudice, we had taught them." Increasingly the foundation of their race prejudice was "the income which they enjoyed" and they formulated "their anti-Negro bias consciously or unconsciously. . .in order to protect their wealth and power."[63] Second, the color line would continue because colonial profits reinforced this same tendency:

> The day of the very rich is drawing
> to a close, so far as individual white
> nations are concerned. But there is a
> loophole. There is a chance for exploi-
> tation on an immense scale for inordinate
> profit, not simply to the very rich, but
> to the middle class and to the laborers.
> This chance lies in the exploitation
> of darker peoples.[64]

For Du Bois, the economic organization of the United States and indeed all other Western capitalism was the other major tension eroding the founding principles. At first he saw the economic tension as secondary to the racial. Later, as he traveled and his ideals matured, he wrote that

> I see more clearly than yesterday that
> back of the problem of race and color,
> lies a greater problem which both
> obscures and implements it: and that
> is the fact that so many civilized
> persons are willing to live in comfort
> even if the price of this is poverty,
> ignorance and disease of the majority
> of their fellowmen: that to maintain
> this privilege men have waged war until
> today war tends to become universal and
> continuous, and the excuse for this war
> continues largely to be color and race.[65]

The emphasis on the protection of private property in The Federalist impeded human progress and, thus, needed

253

revision.[66] Production must fit human needs, not the
needs of private profit. It meant that more would be
needed than a return by America to her republican
ideals. Greed had irrevocably tainted the founding
principles. America no longer respected honest labor.
It had become a land of money-grubbers and "the outlook
is not what a man does but what he is able to get for
doing it."[67] America had become a nation where "we
almost fear to question if the end of racing is not
gold, if the aim of man is not rightly to be rich."[68]
Capitalism and the Industrial Revolution commenced an
economic marvel and ended a 'Frankenstein's monster'
of "drab uniformity and uninteresting drudgery" where
even "its creators do not understand it, cannot curb
or guide it."[69] Thus

> the shadow of hunger, in a world which
> never needs to be hungry, drives us to
> war and murder and hate. But why does
> hunger shadow so vast a mass of men?
> Manifestly because in the great organi-
> zation of men for work a few of the
> participants come out with more wealth
> than they can possibly use, while a
> vast number emerge with less than can
> decently support life.[70]

Before political and social democracy could triumph,
industrial democracy would have to be triumphant.
There was no chance for human progress in a world
dominated by hunger and exploitation. Countries would
have to learn how to plan their economies so that all
individuals could share in the decisions of what to
produce and how those products should be distributed.
The ruling of men "is the effort to direct the individual actions of many persons to some end. This end
theoretically should be the greatest good of all. . ."[71]
Economics, as part of life, is also part of this process and industry too must be directed toward the
common good and the true public interest.[72] It must
"minister to the wants of the many and not to the
few."[73] There would still be menial tasks and people
would have to perform them, but a sense of worth and
respect would surround work. No task would be beneath
human dignity.

In this democratization of industry, Du Bois
argued that the Negro should also lead. It seemed
obvious to Du Bois that the Negro would remain

254

politically and socially segregated for decades. It was the group least integrated and indoctrinated into the American industrial system. But this social and political exclusion of the Negro from the American polity could serve as the basis of human progress. As the most alienated group it had the least stake in the existing order. The Negro would lead the way in the fulfillment of the original ideals of the Declaration of Independence before those ideals became corrupted by the constitutional defense of property. Du Bois still believed in agitation and protest for full civil rights and "in the ultimate uniting of mankind and in a unified American nation, with economic classes and racial barriers leveled. . ."[74] But his conceptualization of the roots of the dilemma reached beyond the organization of the American polity. Now human brotherhood was the ideal "and is to be realized only by such intensified class and race consciousness as will bring irresistible force rather than mere humanitarian appeals to bear. . ."[75] Negroes should attempt to develop their own economy "an economic nation within a nation, able to work through inner cooperation, to found its own institutions, to educate its own genius. . ."[76] They should organize as consumers to combat the unequal effects of supply and demand on their community. Profit and exploitation of labor would not be part of future economic organization. Unemployment and risk would be a thing of the past. It would be a carefully planned and organized economy that would demonstrate the genius of the Negro race, force their acceptance as equals by whites and finally "be a realization of democracy in industry led by consumer's organizations and extending to planned production."[77] When the color line disappeared Blacks would retain solidarity and not splinter into antagonistic classes. They could show America and the world the way to economic as well as civil democracy. They would be living proof that no one should or needs to dominate or make their living off the labor and deprivation of another human being.

Thus from a starting point of close identification with eighteenth century liberalism, Du Bois reached a radical reinterpretation of America's founding ideals. Madison's sociopolitical equilibrium was for the ages; that of Du Bois was for humanity as it evolved through a process of continual change. Du Bois seems to represent the juncture between Madison and Marx--an individualist who believes in the community of all and

in the individual's dependence on others for his or
her own personal fulfillment. Do Bois saw his work as
the link between democracy, economics and humanistic
individualism and how the blight of racial conflict
destroys the human soul. What The Federalist sought
to separate, politics from individual morality, W.E.B.
Du Bois sought to bind together for the formation of a
new individualism for "there must be a loftier respect
for the sovereign human soul that seeks to know itself
and the world about it; that seeks a new freedom for
expansion and self-development; that will love, hate,
and labor in its own way, untrammeled alike by old and
new."[78] Even in his last years Du Bois believed in
the triumph of these ideals and held firm to this concept of the human condition. This is a beautiful world
and the United States "is still a land of magnificent
possibilities."[79] It is a "wonderful America, which
the founding fathers dreamed until their sons devoured
it in greed."[80] If America would forego racism and the
adoration of wealth, the possibility for development
would be almost limitless. The choice, Du Bois argued,
was between a polity that fosters humanism and one that
ossifies the existing distribution of power.

NOTES

[1] Chief Justice Earl Warren, as quoted in A. Leon Higgenbotham, Jr., _In the Matter of Color_ (New York: Oxford University Press, 1978), p. 388.

[2] W.E.B. Du Bois, "Of Our Spiritual Strivings," in his _The Souls of Black Folk_ (New York: Washington Square Press, 1970), p. 10.

[3] W.E.B. Du Bois, "Address to the Nations of the World," in _W.E.B. Du Bois Speaks_, Vol. 1. Edited by Philip S. Foner. (New York: Pathfinder Press, 1970), p. 125. (Hereafter cited as _Speaks_.)

[4] Racial pride was extremely important to Du Bois and was a constant in the evolution of his ideas. He wanted to be seen as an individual, not as a Negro. But in order for the Negro to be accepted as an individual he or she had to push for their rights and pushing for rights necessitated self-confidence in their dignity and worth. Only as a unit could they survive economic and social humiliation and make their just demands heard.

[5] Du Bois, "We Claim Our Rights," _Speaks_, I, p. 171.

[6] W.E.B. Du Bois, "Credo," in his _Darkwater_ (New York: Harcourt, Brace and Howe, 1920).

[7] _Ibid._, p. 3.

[8] _Ibid._, p. 4.

[9] W.E.B. Du Bois, _The Autobiography of W.E.B. Du Bois_ (New York: International Publishers, 1968), p. 57.

[10] Du Bois, "Of The Ruling Of Men," _Darkwater_, pp. 140-141.

[11] Du Bois, "Of Work And Wealth," _Ibid._, p. 103.

[12] Du Bois, "What The Negro Has Done For The United States And Texas." _Speaks_, II, p. 87.

[13] James Madison, _Federalist_ No. 10, in _The Federalist_. Edited by Jacob E. Cooke (Middletown, Connecticut: Wesleyan University Press, 1961), p. 59.

[14] W.E.B. Du Bois, _Dusk of Dawn_ (New York: Harcourt, Brace and World, 1940: reprint edition, New York: Schocken Press, 1968), p. 296. (Hereafter cited as _Dusk._)

[15] Du Bois, _Souls_, p. 3.

[16] Du Bois, _Dusk_, p. 27.

[17] Du Bois, "The Quest For The Golden Fleece," _Souls_, p. 126.

[18] _Ibid._, p. 125.

[19] Madison, _Federalist_ No. 39, p. 251.

[20] _Ibid._, p. 250.

[21] Du Bois, _Autobiography_, p. 80.

[22] Madison, _Federalist_ No. 10, p. 59.

[23] Du Bois, "The Value Of Agitation," _Speaks_ I, pp. 174-175.

[24] Du Bois, _Dusk_, p. 134.

[25] Du Bois, "Of The Sons Of Master And Man." _Souls_, p. 144.

[26] Hamilton, _The Federalist_ No. 1, p. 3. See also Carl F. Becker. _Freedom and Responsibility in the American Way of Life_ (New York: Vintage Books, 1945), p. 76.

[27] _Federalist_ Nos. 9 and 10.

[28] _Federalist_ No. 10.

[29] _Federalist_ Nos. 49, 63, 68, 71.

[30] Hamilton, _Federalist_ No. 23, p. 147.

[31] Madison, _Federalist_ No. 10, p. 58.

[32] Becker, p. 84.

[33] It often seems in _The Federalist_ that the term faction is used, almost as a euphemism, for the masses

of individual citizens. This would agree with Mac-
Pherson's view of the citizenship distinction made by
Locke. For a full explication of this position see
C.B. MacPherson. The Political Theory of Possessive
Individualism (London: Oxford University Press, 1970.)
Also David Schuman, in A Preface to Politics (Lexing-
ton, Massachusetts: D.C. Heath and Company, 1977)
extends the logic of MacPherson's argument to additional aspects of The Federalist. The Constitution
seeks to control the effects of faction. In so doing
it implicitly controls citizens, for who else is there
to be components of these factions? Because of the
ambiguity of human nature, one can never assume lack
of self-interest in human activity. Faction represented to Madison that self-interested activity in
danger of overwhelming 'right' reason or considered
judgement. The effects of faction are controlled by
rendering them impotent; i.e., by making combinations
of factions difficult and their control over the
entire government almost impossible.

However, by rendering factions impotent the Constitution also tends to render most citizens impotent. In
effect, they are just as controlled as are the effects
of faction. They may speak freely and vote freely but
they are prevented by the structures set up through
the Constitution from combining with sufficient force
to make their voices and votes genuinely effective.
Becker speaks of the many ways in which the Constitution hamstrings majorities (Freedom...p. 75.) Further Paul Eidelberg, The Philosophy of the American
Constitution (New York: Free Press, 1968), writes that
"For the Founders, the primary purpose of laws and
institutions is to prevent evil." (p. 249). The
institutional attempt to control evil is a form of
control over the effectiveness of individual actions.
And The Federalist itself provides some support for
this argument. In Federalist No. 9, Hamilton writes
that only the new discoveries which allow the control
of the effects of faction have prevented the cause of
republican government from being indefensible. Again
the implication of controlling the effects of faction
is control over the political efficacy of citizens.
And in Federalist No. 51, Madison argues that "In
framing a government which is to be administered by
men over men, the great difficulty lies in this: you
must first enable the government to control the
governed." This passage seems to suggest that good
government necessitates that control of the people's
potential passions is of greater priority than is

control of potential governmental excesses.

[34]Martin Diamond. "The Declaration and the Constitution: Liberty, Democracy, and the Founders." The American Commonwealth 1976. ed. Irving Kristol and Nathan Glazer (New York: Basic Books, 1976), p. 54. In referring to Montesquieu, Diamond writes that "His political science is a political science of institutions..." It is through these institutions--or structures--that the dangers facing republican government will be thwarted.

[35]Madison, Federalist No. 10, p. 59.

[36]Ibid., p. 65.

[37]Federalist Nos. 63 and 71.

[38]There are both similarities and differences between the ideas of Du Bois and Madison on education and human nature. Both believe that humanity possesses the capability of oppressing one another and both believe in the necessity of educating citizens. However, Madison seems to have viewed human nature as basically finite--as a given. In Federalist No. 10, he argues that "the latent causes of faction are thus sown into the nature of man..." In Federalist No. 6, Hamilton concurs when he writes that "Has it not, on the contrary, invariably been found that momentary passions, and immediate interests, have a more active and imperious control over human conduct than general or remote considerations of policy, utility, or justice?" The Federalist also seems to tell us that great politicians are rare because of the domination of self-interest and vexatiousness in human nature. Carl Becker (Freedom..., p. 8) would agree when he writes that "government springs form their (men's) vices, and is therefore a necessary evil." And it is the defects of human nature that have caused the failure of earlier popular governments and which worry Hamilton in Federalist No. 9.

For Madison and the other authors of The Federalist, humanity's oppressive, self-interested and unreasonable tendencies can be mitigated. First by institutions to control their effects and second through education. Education, however, can only do so much. It can produce a greater quantity of human knowledge, better institutions, and possibly even a greater tendency to use reason instead of passion. But education cannot

change the basic tendencies of human nature toward
self-interest and encroachment on his or her neighbor.
In this respect The Federalist resembles Machiavelli's
idea that citizens can be perfected only to a certain
extent and only through the "Laws." This education
to the laws is necessary in order to ward off the
seemingly inevitable degeneration of every governmental system into an abuse of power. Montesquieu
attempts to ward off degeneration structurally, that
is through an institutional framework. The authors of
The Federalist seem to agree with him. People can
become more reasonable but, at least in part, they must
be structured to be more reasonable.

Du Bois, on the other hand, agreed that human
nature contained both good and bad elements. However,
he viewed it as infinite in its possibilities. Without artificial barriers such as race or economic
deprivation individuals can develop to their highest
potential. When all individuals can do this humanity
itself is raised to a higher level. The more educated
humanity becomes the more tolerant and open it will
become and the more it will realize that communal
interest is the only genuine self-interest. In effect
Du Bois seems to believe that human nature can change.

[39] Du Bois, "Human Rights For All Minorities,"
Speaks, II, p. 182.

[40] Du Bois, "Of The Ruling Of Men," p. 144.

[41] Ibid., p. 153.

[42] Ibid., p. 153.

[43] Ibid., p. 140.

[44] Ibid., p. 145.

[45] Du Bois, "Race Prejudice." Speaks, I, p. 214.

[46] Du Bois, "The Negro Citizen." Speaks, II, p. 38.

[47] Diamond, "The Declaration and the Constitution,"
p. 53.

[48] Du Bois, The Gift of Black Folk (Boston: Strat-
ford Publishing Company, 1924), p. 139. (Hereafter
cited as Gift.)

261

[49]Richard L. Merritt. _Symbols of American Community, 1735-1775_ (New Haven: Yale University Press, 1966) and Higgenbotham.

[50]See C.B. MacPherson. _The Political Theory of Possessive Individualism._ Some supplemental evidence can also be found in Lee Benson. _Turner and Beard_ (Glencoe: Free Press, 1960).

[51]Higgenbotham, p. 6.

[52]Du Bois, "An Appeal To The World." _Speaks_, II, p. 211.

[53]W.E.B. Du Bois, _Color and Democracy_ (New York: Harcourt, Brace, 1945), p. 99.

[54]Becker, p. 84.

[55]Higgenbotham, p. 6.

[56]Du Bois, _Gift_, p. 136.

[57]_Ibid._, p. 137.

[58]_Ibid._, p. 137.

[59]Du Bois, "A Pageant In Seven Decades." _Speaks_, I, p. 37.

[60]Du Bois, _Autobiography_, p. 222.

[61]Du Bois, "Of Work And Wealth."

[62]Madison, _Federalist_ No. 10, p. 59.

[63]Du Bois, _Dusk_, p. 296.

[64]Du Bois, "Of The Souls Of White Folks," _Darkwater_, p. 43.

[65]Du Bois, _Souls_.

[66]Becker, p. 102.

[67]Du Bois, "Education And Work," _Speaks_, I, p. 68.

[68]Du Bois, "Of The Wings of Atlanta," _Souls_, p. 63.

[69] Du Bois, _Dusk_, p. 149.

[70] Du Bois, "Of Work and Wealth," p. 99.

[71] Du Bois, "Of The Ruling Of Men," p. 134.

[72] _Ibid._, p. 138.

[73] Du Bois, "Of Work And Wealth," p. 104.

[74] Du Bois, "A Negro Nation Within The Nation." _Speaks_, II, p. 83.

[75] _Ibid._, p. 83.

[76] _Ibid._, p. 84.

[77] Du Bois, _Dusk_, pp. 211-213.

[78] Du Bois, "Of The Training Of Black Men," _Souls_, p. 88.

[79] Du Bois, _Autobiography_, p. 419.

[80] _Ibid._, p. 422.

PART IV

The Principles Defended

CHAPTER 12
"Joseph Story's Commentaries: Statesmanship and the Constitution"
Peter Schotten

During the last years of his life, Joseph Story's reputation as an American legal giant seemed secure. For nearly thirty-four years he had served as an Associate Justice on the United States Supreme Court, interpreting his nation's fundamental law.[1] His constitutional interpretation significantly influenced the course of the young nation's political development; his most famous opinion for the Court in Martin v. Hunter's Lessee (1816) is to this day, one of the Supreme Court's three or four most important decisions, providing as it did for an enduring national sovereignty.[2] During the nation's formative years, the imprint of Story's thoughts were to be found almost everywhere. Court reports reproduced Story's circuit court opinions. Classrooms at Harvard Law School were filled with the voice of the Supreme Court Justice whose efforts would be largely responsible for its future success. The halls of Congress heard speeches and saw legislation drafted that bore Story's mark on more than one occasion.[3] Periodicals and banquet halls bore witness to a variety of articles written and speeches made[4] while the pages of numerous legal treatises displayed the range of Story's legal research.[5] Foremost among these treatises were his famous Commentaries on the Constitution of the United States.

Yet, despite these significant accomplishments, during the last years of his life, Story's private letters reveal an anguish and despair that seemed quite at odds with his life's achievements. Thus, shortly before his death, Story wrote Charles Sumner of his despondency. "In every way which I look to the future, I can see little or no hope for our country. We are rapidly on the decline." In this same manner, he concluded that "You, as a young man, should cling to hope; I as an old man, know it is all in vain."[6]

Story's despair was not a function of age simply, nor was it a concern with a single political event. Rather, Story saw present in the polity a decline of statesmanship, an increase in partisan politics, and the rise of political disputes that, taken together, seemed to present the United States with political problems of the first magnitude. Slavery, and the sectionalism bred and exacerbated by that institution, seemed under these circumstances to be incapable of political resolution. The Founder's uniquely rational attempt to construct the first large, enduring, republican nation in modern history was threatened in its political infancy. In existence only a little more than fifty years, that political experiment seemed to be on the verge of extinction. Endangered were not only the efforts and good reputation of the nation's Founders; in jeopardy too were the efforts of that first generation of Americans who sought to preserve the new nation by declaring and instituting its constitutive principles. Story, like his colleague and close friend John Marshall, could be counted a member of that generation. Like Marshall, Story's legal and political efforts undertaken throughout his life admitted our overarching and unifying principle. Story sought, above all else, to perpetuate a correct interpretation of the document he thought to be at the center of American political life. The centrality of the Constitution for the right ordering of this republican polity, he argued repeatedly, was necessary for the preservation of the American experiment in self-government.[7] There was, therefore, good reason for Story's despair toward the end of his life; his career's work, inextricably bound to his nation's welfare, now all seemed to have been made in vain.

Originally, Story's devotion to law and politics was the product of both a liberal education and independent reflection. Story had surveyed the age in which he lived and compared it to previous times. He thought it was an era that had produced neither great thought nor great literature. Furthermore, because many proclaimed its eminence too brashly, Story believed that there existed an inflated view of its merits. In at least one area, however, he made an exception. There was a great breakthrough in the science of politics to be noted and celebrated. The United States Constitution represented not simply the re-emergence of republicanism in the West, but an attempt to create a republican form of government liberated from the persuasive and damaging defects of previous republics. The founding of such a government was, quite literally, a great experiment. Helping preserve a government that was intended to be both republican and enduring, therefore, represented for Story the most noble political calling. Story was fully conscious of the importance of this task and never evaded its demands. After all, as he observed, "it is

scarcely too much to affirm, that the cause of liberty
throughout the world is in no small measure suspended
upon this great experiment of self-government by the
people."[8] "We stand," he further noted, "the latest,
and, if we fail, probably the last great experiment in
self-government by the people."[9]

I

Joseph Story's statesmanship began with his recognition of the Founding Fathers as uncommonly wise men
who had provided for republican government in a way
that would be extraordinarily difficult to improve
upon. They were "architects of consummate skill and
fidelity" who had set forth fundamental principles of
government. Therefore, an unwavering commitment to the
fundamental principles of American government, stated
or implied by the Constitution, was required in order
to conserve the novelty of the experiment. Of course,
such principles initially required correct explication
and application. Story's Supreme Court opinions, by
addressing fundamental questions on such issues of
national sovereignty and the extent of property rights
under the Contract and Commerce Clauses, helped advance
the Founder's vision of a commercial republic presided
over by an energetic central government. It was,
however, Chief Justice John Marshall's constitutional
interpretations that were to be praised above all
others. They had gained the enduring respect not only
of Story but, in his informed opinion, of the nation
and of posterity as well.

The great problem Story saw in declaring the Constitution to be a work of unchanging political wisdom
was that such a teaching took place in a nation
governed by volatile public opinion and characterized
by constant change. The United States, he contended,
was a nation generally hostile to fixed political
principles. This conclusion grew out of Story's
analysis of various kinds of regimes. Other nations,
he noted, "have a monarchy gifted with prerogatives; or
a nobility graced with wealth and knowledge and hereditary honors; or a stubborn national spirit, proud of
ancient institutions, and obstinate against all reforms."[10] Monarchies, he pointed out, typically
erected formidable barriers to change, including
ecclesiastical and civil establishments which commanded
veneration for their antiquity, as well as an aris-

tocracy which perpetuated the accumulation of wealth in a few families. Story contended that such obstacles to change meant "ages sometimes elapse" before reforms are introduced, and more ages pass "before they are sanctioned by public reverence."[11] Such barriers to change did not exist in the United States. There were no hereditary honors nor privileges. Neither were there any ancient civil or religious institutions. Primogeniture and entail had been dispensed with. "Property," Story added, "is continually changing like the waves of a sea."[12] And with these changes in the amount of property, the public opinions of citizens also changed frequently. Describing Americans as "a most busy, inquisitive, and one might almost say, meddlesome people in public affairs," Story asserted that this was necessarily because they discussed and voted upon public issues; indeed "we insist upon a voice in all matters; and we are quick to act, and slow to doubt upon any measure, which concerns the Republic."[13] From these factors, he argued, follows the realization that it was specifically republican government that was exposed to the inconvenience of "too little regard for what is established, and too warm a zeal for untried theories."[14]

The implications for statesmanship which followed from this insight were significant. Statesmen, Story thought, would be those political leaders able "to get rid of dangerous and critical excitements, and to forward wise measures, without shocking popular prejudices."[15] The problem was that, in a republic, especially this young and democratic republic, it seemed that popular prejudices were in favor of untried political theories or of novel constitutional interpretations, especially when such theories and interpretations were bolstered by particular interests. At the highest level of constitutional law, Story believed that such novel theories and speculations should never be encouraged; a correct interpretation of the Constitution was a matter of principle, not of interests. Indeed, it would be no exaggeration to suggest that the defining characteristic of Story's public life can be understood as an effort to remove the Constitution, properly interpreted, from that broad category of public concerns and issues about which speculation and controversy were encouraged in a republican government. Fully concurring with Madison's observation in _Federalist_ 49 that "the most rational government will not find it a superfluous advantage to have the prejudices of the community on its side," Story sought to replace debate over the Constitution's fundamental principles by a reverence for those principles.

In order to achieve this habitual reverence, Story explicitly taught that the Founders were entitled to the deep, enduring and grateful respect of their countrymen for the principles they enshrined in the Constitution. "He who founds a hospital, a college, or even a more private and limited charity, is justly esteemed a benefactor of the human race," noted Story. "How much more do they deserve our reverence and praise," he continued, "whose lives are devoted to the formation of institutions which. . .may continue to cherish the principles and the practice of liberty in perpetual freshness and vigor!"[16] In addition to his praise of the Founders, Story spoke with highest regard for the regime of laws they had created; law abidingness comprehended a significant social responsibility for all citizens. The American nation, Story wrote, "could be preserved no longer than a reverence for settled uniform laws constitutes the habit. . .of the community."[17] The backbone of that system of law, of course, was the Constitution; it above all else required universal respect. It was on this basis that Story distinguished party leaders, i.e. partisans, from statesmen. Statesmen, Story noted, would not use the Constitution for their own expedient ends, but would "approach it with a reverent regard."[18] Understood in this light, it is little wonder that at the end of his famous Commentaries on the Constitution, Story stressed the importance "of impressing upon Americans a reverential attachment to the Constitution, as in the highest sense the palladium of American liberty."[19] A reverence for the Founders, for a government of laws, and most specifically, for the Constitution, comprised something like a vital political religion necessary for the salvation of the great republican experiment.

II

Story is best remembered for his Commentaries on the Constitution of the United States, the work that comprises the greatest legacy of his thought. Presenting a comprehensive analysis of the Constitution, the treatise was published in January, 1833, during the most stormy and troubling days of the South Carolina nullification crisis. Not counting the preface,

269

as well as a dedicatory letter to Chief Justice Marshall, The Commentaries were divided into three books. Specifically, Book I comprehended a "History of the Colonies," commencing with a discussion of the origin of the colonies, proceeding through a discussion of their settlement, charters and history, and concluding with a two chapter review and set of conclusions setting forth Story's historical findings. The work's second Book examined "the History of the Revolution and the Confederation." It carefully evaluated the relationship of the states to one another during the Revolutionary War. This second Book also analyzed the origin, substance, decline and fall of the Articles of Confederation. In the third and longest Book, entitled "The Constitution of the United States," Story discussed in great detail the Constitution proper; each clause of that document was examined with his usual precision. Here Story carefully presented a broad interpretation of national powers, supplementing his presentation with relevant Supreme Court decisions. In addition to this clause by clause analysis, the third Book also contains chapters on the origin and adoption of the Constitution and whether or not it could be considered a compact, who is to be the final judge or interpreter of the Constitution, and, the rules required to interpret the Constitution correctly. At the conclusion of Book III, Story presented his closing remarks intended to emphasize the importance of preserving the union.

In the Introduction, Story indicated that the Commentaries owed their existence to two great sources: The Federalist Papers ("an incomparable commentary of three of the greatest statesmen of their age"), and the opinions of Mr. Chief Justice Marshall. Although suggesting that his work represented an improvement in organization over the Federalist, Story made no claim of originality. Rather he sought to transfer "into my own pages all which seemed to be of permanent importance in that great work, and have thereby endeavored to make its merits more generally known." Furthermore, he also made clear that he had "not the ambition to be the author of any new plan of interpreting the theory of the Constitution, or of enlarging or narrowing its powers by ingenious subtitles and learned doubts." Story asserted that the exposition found in the Commentaries were less his own than those of the Framers, or of those who had been called upon to administer under the Constitution. "My own object will be sufficiently attained," he continued, "if I shall have succeeded in bringing before the reader a true view of its powers, maintained by its founders and friends, and confirmed and illustrated by the actual practice of government."[20]

Story's defense of broad national powers, including those of the Supreme Court, developed in Book III, comprises an important work that merits consideration that we will be unable to extend here. Rather, we will concern ourselves with an even more fundamental premise advocated by Story and which he thought essential to the success of the entire work. That premise was indelibly written into the Constitutional law of the United States almost seventeen years before in his opinion for the Court in the case of Martin v. Hunter's Lessee; there he asserted that "The Constitution of the United States was ordained and established, not by the States in their sovereign capacity, but emphatically as the preamble to the Constitution declares, by 'the people of the United States.'"[21] This conclusion forms the foundation upon which Story's more practical constitutional analysis was built.

Interestingly, Story attempted to prove this fundamental conclusion historically, within the pages of the first two of the Commentaries' three Books. Story's turning to history represented an admission that basing political judgments simply upon the text of the Constitution would prove inadequate in that it would insufficiently address the contemporary states' rights argument. As was previously noted, The Commentaries were written in the heat of the South Carolinian nullification crisis, at a time when it appeared that State's ultimate reaction of the Tariff of 1828 would culminate in active resistance or perhaps rebellion. South Carolina's political position received active support from eminent State political figures such as Robert Hayne, John C. Calhoun and James Hamilton. These men all posited a "strict" or illiberal interpretation of the powers granted to the national government by the Constitution. Furthermore, each based his understanding of the constitutional doctrine of "nullification" or "interposition" on a specific pre-constitutional or historical understanding. That is, Hayne, Calhoun and Hamilton all believed that the states constituted the original contracting parties to the Constitution and they, therefore, had founded the government of the United States. From this it followed that should a state disagree with the natioal

271

government over the constitutional propriety of the latter's actions, the state retained the right to judge the legality of the disputed law, and oppose its implementation within its own boundaries. Calhoun stated this thesis with precision in his famous Fort Hill Address:

> The great and leading principle is, that the General Government emanated from the people of the several States, forming distinct political communities, and acting in their separate and sovereign capacity, and not from all the people forming one aggregate political community; that the Constitution of the United States is, in fact, a compact, to which each State is a party, in the character already described; and that the several States, or parties, have a right to judge of its infractions; and in case of a deliberate, palpable, and dangerous exercise of power not delegated, they have the right, in the last resort, to use the language of the Virginia Resolutions, "to interpose for arresting the progress of the evil, and for maintaining, within their respective limits, the authorities, rights, and liberties appertaining to them."[22]

Calhoun was emphatic regarding the propriety of interposition as a legitimate political tactic:

> This right of interposition, thus solemnly asserted, by the State of Virginia, be it called what it may, --State-right, veto, nullification, or by any other name,--I conceive to be the fundamental principle of our system, resting on facts historically as certain as our revolution itself, and deductions as simple and demonstrative as that of any political or moral truth whatever; and I firmly believe that on its recognition depends the stability and safety of our political institutions.[23]

272

From Story's perspective, "the right of interposition" could never be the fundamental doctrine of
the American constitutional system. It was, on the
contrary, a dangerous extra-constitutional response
which tended to subvert that system of law outlined
within the Constitution. He not only opposed South
Carolina's doctrine of nullification, but he also
opposed the very idea of nullification or interposition
in any political setting.[24] It was a doctrine that
has reared its head on several occasions in American
history and Story's response to it is instructive of a
reasoned interpretation in light of the Founders'
intentions.

Calhoun asserted that the idea of state interposition rested on facts "historically as certain as
our revolution itself." Story's Commentaries sought
systematically to refute that view of history, and
similar contemporary accounts, by substitution an
historical analysis of his own. He summarized the
precise legal and political relationship of the
colonies to one another prior to the Revolutionary War.
The people of the colonies were not one people in that
"they had no direct political connection with each
other." However, they did possess a common origin and
common allegiance in the British Crown. Additionally,
each colonist had the right to inhabit any other colony
and, as a British subject, could inherit lands by
descent in every other colony. Finally, commercial
intercourse among the colonies was also regulated by
English law and could not be obstricted by acts of the
colonial legislatures.

The precise relationship among the colonies was
therefore ambiguous. They all maintained a strict
legal relationship to the Mother Country, yet shared
no exact political relationship with each other. However, as Story argued, this state of affairs gradually
changed with the turbulent events that preceded the
Revolutionary War. The 1765 Stamp Act Congress, for
example, saw representatives from a number of colonies
meeting together, in an attempt to secure what they
viewed as the traditional rights of Englishmen, even
though "An utter denial of all parliamentary authority
was not generally maintained until after independence
was in full contemplation of most of the colonies,"[25]
and it became increasingly "obvious that the great
struggle in respect to colonial and parliamentary
rights could scarcely be decided otherwise than by an

273

appeal to arms."[26] "Great Britain was resolutely bent upon enforcing her claims by an open exercise of military power," Story pointed out, "and, on the other hand, America scarcely saw any other choice left to her but unconditional submission or bold and unmeasured resistance."[27]

Story's reference to "America" is critical. By his usage of the term he pointed to the people of America, a people whose very existence came to be defined by their opposition to British rule. Whereas before "the people" of the colonies could be considered one people only in some respects by this action they became one people in the most fundamental sense.

This idea was further developed by Story in the second Book of his Commentaries. Because no redress of grievances had followed the many appeals to the King and Parliament made by the Colonists, it became obvious that closer cooperation and indeed union was necessary to vindicate their rights and protect their liberties. After all, Story contended, "If a resort to arms should be indispensable, it was impossible to hope for success but in united efforts."[28] The need for a "national organization" therefore made necessary the Continental Congress of 1774. About this development of Congress Story made a number of points crucial for his larger argument.

First, the Congress of delegates that assembled on September 4, 1774 in Philadelphia constituted a government. Story is unequivocal on the importance of this point. This Congress, in his opinion, exercised "de facto and de jure a sovereign authority."[29] Secondly, Story asserted that the government which had been formed was a revolutionary government and was conducted upon revolutionary principles. It could only be understood and interpreted in the context of a revolutionary transformation of the polity. It exercised no authority under English law. Indeed, it existed in contradiction to English law; but, standing as a government, its authority was not derived from legal status of the colonies within the British Empire. The logic of his argument was that Congressional authority stemmed from the consent of the people. The authority to govern could most properly be understood "not as the delegated agents of the governments de facto of the colonies, but in virtue of original powers derived from the people."[30] "It was organized under the auspices and with the con--

274

sent of the people, acting directly in their primary, sovereign capacity, and without the intervention of the functionaries to whom the ordinary powers of government were delegated in the colonies. . . ."[31] Such a government, Story contended, "terminated only when it was regularly superseded by the confederated government under the articles finally ratified, as we shall hereafter see, in 1781."[32]

Proceeding with his argument, Story pointed to the deeds of the first and second Continental Congress of 1774 and 1775 as acts of a national government.[33] This historical sequence led to an analysis of the Declaration of Independence that was central to Story's argument. His argument, although hardly simple, can be reduced in complexity. A nation existed prior to the Declaration. Story explained that the nation had come into existence "as soon as Congress assumed power and passed measures which were in their nature national, to that extent the people, from whose acquiescence and consent they took effect, must be considered as agreeing to form a nation."[34] In this connection, Story again mentioned the Congress of 1774 as possessing those powers necessary to adopt appropriate measures for insuring the rights and liberties for all the colonies. The Congresses of 1775 and 1776 possessed more powers and more closely assumed the character of a national government.

The Declaration itself pronounced by the legitimate representatives of the people, represented an act of the whole people. Story noted that "It was emphatically the act of the whole people of the united colonies, by the instrumentality of their representatives, chosen for that among other purposes." "It was not an act competent to State governments," continued Story, "or any of them as organized under their charters, to adopt."[35] Their charters could not have legally provided for such an action, only the people could have such authority. "It was an act of original, inherent sovereignty by the people themselves, resulting from their right to change the form of government, and to institute a new one, whenever necessary for their safety and happiness."[36]

After the adoption of the Declaration no doubt could remain about the legal status occupied by the colonies. The united colonies were declared free and independent, absolved from all allegiance to the

British crown. According to Story, "The Declaration of Independence has accordingly always been treated as an act of paramount and sovereign authority, complete and perfect per se, and ipso facto working an entire dissolution of all political connection with, and allegiance to, Great Britain."[37] This, Story noted, was not merely "a practical fact, but a legal and constitutional view of the matter by courts of justice."[38] This argument cast the Declaration in a different light and changed the conceptual focus of the founding period.

After the Declaration, therefore, it was not difficult for Joseph Story to argue that the people, indeed one people, later founded the Articles of Confederation in order to replace the revolutionary government which had existed under the various Continental Congresses. Story also emphasized in this connection that because the Articles were never ratified by the people the Articles exhibited a serious weakness at its founding.[39] This defect, however, was remedied by the Philadelphia Convention in 1787, when it was stipulated that the proposed Constitution be endorsed by the people through their chosen representatives acting in special state conventions as opposed to being ratified by the various state legislatures. The 1787 convention produced the document creating the nations' third and most enduring framework of government.

III

The historical teaching of Joseph Story's Commentaries was that the people of the United States preceded the government of the United States. Not only did the corporate body of the people of the United States exist prior to the adoption of the United States Constitution, but that body's consent was required to create the nation's first government, the Congress of 1774. Yet, upon reflection, it does seem odd that a people, whose nationality defines their identity, could exist an entity before the founding of their nation. To make practical sense of Story's historical argument, therefore, presents us with some complexities. Only when it is recognized that Story's historical investigation points to philosophical considerations beyond his historical argument can one understand the true character of the thesis advanced in his Commentaries on the Constitution.

276

That such considerations were not more clearly
delineated suggests that Story intended for his work
to engender a deeper public respect for the Constitution as well as to influence statesmen. Wishing to
"inspire in the rising generation a more ardent love
of their country, an unquenchable thirst for liberty,
and a profound reverence for the Constitution and the
Union. . . ,[40] he therefore sought to eschew "meta-
physical refinements" in his work. Thus, although his
history was conspicuously without resort to first
political principles, Story's investigation was clearly
a history informed by such principles. More specifically, Story's historical analysis gains important
implications when seen in the light of the modern
natural rights political theory which commanded both
his study and respect. Understood in this manner,
his argument that the people of the United States preceded government tacitly, although emphatically,
illustrates his view that the people of the United
States existed prior in theory, or principle, to
government. Story's survey of American history is
clearly a most straightforward Lockean formulation of
the origin of regimes.

Once it is recognized that Story's explanation of
the foundation of the American political order presents
itself as an inconspicuous, though interestingly
practical adaptation of Locke's political theory, its
true character can accurately be seen. With Locke,
Story argued that political life existed to secure
certain pre-political rights.[41] Finally, note Story's
observation:

> There can be no freedom, where there
> is no safety to property, or personal
> rights whenever legislation renders
> the possession or enjoyment of property
> precarious; whenever it cuts down the
> obligation and security of contracts;
> whenever it breaks in upon personal
> liberty, or compels a surrender of
> personal privileges, upon any pretext,
> plausible or otherwise, it matters
> little, whether it be the act of the
> many, or the few, of the solidary
> despot, or the assembled magnitude;
> it is still in its essence tyranny.[42]

Also following Locke, his demonstration of the priority

277

of the American people in time and principle to their government logically led to the demand that legitimate government be based upon the consent of the governed. As has been noted Story argued that even the revolutionary government (although founded at a time when "Men had not leisure in the heat of war nicely to scrutinize or weigh such subjects; <u>inter arma silent legas</u>") was grounded in the people's acquiescence.[43] The consent he demanded from civil society did not differ from Locke's belief that the creation of government required "the will and determination of the majority."[44] Therefore, according to Story, the Declaration of Independence is to be understood as a "great and glorious change in the organization of our government (which) owes its whole authority to the efforts of triumphant majority."[45] He further wrote that the minority of colonists who opposed the majority's decision seemed cut off from the protections afforded by the nation; they appeared to be almost in a state of war with the majoirty; "the dissent on the part of the minority was deemed in many cases a crime, carrying along with it the penalty of confiscation, forfeiture, and personal and even capital punishment; and in its mildest form was deemed an unwarrantable outrage upon the public rights, and a total disregard of patriotism."[46]

Joseph Story's history, therefore, was a practical, straightforward attempt to present a historical interpretation of the American political order consistent with the tenets of Lockean political theory. That is, Story sought, through his history, to reveal that the foundations of the American nation were directly rooted in the requirements of modern natural rights political philosophy. Presented in this manner, there was an important conclusion that followed from Story's Lockean analysis. The practical aspect of the priority of the American people to their government was the philosophical view that the states had no significant role to play in the nation's early history; <u>never</u> were they sovereign.[47] In the act of severing their ties with Britain, the people as a whole formed a government based upon their consent; from this it followed that there were never thirteen separate American peoples. For Story the people of the United States were emphatically <u>not</u>, nor could they ever be, the people of the separate states.

Such an assertion was particularly significant

during the South Carolina nullification crisis.
Because South Carolina's interposition argument was
presented as a just legal and political doctrine, a
practical response was required. Here Story presented
a number of objections. For example, he sought to
prove that the Constitution "as a permanent form of
government, as a fundamental law, as a supreme rule,
which no state was at liberty to disregard, suspend,
or annul, was constantly admitted and insisted on, as
one of the strongest reasons why it should be adopted
in lieu of the confederation."[48] Specifically, Story
agreed with Locke that "every Man, by consenting with
others to make one Body Politic under one Government,
puts himself under the Obligation to everyone of that
Society, to submit to the determination of the majority, and to be concluded by it. . . ."[49] Stressing
each citizen's obligation to obey the law of the land
constituted Story's most immediate political concern
in 1833. Stated simply, although the Constitution
affected citizens and required their respect it made
no provision for state nullification. Furthermore,
none was needed, for the Constitution created rule by
popular majority.[50]

    In addition, Story attempted to show that nulli-
fication failed as an extra-constitutional political
doctrine as well. Here his historical analysis also
came into play. He pointed toward a government
originally established by the consent of a popular
majority. From this followed, to paraphrase Jefferson,
the idea that government could only be legitimately
altered or changed by the consent of the governed. A
majority of the whole people governed in both a
philosophical and constitutional sense. Building upon
his examination of the American Revolution, Story
observed that revolutions in general, in so far as they
had not been produced by positive force, had been
founded on the authority of the majority.[51] But if
constitutional change as well as revolution, that most
radical of extra-constitutional change, required a
majority to establish its political dignity then surely
nullification had to be governed by this same consideration. In light of this point, it is crucial to observe
that the majority of any one state, or even of any
section or region, could not constitute a majority of
the whole people. The question of numbers was decisively against South Carolina in 1832. "The people of
the United States," wrote Story, "have the right to
abolish or alter the Constitution of the United States;

but that the people of a single State have such a right is a proposition requiring some reasoning beyond the suggestion that is implied in the principles upon which our political systems are founded."[52] Thus, given Story's interpretation, it seemed that the teachings of John Locke which bestowed legitimacy upon the United States ruled against the intermittent although persistent case put forward for state sovereignty, a case which would not cease until the conclusion of the Civil War.

IV

The ending of the Civil War not only helped assure the continuity of the United States, but it permitted a further industrial and economic development to a degree unimagined in previous eras. Yet, as Professor Diamond has suggested, despite many social and economic changes, no important nation has changed less politically over these past two centuries than has the United States. It would seem that the individualistic, commercial and free people that we are, and the energetic government that actively helps provide for our welfare, well corresponds to the nation most of our Founders hoped would develop. Significantly, it is perhaps their most important expectation that has best endured; that of a Constitution, respected by its people, interpreted by its nation's courts, shaping and providing continuously for the existence of that nation while helping resolve its most divisive political problems.[53]

In his Commentaries, Joseph Story's interpretation of American history sought to help realize this expectation. To be sure, his interpretation was not entirely novel. It was built, by his own admission, upon the writings and opinions of a number of men, including Nathan Dane, James Wilson and John Jay. Yet, having made this acknowledgment, it is equally important to recognize that no constitutional commentator before Joseph Story presented such an interpretation of American history so systematically or comprehensively. To this task, he brought a reputation as a legal giant. So prevalent was his influence that Henry Steele Commanger, no blind partisan of Story's work, could assert "that with the possible exceptions of Coke, Blackstone and Mansfield no English or American jurist exercised an influence on the development of the law greater than that which Story commanded."[54] And it

280

should be noted that Story's work bore fruit, not only in his association with nationalists such as Daniel Webster, but also in the influence of his teaching upon future statesmen. For example, Lincoln's First Inaugural Address reveals an understanding of the American nation which conforms remarkably to Story's teaching on that subject. According to Lincoln:

> The Union is much older than the Constitution. It was formed in fact, by the Articles of Association in 1774. It was matured and continued by the Declaration of Independence in 1776. It was further matured and the faith of all the then thirteen States expressly plighted and engaged that it should be perpetual, by the Articles of Confederation in 1778. And, finally, in 1787, one of the declared objects for ordaining and establishing the Constitution, was "to form a more perfect union."[55]

Story's efforts were not directed solely at statesmen; he attempted to engender a respect for the United States on the part of all its citizens. This desire to foster public virtue was most clearly manifested in Story's association of the nation's highest and most noble acts with the people as a whole. They resisted British tyranny; they established a revolutionary government; they wrote the Declaration of Independence. Story contended that it was not the people of any particular state who had effected these great deeds; it was the people as a corporate body. By this argument, he sought to instill a sense of devotion in the American people for the founding generation, a generation whose acts of national patriotism were praiseworthy and deserved to be honored. The Union of the United States, Story thought, represented the culmination of great deeds and political wisdom.

By means of such teachings Story hoped not simply to insure the perpetuation of the Union but very likely his own fame as well. From his letters we learn of his youthful hope for literary fame. Thus, at the age of almost twenty, Story once wrote a close friend of his "ardent love of literary fame" and of his "hope of 'immortality.'"[56] In later years, even in private

letters, Story would not refer to this kind of fame in
regard to his own life; although, from his comments,
it was obvious that it comprised the proper reward for
those who dedicated their lives to great tasks bene-
fiting their fellow citizens, especially when they did
so in the face of public controversy. A great admirer
of Aristotle, Story was no doubt familiar with Aristotle's teaching that the preservation of a democracy
could present no more difficult task than that of preserving its founding principles.[57] There was honor in
devoting one's life to such a task, and posterity would
praise and celebrate those who dedicated their lives to
such a worthy pursuit. One sees such this opinion
reflected in Story's estimation of his colleague and
good friend John Marshall. As Story often noted,
Marshall has very likely insured his earthly immortality through great achievements, all of which had
helped preserve republican government consistent with
the intention of the Founding Fathers.

But if a steady desire for fame was a force that
drove Story, it was not a thoughtless or unquestioning
one. "In America," he wrote James Kent, "I think we
are in general too cold in the expression of that
approbation of public men which we really feel." Continuing this thought Story concluded that this was an
"error, which. . .does injustice to that honorable
ambition which can hope for no adequate reward, except
from a well-earned fame, cheerfully and publicly
given."[58] The degree to which a democracy could recognize greatness and dedication in its leaders became a
more agonizing problem for Story toward the end of his
life as the Union became racked by increasingly severe
political problems. Too often the reputation of
political leaders seemed to rest upon their immediate
public approval. The passing from power of John
Quincy Adams occasioned one instance of Story's occa-
sional skepticism regarding the worth of a proper
ambition ("Mr. Adams has no more favors to bestow,
and he is now passed by with indifference, by all
fair-weather friends")[59] as did a visit to Alexander
Hamilton's grave. On that occasion he wrote:

> In Trinity Church yard a monument is
> erected to General Hamilton, and I
> passed a half hour in solemnly sur-
> veying it. It is of marble, and you
> ascend by three stone steps; an iron
> balustrade encloses it. . . . The

whole does not exceed in height
twelve feet, and though neat, and
perhaps elegant, it seems hardly
equal to the character of the man of
the opulence of the city. . . . How
transitory is human greatness. The
crowds pass and repass, and scarcely
once give a glance to the monument.
The name is not mentioned. The city
feels not the value of the dust it
encircles. . . . The fame which we
so ardently seek, and so dearly purchase, is a fleeting shadow. It
deludes us while living. But the tomb
closes on greatness, and it is no more.
Perhaps a few wanderers, like ourselves,
gaze on the spot and sigh a sweet and
parting adieu; but the hour of business
is undisturbed and the gaiety of plea-
surers pauses not to consider.[60]

Story's respect for Hamilton was profound, and his
observations point to our worst fears regarding the
inability of a republican regime specifically to acknowledge political greatness, or excellence in general.
As Tocqueville pointed out, in an egalitarian age, distinctions of all kinds are eschewed and general causes,
not human actions, are regarded as the determinant of
significant events. Thus, it was not apparent to
Story (nor is it always apparent to us today) that a
republican regime can properly acknowledge the debt it
owes its greatest benefactors. Yet, despite this
uncertainty, Story labored to foster reverence for his
nation's Constitution and the men who wrote it. As
such, his life helped form a vital link between the
Founding generation of Hamilton and Madison and that
of Lincoln, constitutional statesman par excellence.
To the extent that the survival of the American Experiment in self-government can fairly be attributed
to human wisdom and political prudence and not simply
to accident, force, or chance, Story's efforts were
not in vain. Like those even greater men who preceded
and succeeded him, and who sought to provide for an
enduring nation by writing and helping preserve its
fundamentally important Constitution, Story's efforts
are worthy of the deep respect he systematically
sought to instill in others.

NOTES

[1]Story's appointment to the Supreme Court was approved by the Senate on November 11, 1811. He assumed his seat on the Court on February 3, 1811, a position he held until his death September 10, 1845. After Marshall's death during the 1836 term, Story served as "President" of the Supreme Court.

[2]Wheat. 304 (1816). Note Charles Warren's description of the case:

> On March 20, 1816, Judge Story rendered the opinion of the Court, an opinion which has ever since been the keystone of the whole arch of Federal judicial power....
>
> The vital effect upon the history of the United States of this courageous maintenance of Federal supremacy and of the constitutional powers of the Federal Judiciary can hardly be overemphasized.... Charles Warren. The Supreme Court in United States History (2 vols.; Boston: Little, Brown and Company, 1926), Vol. I, pp. 449-451.

[3]To cite one example Story drafted the 1825 Crimes Act, which revised to the federal criminal code although Daniel Webster has received credit for its passage. Life and Letters of Joseph Story, William W. Story, (2 vols.; Boston: Charles C. Little and James Brown, 1851), Vol. I, pp. 409-411. The Story-Webster collaboration is frequently acknowledged and quite significant. It is highly probable, for example, that Story decisively influenced Webster's famous reply to Hayne. On the Story-Webster relationship, see James McClellan, Joseph Story and the American Constitution (Norman: University of Oklahoma Press, 1971), pp. 280-283.

[4]Many, although by no means all, are reprinted in the Miscellaneous Writings of Joseph Story, ed. William W. Story (Boston: Charles C. Little and James Brown, 1852).

[5]As a young man, Story had written A Selection of

Pleadings in Civil Actions in 1805. He also had edited three additional works. Then, in the years between 1832 and 1845, came the comprehensive Commentaries: On the Law of Bailments, On the Constitution, On the Conflict of Laws, On Equity Pleading, On the Law of Agency, On the Law of Partnership, On the Law of Bills of Exchange, and On the Law of Promissory Notes. In addition, Story during this time published various abridgements, revisions and expanded editions of these works. According to his son, Story "never employed an amanuesis or secretary, generally making even his own indexes, and always personally revising every proof-sheet...." (Life and Letters, II, p. 344).

[6]Story to Charles Sumner, January 4, 1845, Life and Letters, p. 519.

[7]It is appropriate to mention here that Story's "non-constitutional" writings gave extensive support to his interpretation of constitutional law. Commanger, for example, observes that Story's Commentaries on Bailments, Equity, Agency, Partnership, Bills of Exchange, and Promissory Notes all "went far to arrest the natural tendency toward local law and impose upon the bench and bar of a good part of the nation uniformity of practice." According to Newmeyer, "Motivating his (Story's) fight for the common law of criminal jurisdiction, for an extensive admiralty jurisdiction, and for a broad assertion of the federal appellate jurisdiction, is clearly Story's fear for the permanence of the union in the face of disintegrating tendencies of local self-interest, his conviction of the efficacy of the Constitution as a preventative against such tendencies, and his optimistic visions of national destiny." See Henry Steele Commanger, "Joseph Story" in The Gaspar G. Bacon Lectures on the Constitution of the United States, 1940-50, (Boston: Boston University Press, 1953). p. 53, and R. Kent Newmeyer, Justice Joseph Story: A Political and Constitutional Study (unpublished Ph.D. dissertation, University of Nebraska, 1959), p. 202.

[8]Joseph Story, "The Value and Importance of Legal Studies," in Miscellaneous Writings, p. 543.

[9]Joseph Story, "History and Influence of the Puritans," Miscellaneous Writings, p. 473.

[10]"Progress of Jurisprudence," in Miscellaneous

Writings, p. 228.

[11] Ibid., pp. 228-229.

[12] "Speech on the Apportionment of Senators,"
Miscellaneous Writings, p. 185.

[13] "Statesmen, Their Rareness and Importance:
Daniel Webster, The New England Magazine, Vol. VII
(Aug., 1834), p. 89.

[14] "Progress of Jurisprudence," in Miscellaneous
Writings, p. 229. See also "The Science of Government"
in that same work, p. 626.

[15] "Statesmen," New England Magazine, p. 93.

[16] Joseph Story, Commentaries on the Constitution
of the United States (2 vols.; 5th edition; Boston:
Little, Brown and Company, 1891), I. Sec. 507, p. 381.

[17] "The Value and Importance of Legal Studies,"
in Miscellaneous Writings, p. 511.

[18] "The Science of Government," Miscellaneous
Writings, pp. 622-623.

[19] Commentaries on the Constitution, I, p. xi.

[20] Ibid., pp. ix-xi. The Commentaries were written,
Story wrote James Kent, "to recommend the Constitution
upon true, old and elevated principles." Story to
Kent, Oct. 27, 1832, Life and Letters, II, p. 109.
Although Story's constitutional interpretation was
fundamentally similar to that propounded by the
Federalist, there were a few differences (perhaps most
significantly on the utility of a Bill of Rights).
Story's heavy dependence on the Federalist owes not
simply to the brilliance of that work but also to the
fact that James Madison's Notes on the Constitutional
Convention were not available in 1833.

[21] Wheat, at 324.

[22] The Works of John C. Calhoun, ed., Richard K.
Cralli (6 vols.; New York: D. Appleton & Co., 1854-56)
VI, pp. 60-61.

[23] Ibid., p. 61.

[24]While a Congressman, Story apposed a similar rebellious spirit in this native Massachusetts brought in over the government's embargo policy. See especially letters written by Story to William Fettyplace, January 14, 1808, and to Samuel Fay, January 9, 1809 in Life and Letters, I pp. 176 and 182 as appropriate.

[25]Commentaries on the Constitution, I sec. 194, pp. 140-141.

[26]Ibid., sec. 197, p. 143.

[27]Ibid.

[28]Ibid., sec. 200, p. 145.

[29]Ibid., sec. 201, p. 145.

[30]Ibid.

[31]Ibid.

[32]Ibid.

[33]Ibid., secs. 203-204, pp. 145-148.

[34]Ibid., sec. 213, p. 156.

[35]Ibid., sec. 211, p. 154.

[36]Ibid.

[37]Ibid., p. 155.

[38]Ibid.

[39]Ibid., sec. 217, p. 161. Cf. Hamilton in Federalist 22: "It has not a little contributed to the infirmities of the existing federal system, that it never had a ratification by the PEOPLE. Resting on no better foundation than the consent of the several Legislatures; it has been exposed to frequent and intricate questions concerning the validity of its powers; and has in some instances given birth to the enormous doctrine of a right of legislative repeal. Owing its ratification to the law of the State, it has been contended, that the same authority might repeal the law by which it was ratified. However gross a heresy it may be, to maintain that a party to a compact

has a right to revoke that compact, the doctrine itself
has had respectable advocates. The possibility of a
question of this nature, proves the necessity of laying
the foundations of our national government deeper than
the mere sanction of delegated authority. The fabric
of American Empire ought to rest on the solid basis of
THE CONSENT OF THE PEOPLE. The streams of national
power ought to flow immediately from that pure original
fountain of all legitimate authority."

[40]Ibid., II, sec. 1914, p. 657.

[41]Ibid., I, sec. 330, p. 238. Story's Lockean
desire to secure the rights of life, liberty and
property is also clearly expressed in his Speech on
the Apportionment of Senators" as well as in his "The
Science of Government," both in Miscellaneous Writings,
pp. 184-185 and 619-620, as appropriate. Also note
Story's condemnation of slavery on the basis of natural
rights in "Piracy and the Slave Trade," in the same
work, p. 140.

[42]"The Value and Importance of Legal Studies,"
Ibid., pp. 511-512.

[43]Commentaries, I, sec. 217, p. 161.

[44]John Locke, The Second Treatise of Government,
sec. 96.

[45]Commentaries, I, sec. 329, p. 237.

[46]Ibid.

[47]Commentaries, I secs. 207 and 215, pp. 149, 157-
158.

[48]Ibid., sec. 359, p. 259. See above, note 37.

[49]Locke, Second Treatise, Sec. 97.

[50]Commentaries, I, secs. 363, p. 264. Also see
secs. 379 and 381, pp. 280-281, 283.

[51]As suggested, Story explicitly interpreted
Locke's discussion of a people's right to rebellion as
meaning a majority of the whole people's right to
rebellion. Not considered in this formulation is the
right of new people (admittedly a minority of the

whole) to form a new society and government. Of course, this was not the argument maintained by South Carolina in the early 1830's. On the ambiguity and complexity of this problem, discussed here in the context of a chief magistrate acting unlawfully, note Locke, Second Treatise, sec. 209.

[52] Ibid., sec. 359, p. 259. Cf. Locke, Second Treatise, sec. 211-243.

[53] The pervasion of constitutionality as a sign of a social policy's legitimacy should never be underestimated; in the United States we are constantly asking "is this or that program permitted"? Sometimes this question is posed to the exclusion of asking if that same program is good or in the public interest. Ironically, it is the very fact that the idea of constitutionality is so engrained in fabric of American politics that has allowed courts to decide increasing numbers of cases, often in areas about which the Constitution has little to say. The immediate effect of such a state of affairs is, of course, both to trivialize the Constitution and subject the judiciary to an increasing amount of well-deserved criticism. On the increasingly active role of the judiciary, see Donald Horowitz, The Courts and Social Policy (Washington, D.C.: The Brookings Institute, 1977), pp. 1-21.

[54] Commanger, "Joseph Story," p. 80.

[55] The Collected Works of Abraham Lincoln, ed. Roy Basler (8 vols.: New Brunswick: Rutgers University Press, 1953), IV, p. 265.

[56] Story to Charles P. Sumner, Life and Letters. I, p. 72.

[57] Aristotle, The Politics, 1319b.

[58] Story to James Kent, August 15, 1820, Life and Letters, I, p. 379.

[59] Story to Mrs. Story, February 25, 1829, Life and Letters, I, p. 562. Cf. "Statesmen," New England Magazine, p. 95.

[60] Story to Samuel P. Fay, May 18, 1807, Life and Letters, I, p. 144.

CHAPTER 13
"William Howard Taft, 'The Progressives' and the Inter-
pretation of the Modern Presidency"
Peter Schultz

Introduction

It seems safe to say that the birth of the "modern
presidency" is to be explained as part of the attempt
of the "Progressives" to adapt the American constitutional system to the twentieth century, or to the tasks
of the modern or positive state. This was true not only
of Woodrow Wilson, but of Theodore Roosevelt as well.[1]
As Roosevelt argues in his Autobiography,[2] America had
reached "the stage where what was needed for our people
was a real democracy."[3] Thoughtful men, not bound by
an outdated constitutional faith, had come to realize
"that Government must now interfere to protect labor,
to subordinate the big corporations to the public welfare, to shackle cunning and fraud exactly as centuries
before it had intervened to shackle the physical force
which does wrong by violence."[4] Roosevelt's stewardship theory of presidential power was the necessary
part of this modernization, or democratization, of the
American constitutional system.

Today more than ever, however, we are willing to
question the constitutional philosophy of the Progressives. The "modern presidency" it seems has run amuck;
it is for all practical purposes indistinguishable from
the "imperial presidency."[5] And yet the Progressive
tradition still rules our theoretical concepts about
the presidency. For if they were wrong not to follow
the wisdom of the Founders of the Constitution with
regard to presidential power, nonetheless it is still
thought that their understanding of the Constitution
itself was correct. The Progressives argued that the
Constitution of the Founders cannot accommodate a
powerful presidency and their intellectual descendents
still tend to agree.[6] It is only in the wake of Water-
gate and the "post-imperial presidency" that it has
once more become an academic commonplace to speak of
constitutional restraints on presidential power.
Central to this rediscovered wisdom of the Founders
is the notion that the Constitution does, after all,
make a difference in presidential behavior. Some
heirs of the Progressive tradition have recommended a
return to the constitutional law or the legislature.[7]
But were the Progressives correct about the Founders'
intentions vis-a-vis the executive? If the Progres-

sives misconstrued the Founders' conception of the presidency, a simple rejection of the Progressive tradition may or may not constitute a return to the original understanding of a constitutional presidency. This is the question that needs to be raised, both in order to better understand the Constitution and the continuing perplexity over the presidency today.

There is little doubt that the identification of the constitutional presidency with a narrowly constrained and subordinate executive has drawn strength from the prevailing understanding of William Howard Taft and his relationship to Theodore Roosevelt, an understanding which arose out of the Progressive era. According to this view, Taft was above all else a "constitutionalist," and for this reason one of the leading proponents of a narrow interpretation of presidential power.[8] Moreover, he is seen to have been in complete opposition to Roosevelt's stewardship theory because the latter's theory attributes to the President the power to act for the public good even when the law of the legislature is silent, and sometimes against them. In sum, it is a generally accepted view that Roosevelt was correct when he characterized Taft's view of presidential powers as "narrowly legalistic," and as making "the President the servant of the Congress rather than of the people, and (able to) do nothing, no matter how necessary it be to act, unless the Constitution explicitly commands the action."[9]

The critical point about Taft's theory of executive power is not that he disagreed with Roosevelt about the necessity or usefulness of an energetic and independent executive. As we shall see, he did not. In truth, Taft defended both executive energy and independence, but did so on the basis of the Constitution itself. What is most important in Taft's understanding of a Constitutional presidency is the recovery of a theory of executive power consistent with the Founders' intentions. Such a theory offers both a plausible alternative to the Roosevelt-Wilson understanding of the Constitution and also to the Jeffersonian understanding of presidential prerogative.

Taft's Understanding of Presidential Power

The flaws in the Progressive interpretation of Taft's theory of presidential powers are clearly

291

revealed in a closer reading of his oft quoted but infrequently studied monograph, Our Chief Magistrate and His Powers.[10] At the outset, where Taft assesses the action of the constitutional convention with regard to the presidency, he argues that the Constitution creates an executive with "wide powers, not rigidly limited."[11] Toward the end of the same work, he argues that "the grants of Executive power are necessarily in general terms in order not to embarrass the Executive in the field of action plainly marked for him."[12] Taft concludes by arguing that

> The Constitution does give the President wide discretion and great power, and it ought to do so. It calls from him activity and energy to see that within his proper sphere he does what his great responsibilities require. He is no figurehead. . . .[13]

According to Taft, therefore, the Constitution grants the President general powers and wide discretion in sum, great responsibilities. But what are the sources of this discretion and power? Taft, following Article II of the Constitution, enumerates them as follows: the veto power, the power "to take care that the laws be faithfully executed," and the commander in chief clause. Let us examine Taft's understanding of these powers, beginning with the veto power.

The President's veto power, he writes, is indicative of the Founders' conception of the office, i.e., that they rejected the view that "the Executive should be the mere agent of the Legislature to carry out their will."[14] Rather, the President was intended to play "an important part in the machinery of making laws."[15] Furthermore, the veto power is "purely legislative", meaning that "the reasons which control (the President's) action must be much like those which affect the actions of the members of Congress."[16] The Constitution itself indicates as much by making "the President's veto turn on the question whether he approves the bill or not," thereby allowing and even requiring that the President pass "on the merits of a bill," just as if he were a member of Congress.[17] So, the veto power as granted by the Constitution requires the President to concern himself with the merits of proposed legislation. That power draws the President into the legislative process; or, as Taft says, makes

292

the President "an important part in the machinery of making laws."[18] In brief, the veto power is a "great power" which confers "wide discretion" on the President.

According to Taft, however, the President's legislative discretion is not unlimited. Most importantly, the President must "veto a bill no matter how much he approves of its expediency if he believes that it is contrary to the constitutional limitations imposed on Congress."[19] This is the President's duty, Taft argues, both because the President pledges to defend the Constitution and because the courts alone cannot withstand the constitutional excesses of the legislature. Therefore, the President "cannot escape his obligation (in this regard) when the question. . . is whether. . .a bill. . .violates the Constitution."[20] In fact, Taft argues that the President's duty here is "as high and exacting. . .as the duty of the Supreme Court."[21] Interpreting the Constitution is, implicitly, not an exclusively judicial concern.

Similarly, Taft argues that the Constitution confers great power and wide discretion on the President by making him chief executive, specifically by vesting him with the responsibility to "take care that the laws be faithfully executed." As Taft says, this is the President's "widest power and (his) broadest duty."[22] This is so for several reasons.

First, in order to execute the laws, the President or his subordinates must interpret them. As Taft points out, "In order that (the President) or his subordinates shall enforce a statute, they must necessarily find out what it means, and on their interpretation enforce the law."[23] The scope of the executive's discretion here varies according to the law in question, but in most cases where there is doubt, "executive interpretation is final."[24] There exists then "a wide field of action"[25] in which the executive says what the law is. In fact, "statutory construction is practically one of the greatest executive powers."[26] The scope and character of this power he characterized as follows:

> Someone has said, 'Let me make the
> ballads of the country, and I care not
> who makes the laws.' One might also
> say, paraphrasing this, 'Let anyone

make the laws of the country, if
I can construe them.'[27]

For Taft, the duty to execute statutory law necessarily
confers on the President a substantial measure of discretion.

There is, however, another dimension to the
President's duty to faithfully execute the laws, viz.,
to execute the treaties of the United States which
are, "under the Constitution, laws of the United
States, having the same effects as Congressional en-
actments."[28] Here Taft is relying on Article VI of
the Constitution, which says that "This Constitution,
and the Laws of the United States. . .made in pursuance
thereof; and all Treaties made, or which shall be made,
under the Authority of the United States, shall be the
supreme Law of the Land. . . ."[29] Moreover, Taft
argues that in executing treaties the President may
act without consulting Congress, and even in the absence of legislation facilitating or regulating the
performance of this duty.[30]

Thirdly, and most insightfully, the President's
duty as chief executor of the laws extends even beyond
"express Congressional statutes and provisions having
the force of law in treaties" to "any obligation
inferable from the Constitution, or any duty of the
President or the Attorney-General. . .derived from the
general code of duties under the laws of the United
States."[31] Here, Taft relies on the decision and
language of the Supreme Court in the case in re
Neagle.[32] To quote Justice Miller's opinion in Neagle:

> Is this duty (to execute the laws)
> limited to the enforcement of acts
> of Congress or of treaties of the
> United States according to their
> express terms, or does it include
> the rights, duties, and obligations
> growing out of the Constitution it-
> self, our international relations,
> and all the protection implied by
> the nature of government under the
> Constitution?[33]

Both Taft and Justice Miller affirm that the President's
duty to execute the "laws" extends beyond the written
law itself.

The question then arises, How far does this authority extend? What kinds of activities does this interpretation of executive power protect or justify? The answer Taft gives is both complex and subtle. First, the President's authority in this regard extends to protecting American citizens, both at home and abroad. Thus, Taft argues that "the President has the authority to protect the lives of American citizens and their property with the army and navy."[34] This power "grows out of (the President's) control over our foreign relations and his duty to enforce. . . the obligation of the government to its own citizens."[35] The President is not authorized, "to order the army and navy to commit an act of war," as this would be "a usurpation of power on his part."[36] For Taft, the President's power to protect American citizens and their property is limited to "police" actions, defined as limited military actions in countries where the "peace is often disturbed and law and order are not maintained."[37] In such cases, the President may take military action because injuries to American citizens and their property cannot be remedied "through diplomatic complaints and negotiations."[38]

Secondly, the President's responsibility in this regard authorizes him to preserve the status quo in some situations even though, strictly speaking, he is without legal authorization to do so. For example, although Congress failed to renew Roosevelt's authority to control the Canal Zone in Panama during the building of the canal, Taft advised him without hesitation, "that his statutory authority was to build the Canal, and his constitutional duty to take care that the laws be faithfully executed required him to maintain the existing government and continue the status quo which was necessary to the construction of the Canal."[39] By any standard this is a conception of presidential powers broadly conceived.

It is clear that for Taft the constitutional duty to execute the laws, while not unlimited, confers great power and wide discretion upon the President. The President's duty in this regard is not narrowly legal, nor is the President subordinated to Congress by virtue of this responsibility.

Finally, Taft also interprets the commander in chief clause in the same way. Because of his consti-

295

tutional position as commander in chief, the President
may "order the army and navy anywhere he will, if the
appropriations furnish the means of transportation."[40]
Moreover, Taft argues that Congress' power in this regard is limited, and to some extent subordinate to that
of the President. For example, Congress may not itself
"determine the movements of the army and navy," or
place this power beyond the President's control in one
of his subordinates.[41] As Hamilton argued that the
President is the "first general and admiral" of the
nation, so too did Taft who saw the President as having
"the supreme command and direction of the military and
naval forces" of the nation, both in peace and in
war.[42]

Unlike Roosevelt, Taft does say that the President's discretion as commander in chief is not unlimited. He does not argue that the President as
commander in chief has the "power to do anything,
anywhere, that can be done with an army or navy."[43]
More importantly, the President may not wage on his
own authority, "a war of aggression against a foreign
country,"[44] or even commit an act of war against a
foreign country, or at least those countries capable
of executing its responsibilities to American citizens.
To wage war, Taft argues, "the power of Congress must
be affirmatively asserted. . . ."[45]

It should be clear that Taft, although a constitutionalist, did not construe the executive power of
the United States narrowly or as subordinate to the
legislative power in every regard. It would be fair
to say that Taft, like Roosevelt, thought that the
President possesses a kind of prerogative, that is,
the power to act for the public interest where the
laws or the legislature is silent, and even at times
against them. As Taft says near the end of Our Chief
Magistrate,

> I. . .hope that I have shown that
> (the executive power) is limited, so
> far as it is possible to limit such
> a power consistent with that discre-
> tion and promptness of action that
> are essential to preserve the inter-
> ests of the public in times of
> emergency, or legislative neglect
> or inaction.[46]

296

But while Taft is willing to admit that the President's constitutional authority encompasses an area of executive prerogative, he also argues that his prerogative is limited. Those limits are established by what Taft conceives to be the President's over-riding constitutional responsibility, viz., to preserve the peace of the nation. For Taft, this is the President's most important constitutional responsibility, his highest political duty.

> The President is made Commander-in-Chief. . .evidently for the purpose of enabling him to defend the country against invasion, to suppress insurrection and to take care that the laws be faithfully executed . . . In other words, he is to maintain the peace of the United States.[47]

In sum, the executive power of the United States is nothing less and nothing more than the power to preserve to the nation the blessings of peace, or of law and good order. As noted above, a part of this responsibility is protecting all citizens, even "embryonic" citizens, anywhere.[48] And, because this responsibility is executive, both in the sense of being constitutionally entrusted to the President and in the sense of requiring the exercise of discretion, neither Congress nor the courts may determine the President's actions in this regard. This is not, however, to say that President's power is unlimited. His power is limited because his responsibility is limited, or defined by the Constitution. The President's most important responsibility is for the peace of the nation, and all his powers, even that of commander in chief, must be interpreted in light of this responsibility. The obvious tension in these seemingly irreconcilable principles--of broad powers but distinctly limited in application--is reconciled within the constitutional understanding of limited government with enumerated powers.

Taft, The Constitution and the Modern Presidency

As we have seen, Taft conceived presidential power to be at once broad and limited. Two further questions arise out of this discussion. First, what evidence is there, constitutional or otherwise, to support Taft's interpretation? Second, would Taft's interpretation satisfy either Theodore Roosevelt or Woodrow Wilson, i.e., the earliest proponents of the modern presidency?

The constitutional evidence to support Taft's interpretation is strong. As Taft emphasizes, the President is both the chief executor of the laws and the supreme commander of the force of the nation. That is, the President possesses both the right and the power, under the Constitution, to enforce the nation's laws and to preserve the peace of the nation. To say then that the Constitution makes the President responsible for the peace and good order of the nation logically follows.

Moreover, there are two other parts of Article II which lend support to Taft's argument. First, the President is granted the pardoning power,[49] a power which has been interpreted as necessary for guaranteeing the peace of the nation.[50] Second, in his oath of office, the President promises to "preserve, protect and defend the Constitution of the United States,"[51] language which suggests that the President, above all other officers, is the protector of the nation and of its laws.

Beyond the constitutional evidence, there is a striking similarity between Taft's argument in Our Chief Magistrate and Hamilton's argument in his "Pacificus" papers.[52] Hamilton had argued there that the President is constitutionally entitled to issue proclamations of neutrality, insofar as neutrality is consistent with the nation's treaties. According to Hamilton, such proclamations are a part of the executive power, because the President is the interpreter of the nation's treaties, "where the judiciary is not competent to do so."[53] But, even more importantly in the present context, is Hamilton's response to the objection, that because the legislature is authorized by the Constitution to declare war, only Congress can judge "whether the nation is or is not under obligation to make war."[54] Hamilton's response deserves to be quoted at length.

> The answer is, that, however true this
> position may be, it will not follow
> that the executive is in any case
> excluded from a similar right of judg-

298

ment in the execution of its own
functions. If, on the one hand, the
Legislature have a right to declare
war, it is on the other, <u>the duty of
the executive to preserve the peace</u>
till the declaration is made; and in
fulfilling this duty, it must necessarily possess a right of judging
what is the nature of the obligations
which the treaties of the country
impose on the government; and when it
has concluded that there is nothing
inconsistent with neutrality, it becomes both its province and its duty
to enforce the laws incident to that
state of the nation.[55]

According to Hamilton, then, it is the President's
duty to preserve the peace of the nation, whereas it is
the legislature's responsibility to declare war. In
fulfillment of his responsibility, the President possesses a wide discretion, including interpreting the
nation's treaties. As Hamilton concluded, in language
which is strikingly similar to that of Taft,

(It) is the province and duty of the
executive to preserve to the nation
the blessings of peace. The Legislature alone can interrupt them by
placing the nation in a state of war.[56]

Additionally, as Hamilton makes clear, while the President is bound by the nation's treaties, he is not
simply subordinate to Congress. He has a constitutional responsibility to preserve the peace and he
may use his powers to fulfill that responsibility, at
least until Congress has acted.

It seems fair to conclude then that Taft's understanding of presidential power and responsibility is
supported by the Constitution itself and at least one
interpretation of that document by one of its principle defenders of the founding generation. But would
Taft's interpretation, even as explained here, satisfy
either Roosevelt or Wilson? That is, does Taft's conception of presidential power and responsibility,
however faithful to the Constitution, meet those concerns which led Roosevelt and Wilson to espouse what
has come to be known as "the modern presidency"? We

299

think the answer to this question is "no."

To see why this is so, it must first be emphasized that, according to Taft, the President's most important constitutional and political duties are best characterized as duties of restraint. For Taft, and to a large extent for Hamilton as well, executive power or energy is most visible as a check or restraint on congressional and even popular excesses. This is clearly the case, for example, with regard to the President's legislative power, i.e., the veto power. That the President's greatest legislative power is his veto power means that he is better equipped by the Constitution to check Congress than to lead it.

Thus, Taft does agree with Roosevelt and Wilson that executive energy is necessary and beneficial, but he understands this energy differently. The difference is critical. Executive energy is necessary and beneficial because it allows the President to withstand both the fiscal and constitutional excesses of the legislature.[57] In fact, Taft argues that from his vantage point the President can see these excesses more clearly, and because he represents the whole people, i.e., is dependent on no particular constituency, he is better able to resist them.[58] To be sure, Taft did recognize the need for presidential leadership, but like the Founders, he emphasized the need for restraint as well.

Furthermore, even the President's executive responsibilities may be seen as responsibilities of restraint, e.g., his responsibility as commander in chief. For although the President's power in this regard is political, he is duty-bound to ensure that the nation is not led into war unnecessarily, either by the demands of the military or by those of the people's representatives in Congress. Under the Constitution, the first responsibility of the commander in chief is to keep the nation out of war, hence, a civilian supreme commander. Of course he is also responsible for the security of the nation. But this latter responsibility should be fulfilled in ways consistent with the former. In brief, only very grave threats to the nation's security could justify presidential war-making. It is especially in such circumstances that congressional approval should be sought.

When seen in this light, the differences between

300

Taft, on the one hand, and Roosevelt and Wilson, on the other, are clarified. For Taft, the President's constitutional responsibilities are not simply leadership functions, if "leadership" means translating the popular will into law or action. For Taft, the President is constitutionally obligated to measure the popular will by the Constitution. A distinction explicitly raised in The Federalist but largely ignored by Progressive reformers. Roosevelt and Wilson, for example, have a tendency to argue that the President should "measure" the Constitution by the popular will.[59]

At its roots, then, Taft's understanding of presidential power and Constitutional responsibility is in tension with the "real democracy," of Roosevelt and Wilson.[60] It is for this reason that Taft's reading of the Constitution proved unacceptable to Roosevelt and Wilson. However much he distorted Taft's interpretation of presidential power, Roosevelt sensed this when he described Taft's position as follows:

> Mr. Taft's position is the position
> that has been held from the beginning
> of our government, although not so
> openly held, by a large number of
> respectable and honorable men, who,
> at bottom, distrust popular govern-
> ment, and, when they must accept it,
> accept it with reluctance, and hedge
> it around with every species of re-
> strictions and checks and balances,
> so as to make the power of the people
> as limited and as ineffective as
> possible. . . . Essentially this
> view is that the Constitution is a
> straightjacket to be used for the con-
> trol of an unruly patient--the people.[61]

Now, if one ignores Roosevelt's hyperbole, which suggests that Taft not merely distrusted but opposed popular government, this is a fair assessment of Taft's understanding of the American political order. But it is not a bad description of the framers' understanding as well, who certainly were "respectable and honorable men." Certainly, the framers distrusted popular government and saw the Constitution as serving to control popular excesses. In The Federalist Hamilton defends the creation of an energetic and independent executive, armed with a qualified veto power, as a

necessary and beneficial check on the legislature and
even on the people. According to Hamilton, such an
arrangement is essentially beneficial in times of
popular unrest, when it is necessary for the government "to withstand the temporary delusions of (the
people) to give them time and opportunity for more
cool and sedate reflection."[62] What joins Taft and
Hamilton and distinguishes both from Roosevelt and
Wilson is their agreement that presidential power was
intended as much to allow the President to frustrate
popular desires as to fulfill them. Taft was in
accord with Hamilton further in his notion that the
timely performance of this presidential duty was
essential to the political and constitutional well-
being of the nation. For Roosevelt, and the Progressives in general, such undemocratic responsibilities
are no longer necessary or beneficial. The government
in general and the President in particular must become
"stewards" of the people, because in "a rich and
complex society" democracy is impossible unless the
government sides with the many against the few.[63]

It is doubtful that the Progressive tradition has
understood Taft's argument in part because it has not
understood Hamilton's conception of presidential power
under the Constitution. If they had understood Taft's
interpretation of presidential power correctly the
Progressives would still have rejected it. However
broad it might be, Taft's understanding appears to be
fundamentally flawed because it cuts against the grain
of the modern democratic argument. For Taft, it is
fair to say, democratic government is and will remain
a problem, or more candidly, a deficient political
order which must be restrained, checked, even modified.
And one might also say that the message Taft conveys
to us today is this:

> If we are to have constitutional, as
> opposed to presidential government,
> then we must recover the Framers'
> understanding of democracy. However,
> to so defend constitutional government,
> one must be aware of the problematic
> character of democracy. Repairing the
> Constitution to offset an overblown,
> even imperial, presidency, will be in-
> sufficient unless we also recover the
> democratic teaching which underlies
> the Constitution.

NOTES

¹See Pearson's essay on Woodrow Wilson in this collection.

²Theodore Roosevelt, _Autobiography_ (New York: MacMillan Co., 1913).

³_Ibid._, p. 464.

⁴_Ibid._

⁵Arthur M. Schlesinger, Jr., _The Imperial Presidency_ (Boston: Houghton-Mifflin, Co., 1973); Louis Henkin, _Foreign Affairs and the Constitution_ (Mineola: Foundation Press, 1972).

⁶_Ibid._

⁷This caveat is necessary given the fact that the leading exponent of a return to a constitutional presidency as understood by the framers, Arthur M. Schlesinger, Jr., fails to establish a strong presidency, _within_ the Constitution, by relying on a "Lockian-Jefferson" notion of prerogative. Such a notion allows the President the right to _usurp_ the powers of other departments of government, whenever he deems it necessary or in the public interest, broadly defined. See Lucius Wilmerding, Jr., "The President and the Law," _Political Science Quarterly_ 57 (September, 1952), pp. 321-338.

⁸For example, see Roosevelt, _Autobiography_, p. 395; Wilfred E. Binkley, _President and Congress_, 3rd ed. (New York: Vintage Books, 1963), 224ff; James MacGregor Burns, et al. _Government by the People_, 6th ed. (Englewood Cliffs: Prentice-Hall, 1966), p. 420; and Robert Sherrill, et al., _Governing America_ (Chicago: Rand McNally, 1978), p. 277.

⁹Roosevelt, _Autobiography_, p. 395.

¹⁰William Howard Taft, _Our Chief Magistrate and His Powers_ (New York: Columbia University Press, 1916). Reprinted as _The President and His Powers_ (New York: Columbia University Press, 1967).

[11] Ibid., p. 4.

[12] Ibid., p. 140.

[13] Ibid., p. 157, emphasis added.

[14] Ibid., p. 3.

[15] Ibid., p. 16.

[16] Ibid., pp. 14-15.

[17] Ibid., p. 16.

[18] Ibid.

[19] Ibid., p. 19.

[20] Ibid.

[21] Ibid.

[22] Ibid., p. 78.

[23] Ibid.

[24] Ibid., p. 79.

[25] Ibid.

[26] Ibid., p. 78.

[27] Ibid.

[28] Ibid., p. 85.

[29] U.S. Constitution, article IV.

[30] Ibid., pp. 85-88.

[31] Ibid., pp. 88-89.

[32] 135 U.S. 1.

[33] Taft, Our Chief Magistrate, pp. 91-92.

[34] William Howard Taft, "The Boundaries Between the Executive, the Legislative and the Judicial Branches of the Government," Yale Law Journal 25 (June 1916),

p. 610.

[35] Ibid.

[36] Ibid., p. 611.

[37] Ibid.

[38] Ibid.

[39] Taft, _Our Chief Magistrate_, pp. 93-94.

[40] Ibid., p. 94. Compare this statement with a similar one by Roosevelt in his _Autobiography_, pp. 552-553.

[41] Ibid., pp. 127-128.

[42] Alexander Hamilton, _Federalist_ No. 69. _The Federalist Papers_. Edited by Jacob E. Cooke. (Middletown, Connecticut: Wesleyan University Press, 1961), pp. 465-66.

[43] Youngstown Sheet and Tube Co. v. Sawyer, 343 U.S. 579, 642 (1952) (Jackson, J., concurring).

[44] Taft, _Our Chief Magistrate_, p. 95.

[45] Ibid.

[46] Ibid., p. 156.

[47] Ibid., pp. 128-129.

[48] Taft refers to the Supreme Court's recognition in the Neagle case of the legitimacy of the action a captain in the United States' Navy, who compelled the surrender of one Kotza, a Hungarian who had made a declaration of his "intention to become a citizen of the United States," and who was deemed to be for that "an 'embryo' American citizen." Ibid., pp. 92-93.

[49] U.S. Constitution, article II, sec. 2.

[50] See Hamilton's argument in _Federalist_ No. 74. Also, consider the case of Murphy v. Ford, 390 F. Supp. 1372 (1975), where in upholding President Ford's pardon of Richard Nixon, the court reasoned as follows: "By pardoning Richard Nixon, who many believed was the

leader of a conspiratorial insurrection and rebellion
...President Ford was taking steps, in the words of
Alexander Hamilton in the Federalist, to 'restore the
tranquility of the common wealth' by a 'well-timed
offer of pardon' to the putative rebel leader."

[51]U.S. Constitution, article II, sec. 1.

[52]The Works of Alexander Hamilton, ed. Henry Cabot
Lodge, Vol. 4 (New York: G.P. Putnam's Sons, 1885),
pp. 432-444.

[53]Ibid., pp. 441-442.

[54]Ibid., p. 440.

[55]Ibid.

[56]Ibid., p. 443.

[57]Taft, Our Chief Magistrate, pp. 19-28.

[58]Ibid.

[59]This tendency is stronger in Roosevelt than in
Wilson, partially because of the latter's respect for
the American federal system. For Wilson, the question
of federalism, or "states' rights," is not "a mere
question of choice, a mere question of statesmanship,
but also a question, a very fundamental question, of
constitutional law." Woodrow Wilson, Constitutional
Government in the United States (New York: Columbia
University Press, 1964), p. 178, emphasis added.

[60]See note 3, above.

[61]Theodore Roosevelt, Works, National Edition,
vol. 17 (New York: Charles Scribner's Sons, 1926),
pp. 158-159.

[62]Hamilton, Federalist, No. 71, p. 482.

[63]Roosevelt, Autobiography, p. 512.

SECTION V

The Nature of American Democracy

CHAPTER 14

"Reinhold Niebuhr and the Irony of American History:
A Christian Realist's Analysis of the American
Founding."
James F. Pontuso

America has two foundings; what shall we think of
them? This query forms the structure of the argument
found in Reinhold Niebuhr's The Irony of American
History.[1]

The first founding is tangible, visible, concrete,
and has a date--1787. It is the manifestation of the
political philosophy of the Founders. This philosophy
both guided the ordering of offices set out in the
Constitution and informed the Founder's understanding
of government. Its great practical expression is The
Philadelphia Convention; its most coherent theoretical
expression is The Federalist.

The Founders, particularly James Madison, are
given high praise by Niebuhr. By devising a system
based on division of power, checks and balances, and
the balancing of contending interests, Madison more
than any of the Founders established the foundation
that would provide succeeding generations the opportunity to strive for liberty and justice.

This remarkable feat of ensuring justice through a
continuous clash of ambition, interest, and power was,
to Niebuhr, all the more profound because it rested on
an understanding of man's nature very similar to Christian realism. Christian realism views are seen as a
curious compound of spirit and animality, egoism and
altruism, selfishness and selflessness. Any attempt
at political realism must grapple with the paradoxes
and ambiguities of this nature if it is to avoid the
perils of tyranny or irrelevance.

It is not the purpose of this essay to raise the
question whether or nor Madison did, in fact, derive
his understanding of man from an explicitly Christian
precepts. Rather, we shall only note that it is significant that Niebuhr, from his background as a neo-
Orthodox Christian theologian, arrived at a philosophy
of politics almost identical to that of James Madison.

Niebuhr's enthusiasm for the first founding must
be viewed in terms of his criticism of the second.[2]
The second founding of the American polity is a social

founding and rests on a series of "idealistic" arguments about the nature of man. Put simply, the second founding focuses on the essential goodness of man and neglects his existentially evil self. By doing so, it raises the possibilities of perfection and infinite progress. It is a poor way to start the business of building political institutions.

This second founding has no particular moment of coming into being; rather, it draws upon many authors, historical events, and unarticulated experiences which all shape the American ethos. Niebuhr identifies this ethos as the general acceptance by the American people of the optimism of the Enlightenment, confirmed by the fortuity of America's great resources, immense spaces, and unassailable physical configuration. Ironically, the Founders contributed to this second founding by establishing a regime of liberty, in which contending social philosophies could develop, flourish, and eventually challenge the political realism which provided them the opportunity to exist.

The mismatch between the political and social foundings led Niebuhr to both attack and defend the nature of the American political system. In this essay, we shall examine this unique approach to the regime. Then we shall argue that there are several major points of disagreement between Niebuhr's political philosophy and that of the Founders. The differences are significant enough to question Niebuhr's understanding of the founding arguments and raise the possibility that Madison would not have agreed with Niebuhr's defense of the Constitution.

A comparison of their thinking raises further questions about the nature of the founding and the polity itself. If Niebuhr is wrong about Madison's implicit Christian realism, then perhaps the Founders did intend to create a Hobbesian political system based primarily on man's competitive instincts. If that is so, the true irony of the Founders' work is that it has self-destruction built into its fundamental law. Without a common bonds and sense of limit provided by religion, the democratic tendencies inherent in the Constitution could render great public enterprises, heroic feats of defense, and grand strategic designs impossible. Let us begin by examining Niebuhr's critique of America's second founding.

Niebuhr's basic criticism of American culture is that it is a direct heir of the rationalism of the Enlightenment. The Enlightenment, a revolt against the Medieval world view, had as its unifying theme the notion that man is a basically harmless creature. When left to his own devices, he will discover the rational order of things, discard the evil he had acquired from society, and erect a world free from corruption. Imperfect society was the cause of man's imperfections; a perfect society would perfect man's true nature. Sharply at odds with the Medieval notion that man was only spiritually perfectable, it taught that political perfection could be attained through man's own work, rather than God's grace. This rationalistic faith in political perfection later took the form of the idea of infinite progress or, under the influence of Marx, belief in a revolutionary event that would suddenly and totally transform the feral man of historical experience into a new man of peace and justice.

It is Niebuhr's argument that this optimistic view of human nature has blinded American social philosophy to the enormous difficulties inherent in any resolution of conflict; which, after all, is a permanent part of the human condition. This social myopia lies at the heart of the irony of American history; the more intensely Americans have tried to realize their ideals, the further away they seem to recede. Anticipated outcomes are contradicted by events, and Americans seem peculiarly unable to learn from experience. American history often looks ridiculous to the outsider. It is not the stumblings of a fool or the villainy of the scoundrel; rather, it is the ridiculousness of childlike innocence.[3]

The innocence of American social philosophy derives from its casual rejection of basic Christian precepts. It is Niebuhr's contention that the abandoned view of Christian realism, implicit in the Founders' political thought, gives a fuller appreciation of human nature and its limitations. Without the revealed truths of religion, the meaning, purpose, and final destiny of man remain shrouded in mystery. While the unaided mind is, as the Enlightenment demonstrated, able to comprehend many things, it is incapable of answering the ultimate questions of existence, and, hence, the true grounds of political association. Revelation acts as a guidepost toward the highest form of understanding, without which neither political or social ideas can be rationally ordered. Revelation does not defy reason, as the Enlightenment philosophies argued, but rather heightens and broadens the scope of reason.

> The truth as apprehended by faith is not something which simple men believe upon authority and wiser men deduce from experience. For there is an element in the truth of faith which defies the wisdom of both the wise and the foolish, more particularly of the wise. But on the other hand a truth of faith is not something which stands perpetually in contradiction to experience. On the contrary it illuminates experience and is in turn validated by experience.[4]

Although divine wisdom is given to man, his nature is so constructed that he will not necessarily accept it. Neibuhr explains this apparent paradox by observing that the same capacity for transcendence which makes acceptance of revelation possible also raises the possibility that man will doubt any explanation which gives meaning to his existence. Man's free will makes thought possible; thought makes man aware of nothingness. Spurred on by this dilemma, man attempts to discover his own nature in order to chart a proper and fitting course for his life. However, the very consciousness which makes it possible for man to ask this question also makes it impossible for him to answer it. Since man's consciousness stands beyond the patterns of nature and since consciousness is forever a mystery to itself, man is simply incapable of constructing any final or complete knowledge of existence. As Niebuhr puts it, "the self which stands outside itself cannot discover meaning in either itself or the world."[5]

The essential "homelessness" of the human spirit gives rise to the persistent problem of anxiety. Man is anxious because he is unsure of how best to order his life, and since every standard of judgment, every notion of right, is beyond the horizon of temporal knowledge, every human action presents a potential moral dilemma,[6] since to live is to act. But because man is a creature "who cannot find a true norm short of the ultimate reality," he must find some provisional justification for his actions. Unwilling to admit that his ideals are a creation of his own will, man invariably reaches beyond himself, projecting his principles as the embodiment of some final or ultimate truth. This quest to be in harmony with the eternal is a response to man's anxiety. In fact, the need for certainty is so strong that it seduces man into believing that his own partial and incomplete understanding of the truth is whole and universal. Hence, man deifies himself, Niebuhr explains, because:

> (he is) unwilling to recognize and
> acknowledge the weakness, finiteness
> and dependence of his position, inclined
> to grasp after power and security which
> transcend the possibilities of human
> existence, and (professes to have) a
> virtue and knowledge which are byond
> the limits of mere creatures.[7]

Man's arduous search for some ultimate standard convinces him that his own partial and incomplete ideals of the good are a true expression of reality. Hence, even the purest of principles are likely to be infused with the "idological taint," of the person who holds them. The "ideological taint," which for Niebuhr is synonomous with original sin, manifests itself crudely as a rationalization for power and privilege or, less overtly, as a defense of the superiority of one's own group, nation, culture, or historical epoch. Under such a delusion, man tends toward self-righteousness. Niebuhr states "when the self mistakes its standards for God's standards it is naturally inclined to attribute the very essence of evil to non-conformists."[8] The political ramifications of this human trait become apparent if one realizes that each group or nation is likely to fashion its own ideal of goodness, making existence on this earth a never-ending conflict between men. In fact, true justice in human terms is possible only in a situation where the power of each group is balanced by countervailing power, a situation which hinders any one group from imposing its will on others.[9]

America, in many ways, is the culmination of the Enlightenment's rejection of Christian wisdom. It is not surprising, Niebuhr argues, that America has displayed all the glaring follies of a culture which is based on the Enlightenment's idealism. These symptoms

311

are visible in the idealistic social philosophy which
has guided American policy, both foreign and domestic.

In foreign affairs, America has wavered between
projecting its own political ideals abroad and iso-
lating itself from the world altogether. The former
policy, best exemplified in the Wilson era, holds that
since all nations are moving toward a higher plateau
of government and society, all nations must adopt
democratic institutions. America's goal has been to
guide these backward nations toward the more advanced
stages of democracy; stages which are already found,
not surprisingly, in America.

For Niebuhr, the Wilsonian philosophy of making
the world safe for (American) democracy is an expression of this self-righteousness because it recognizes
only its own perspective as the proper one, while
failing to take seriously the ideals and concerns of
others. Of course, national pride is not unique to
America. But, America has been uniquely oblivious to
its own pride since there is nothing in the Enlightenment teaching which can account for this weakness in
men's souls.

No more satisfying to Niebuhr is isolationism,
America's response to foreign affairs from the founding
era until World War II. Isolationism, argues Niebuhr,
is merely another manifestation of self-righteousness,
since it rests on the assumption that the world is evil
and that "we" are virtuous--so virtuous that we cannot
soil our hands with the affairs of others.[10] One might
say that the political realism of isolationism of the
first founding was transmuted into a prideful moral
slogan by the second founding's naive idealism and
shallow understanding of men and nations.

III

The innocence of American social philosophy has
not been limited to areas of foreign affairs. It is
also conspicuously present in American attitudes toward
materialism, individualism, social engineering, liberty,
and equality. Each of these areas figures prominently
in Western political and social philosophy; but in
America, Niebuhr sees these perennial issues taking on
a peculiarly American coloration. This American perspective confounds Marxists and exasperates Christian

realism.

Consider the example of materialsm. Charles Beard
argued that the pursuit of economic goals took precedence over all others in the founding of the polity.
Niebuhr would agree--up to a point. Wealth, he notes,
has seldom been sought for its own sake in America.
Rather, it has generally been seen as a proximate means
to a higher end, freeing man from the burdens of harsh
physical labor. The true goal of American materialism
has been the promotion of man's dignity by liberating
him from the necessities of his environment. It is a
position consistent with the Enlightenment; yet one
that seems almost deliberately designed to frustrate
any analysis in terms of Marxism.

For Niebuhr, the question is whether the goal of
economic prosperity, even for the most enlightened
reasons, recognizes the true basis of human dignity.
There can be no doubt that the American economic system
has brought unprecedented wealth to more ordinary persons than any other system in the history of man. Yet,
the net effect of enlightened materialism has not
raised man to a higher level. Instead, it has tended
to glorify the trivial. The pursuit of happiness has
become synomomous with the pursuit of wealth. In turn,
this relentless drive for an ephemeral happiness has
obscured the Christian roots of the political founding.
Cut off as it is from its moral heritage, this idealistic view of the human condition has little need for
the tragic sense of life and leaves people unprepared
to confront the permanency of death, sorrow, pain, and
the paradoxes involved in wielding great political
power in a sinful world.[11]

The greatest irony of American propserity is that
the very technology that has enriched material life
also poses the gravest threat to its continued existence. The weapons of modern war can, for the first
time in history, quickly destroy every vestige of the
world as we have known it. The same technology that
has catapulted America into the front rank of world
powers has left her unusually vulnerable to the very
forces upon which modern military strength is built.
The irony is even further compounded by the fact that
since World War II, America has become permanently
involved in international politics. Her principal
antagonist is both intractable and fundamentally opposed
to her conception of justice. Thus, at the same time,

America must confront the fruits of the second founding,
she is engaged in a potentially deadly confrontation
with a political system possessing even more pretentious
claims to universality and infallibility. Unsuited by
experience and outlook, the United States must bear the
burden of a protracted conflict which makes final peace
and security an illusion.

American individualism is another example Niebuhr
cites in support of his conception of the short-sight-
edness of American social philosophy. Niebuhr does not
deny that the promotion of individual freedom is one of
the essential ingredients of a just society. But
Americans have taken their commitment to individualism
to the point where it threatens to undermine the bonds
of civil association. The ideal of Jefferson's self-
sufficient yeoman farmer has become a modern defense of
the robber baron. The goal of the individual liberty
of the common man has served to protect elite privileges
that serve neither the common man nor the common good.[13]

American individualism tends to destroy the fragile
bonds of community that make the polity viable. After
all, Niebuhr maintains, man is by nature a social and
political animal who needs a careful nurturing of the
virtues which make spiritual and material well-being
possible. An emphasis on eccentric individualism does
not prepare citizens to live in a community that may
demand individual sacrifices for the preservation of
the polity. Nowhere is the tension between the individual and community more conspicuous than when the defense
of the polity becomes necessary. Because the nature of
politics does not permit Americans to evade the ordinary responsibilities of citizenship that affect every
other regime, many young men who have been assured that
only the individual counts, have died upon foreign
battlefields.[14] It is this kind of incongruity between
political reality and social idealism that makes this
giveness in the human condition seem so intolerable
to men of the "second founding."

The experienced incongruities between the ideals
of American social philosophy and the reality of politics is likewise illustrated by the American version of
social engineering. Because of an enlightened optimism
about human nature, there is a strong propensity among
Americans to believe that political reality can be
brought into conformity with the ideal world of its
social philosophy. Perfection, or at least positive

movement toward perfection, can be rationally engineered. This is a theoretical failure expecially evident in American social sciences. When harmony is posited as the norm and conflict is abnormal, the task of the social sciences is to engineer harmony. Unlike European versions of social engineering, however, the American version takes a deceptively benign form as it conceives the engineering as an educational process. Niebuhr believes that this strain of America's second founding can be traced to the work of a single individual; in this case, the writings of John Dewey. Education in Dewey's work becomes the panacea for the ills of the human condition. It is the means by which idealism triumphs over necessity.

What confounds the social scientist's efforts at even the most peaceful attempts at social engineering is that man's free will, the very thing that makes the engineering necessary, ultimately serves to defeat the attempt. The most meticulous and best laid plans run aground on the unexpected events and free choices of men that are at the heart of the human condition. Furthermore, the argument that man is determined solely by his environment implicitly denies the possibility of choice which, in Christian terms, is the basis of man's dignity. The social scientist, to politically coordinate the progress toward an idealistic conception of perfection, must somehow extract himself from the environmental determinism that afflicts the rest of mankind. The intellectual must be an exception to the prevailing patterns of the human condition. The denial of the impossibility of ever reaching such a position has become the corrupting hybris of modern social science. The conceptual error is in turn compounded by the attempt to transfer the methods of the natural sciences. Such a graft will not bear pleasant fruit. While the ends of the natural sciences tend to be less controversial, the ends of politics are inherently objects of conflict. It is in the nature of politics that the pursuit of one measure of justice may necessarily entail the suppression of another aspect of the same justice.[15]

Paradoxically, another theme of American thought runs counter to the social engineering motif--rugged individualism. Nurtured by laissez-faire and the rough and tumble of the early America of dear labor, this tough-minded thinking holds that no planning, indeed no deliberation of any kind, is needed to guide human affairs. Proponents of this school argue that the natural progress of history or evolution will eventually resolve conflicts. Here, American materialism and individualism come together as one. The invisible hand of the marketplace is the enemy of political power that can only intrude to disrupt an otherwise harmonious human existence. Hostile toward the very idea of political power, it is a social philosophy that constantly threatens to veto the demands of the community and throw the polity into the winds of forces and circumstances beyond its control. In a sense, it is almost as centrifugal as another great force in American life, the relentless drive for equality.

Political power can perhaps be made tolerable if it is somehow assumed that it is exercised equally by all citizens. This vaguely Rousseauean ideal is part of the American commitment to equality. The notion of equality, to Niebuhr, is found in both the Christian roots of the American polity and in its corruption by Enlightenment optimism. The Founders' understanding of equality in the Declaration of Independence, Niebuhr argues (somewhat contrary to much scholarly opinion), was based on the belief that all men were created equal in the eyes of God. This religious insight has degenerated into the democratic notion that all ideas are equal, and there is no reasoned basis for choosing one over another. Since each individual's judgment is as good as another on any social matter, there is no transcendent standard of right and wrong. Morality is thus reduced to a Hobbesian contest of individual wills that resemble a war of all against all. Freed from moral restraints, man finds the basis of his vaunted equality is built on quicksand. For the Christian realist, though, equality can only truly exist and flourish when man is recognized as created in the image of God.[17]

The second founding, then, is built on shaky pillars. Individualism is constantly threatened by a hostile world. Social engineering is frustrated by the march of events. Laissez-faire is embarrassed by the constant intrusion of politics. Equality degenerates into a shallow value relativism.

We have seen that Niebuhr thought the second founding was based on the notion of the infinite malleability of human nature and the inevitability of perpetual progress. Both articles of faith die daily before the grim giveness of human willfulness and the daily record of events. What Niebuhr thinks about the second founding is pejorative in the extreme; did he find redeeming features in the first?

IV

Niebuhr's Defense of American Political Philosophy

The weaknesses in America's social philosophy are redeemed by the political philosophy of the Founders. The source of the Constitution's wisdom, Niebuhr contends, is the "Christian realism" of James Madison. According to Niebuhr, Madison's strength was his recognition of human weakness. He realized that men are self-seeking, and that even when they try to be impartial, their own self-interest clouds their judgment. Niebuhr repeatedly quotes with approval Madison's statement that, "As long as any connection exists between man's reason and his self-love, his options and passions will have a reciprocal influence upon each other."[18] Thus, Madison built his Constitutionalism around the axiom that man has both a strong propensity for evil and a great capacity for good. The trick is to construct political institutions that work with the compound of egotism and altruism that fuels the engines of every man. Even a cursory glance at certain numbers (10, 39) of The Federalist reveals a strong resemblance between Madison's republican citizen and Niebuhr's man-in-rebellion-from-God. Certainly, Niebuhr was struck with the parallels.

Niebuhr claims that the Madisonian view of human nature grew out of his tacit acceptance of a Christian world view. This skepticism about the perfectability of man through his own efforts led him to doubt the wisdom of fully trusting any group or individual with unchecked political power. Since it is a natural tendency of everyone to claim a larger share of the earth's goods than is their due, a free government requires that there be as many sources of checks and balances on the exercise of political power as expediency warrants. Thus, in Niebuhr's understanding, does the separation of powers derive from a core element in Christian theology.

Niebuhr describes the operation of the Madisonian understanding of constitutional government in the

317

following way. Power is diffused among innumerable
factions within society. Each group is allowed to seek
its own good (since there is no nationally defined
good), yet is unable to genuinely oppress another group
because no faction has sufficient power through numbers
to act as a tyrannical majority. Public policy is
formed by a series of compromises, as majorities are
formed out of temporary confederacies of minorities.
Since policies must be broad enough to include a maximum of contending interests, the normal result will be
a moderate policy that is rarely threatening to any
strong minority interest.

The net result of the founding political philosophy
is that America has been able to avoid many of the
dilemmas of European politics. The American polity has
approached political problems more pragmatically, not
because of a dramatically different social philosophy,
but because of a radically different political founding.
The ideology of the cultural founding has largely been
ignored by the demands of the political community.
Thus, the nation has been spared what Niebuhr considers
the foolishness of the idealistic philosophy of the
Enlightenment. While its follies are not unheard of in
the land, the political system has tended to mitigate
the harmful effects of Enlightenment illusion.

America has averted the dangers of planning because
power is so dispersed that no coherent plan is possible.
It has escaped the foolishness of those who do not
understand the power of self-interest because its institutions have balanced interest against interest. It has
provided the opportunity for bargaining and compromise
in the pursuit of its ideals by refusing to take either
liberty or equality to their logical conclusion.[19]

Along with his specific defense of the Constitutional system, Niebuhr approves of the Founders' choice
of democracy as the most legitimate form of government.
It is the best regime, he says, because it checks the
pretensions of rulers. Those entrusted with power,
contends Niebuhr, easily become infatuated with their
own importance and enticed to insist on their own vision
of justice and social order. It is not simply that
self-interest seduces the powerful to become corrupt.
Rather, it is the fact that their claim to personal
virtue and wisdom often become dangerous self-delusions.
By dispersing power throughout society, democracy
limits the greedy and egotistical tendencies of those

in authority.

A second asset of democracy is the freedom it accords to the individual. Niebuhr argues that democracy is the most appropriate regime because at the core of his being man is free, and democracy reflects that freedom. Given the fact of human freedom, it is natural that individuals will live their lives in innumerably different ways. Democracy recognizes humanity's infinite variety and uniqueness and, unlike other regimes which attempt to mold human beings into a preconceived notion of perfection, it allows the individual to develop his own personality and particular means of self-fulfillment.

Niebuhr's famous dictum summarizes how democracy both checks man's pretensions and fulfills his aspiration. He states, "Man's capacity for justice makes democracy possible; but man's inclination to injustice makes democracy necessary."[20]

V

Differences Between Niebuhr and the Founders

We have seen how Madison's reflections on human nature closely resemble Niebuhr's Christian anthropology. Both thinkers view man as a composite of egoism and altruism and come to similar conclusions about the proper political institutions for such a creature.

But are their observations derived from the same source? Is Madison's understanding of man really similar to "Christian realism"? One clue is derived from the greater depth of Niebuhr's psychology. Recall that for Niebuhr, man's false pride and provisional morality both derive from the same source, his permanent state of anxiety. Since the ultimate nature of reality is not comprehensible within the horizon of temporal life, man is forced to make judgments about the meaning and purpose of life which are beyond his capacity. Although these judgments represent man's yearning to live within some ultimate principle of purposefulness, they are easily transmuted into self-righteousness and pride since men view ultimate truth from their own limited perspective.

Madison, on the other hand, offers little in the way of articulated understanding of the springs of human conduct (with the exceptions of beautiful cameos like Federalist No. 10). Instead, we have cogent descriptions of the fallen angel in action, and the practical conclusions for good government.

A second clue (and the root of the difference) lies in the fact that the Founders understood themselves to be children of the Enlightenment, a fact illustrated by their claim to have discovered a new science of politics.[21]

The fact that Niebuhr and Madison have different philosophical roots allows us to raise the possibility that superficially apparent parallels mask some fundamental differences in their political prescriptions.

As an example, let us examine the two thinkers' approaches to democracy. Niebuhr's contention that democracy is important because it checks the pretensions of rulers is certainly at odds with Madison's statement that representatives to the national legislatures will "enlarge and refine" the public view. Madison seems to be as concerned with establishing the preconditions for effective leadership as he is with restraining the abuses of power. After all, the equilibrium of contending interests would also take place within each representative district. In most instances, Madison foresaw, a candidate who is broadly popular to many interests but closely allied to no one, would be selected for office. Such an arrangement encourages a sphere of independence between the representative and his constituents. This insulation from popular sentiment makes it possible, although by no means certain, that elected officials will deliberate on concerns affecting the national interest. Madison's scheme does not excessively check the power of rulers, but rather allows representatives to use their own reasoned judgment by disengaging them from the immediate interests of their constituents.[22]

Another important difference between Niebuhr and the Founders concerns their opinions on the means of securing stability within the regime. Madison never squarely meets the problem of how the multiplicity of squabbling factions will finally pull together on great issues of national importance. Niebuhr, on the other hand, realizes that no government and certainly no democracy can rest solely on an equilibrium of contending forces; there must be some common principle which binds the society together and keeps the competition among groups from degenerating into civil war. For Niebuhr, this common bond is found in religion. In this, Niebuhr seems to follow Washington who wrote in his Farewell Address:

> Of all the dispositions and habits which lead to political prosperity, religion and morality are indispensable supports. In vain would that man claim tribute of patriotism, who should labor to subvert these great pillars of human happiness, these firmest props of the duties of men and citizens.[23]

Niebuhr aggres with Washington that religion informs men of their duties; he does not fully accept religion's connection with citizenship. In his usual dialectical manner, Niebuhr argues that religion ought to both attach men to their fellow citizens and make them aware of the broader community of men. Christian duty, explains Niebuhr, starts within national borders but looks toward the ideal of the universal brotherhood of mankind. "Loyalty to the community," he explains, "is . . . morally tolerable only if it includes values wider than those of the community."[24]

Religion can act as the adhesive of society, but Niebuhr certainly does not suggest that it makes men pliant or slavishly obedient citizens. Religion forces men to bring every social institution, every humanly created idea or interpretation of justice, under constant review because of man's inability to know the full truth. Every moral supposition, even though it be in concert with the ultimate reality, is also merely an avowal of some particular culture or historical era. The Christian realist is cognizant of this "ideological taint," and he refuses to wholeheartedly attach himself to any one notion of political or social morality.[25]

Niebuhr's position on this point is far more reminscent of Jefferson than Madison. Although Jefferson's criterion for judging institutions (changes should be made as advances in the arts and sciences increase human wisdom) is quite different from Niebuhr's, Jefferson's suggestion that a constitutional convention be called every so often is far closer to

Niebuhr's argument in favor of constant review than is
Madison's praise of tradition in Federalist No. 49.
Madison warns that if the people are repeatedly asked
to decide on the correctness of the first principles of
government, those principles will eventually lose their
authority. Since these principles are the foundation
on which all the other laws rest, the sentiment in favor
of lawfulness, a hallmark of a decent society, will be
undermined. Further, if questions concerning these
principles are constantly brought to public attention,
the people necessarily will come to think something is
wrong with them. Eventually, Madison argues, the people
will make a mistake and adopt the wrong principles of
government.

Niebuhr also realizes that strength of tradition
in binding together the members of a community. It is
doubtful, though, whether he could fully support
Federalist No. 49 in which Madison argues that later
generations ought to develop what might be called a
blind attachment to the Constitution. Niebuhr's
Christian realism makes him doubt whether any political
system can be wholly good, while Madison actually
believed he had discovered the proper institutions by
which human beings should be governed.[26]

A further disagreement between Madison and Niebuhr
can be seen in their reliance on religion. First of
all, Madison does not depend on religion to support his
political philosophy. In fact, he explicitly rejects
it as an unreliable means of restraining behavior. He
even suggests that religion is upsetting to public
order because it makes men intolerant. He proposes
that factions based on interest be cultivated in
America, for although differences in wealth and occupation are the most durable sources of division in
society, they are more easily resolved than are the
intractable differences rooted in religion and principle. Madison's point seems to be that compromise is
possible on the basis of how much wealth each faction
is to gain but impossible on the basis of dearly held
beliefs.[27]

Of course, Niebuhr's Christian realism is quite
different than the intolerant Christianity of Madison's
era which had flamed the religious wars of Europe.
Niebuhr's novel and more tolerant Christian teaching
rests on a recognition that it is not man's judgment
but God's word which holds mastery in the universe.

Without the revelation of God's grace, human life would be forever lost in sinfulness and self-delusion. Niebuhr's religion is thus purged of self-righteousness and becomes guided by a humble awareness that every judgment, every truth, even one's own, can be jaded by self-love.[28]

Niebuhr reasons that religious awareness is fundamental to order because it promotes the notion of human dignity. Each individual, no matter how lowly his birth or demeanor, must be accorded dignity since everyone is part of the divine creation. Such a principle is especially important in a democracy, Niebuhr concludes, for it is the basis of mutual respect and the precondition for a regime of true equality.

A final disagreement between Niebuhr and the Founders becomes apparent if Niebuhr's questioning of economic abundance is compared to Hamilton's argument supporting it. Hamilton sees economic life as a means to political ends. Not only does the development of great commercial enterprises create the military prowness necessary for national defense, it gives men the opportunity to acquire wealth. Men become attached to the government because they see their own interests tied to its continued durability. Stability is achieved by making men's desires serve the ends of the regime. After all, the rich are rarely revolutionaries and the middle class is moderate because its property is secure.[29]

Niebuhr has two objections to the Hamiltonian ideal of a constantly rising living standard as the bulwark of order. First, Niebuhr wonders what will happen when America's resources are depleted and her economic progress slows. Without some deeper appreciation of existence, Niebuhr argues, Americans will not be able to understand this shock to their way of life. Second, Niebuhr rejects an undue concern for abundance on moral grounds. As stated above, he fears that it trivializes man's life and corrupts the higher aspects of his being.

The difference between Hamilton and Niebuhr is at bottom, however, one based on diverging views of the importance of religion to the community. Niebuhr looks at the bonds of the community as a species of the divine Love; Hamilton views it in terms of social utility. Niebuhr argues that the primary, although not

the only, bond of community is the individual's selfless
concern for the common good. This community of interests draws its substenance from a common religious
awareness. On the other hand, Hamilton, who was a
strong supporter of religion and was cognizant of religion's role as a social cohesive, argued that stable
government cannot rest primarily on piety. Hamilton's
goal was to turn men's self-interest, their striving
for power, honor, and glory toward the good of the
community. What separates Niebuhr and Hamilton is not
so much their understanding of man's self-interest;
rather, it is Niebuhr's vision of existence which
stretches beyond the politics of this life and finally
prevents him from wholeheartedly supporting any regime--
no matter how decent. Because of his religious perspective, Niebuhr is engaged in a continuing dialectic
between the realism of two worlds: the realm of political life and the transcendent kingdom which is always
breaking into the political in unexpected ways.
Hamilton, however, has a zestful and undivided enthusiasm for the "city of the world" with its fiercely
clashing factions and civic morality of republican
virtue. In Federalist No. 9, his zeal becomes effer-
vescent:

> Happily for mankind, stupendous fabrics
> reared on the basis of liberty, which
> have flourished for ages, have in a few
> glorious instances refuted their (the
> critics of republicanism) gloomy sophisms.
> And, I trust America will be the broad
> and solid foundation of other edifices
> not less magnificent, which will be
> equally permanent monuments of their
> errors.

This magnificent edifice is founded not on any
idealistic principle like religion but squarely on the
"new science of politics."[30]

CONCLUSION

The Irony of American History is both an acceptance
and a rejection, a defense and an attack, of American
thought and practice. It is a delicate balance of
criticism and praise, which like much of Niebuhr's work
is not so much contradictory as dialectic in nature.
For example, Niebuhr criticizes American social

324

philosophy for not perceiving man's self-interest, yet he also rejects Hamilton's proposal for building a political community based solely on self-interest. Similarly, Niebuhr exposes the folly of expecting an easy resolution of conflict (and, therefore a spontaneous community of interests), yet contends that patriotism or even loyalty to the Constitution (which Madison proposed as a basis for unity) might easily be turned into unjustified adulation of the nation. One cannot help wonder along with Madison, however, if any regime can withstand the onslaught of constant scrutiny without falling into political decay and degeneracy.

Niebuhr seems closest to the American constitutional system in his support of Madison's balance of contending interests as the best means of attaining social justice. Yet, even on this point questions can be raised about Niebuhr's position. Where and how are the conflicts between groups to be worked out? Niebuhr supplies no mechanism, no institution, by which compromise and conciliation can be made.[31] Niebuhr's Catholic counterpart, John Courtney Murray, insisted that civilized political behavior rests on the right use of reason and that those institutions which form the character necessary to the proper exercise of reason must be promoted. Niebuhr, on the other hand, contends that reason is simply an inadequate means of controlling man's self-interest and that no institution can be trusted to inculcate virtue. "Relations between groups are always political rather than ethical," Niebuhr argues. Having stated this, Niebuhr could be charged with implying that there are no limits (not even rhetorical ones) to political action which reason alone can supply. Without cultivating reason, which is in itself a form of moderation and restraint, the contest for political advantage can easily degenerate into a quest for power, which, as Murray warns, may become very uncivilized indeed.[32] Reason, as Madison and Niebuhr rightly saw, certainly is the servant of the will. But, as experience and philosophy teaches, right reasoning or virtuous subjects helps check the baser and more unlawful passions of men striving to live together as citizens. (The irony of Niebuhr's critique of the "reason" of the Enlightenment is that Niebuhr himself is a product of Enlightenment Philosophy. Indeed, Protestant Theology itself may be regarded as a forerunner of the age of the philosophes. Unlike Murray, who can criticize the "new science of politics" from the perspective of the medieval notion of Right

Reason, Niebuhr subtly opens the door for self-interest and power to dominate politics. This strange hiatus in Niebuhr's usual dialectical approach to reason and will is perhaps explained by the fact that Niebuhr is looking at the Enlightenment from the perspective of its logical progeny, not as a fierce warrior from another culture.)

Despite his petty differences with the American constitutional system, it cannot be doubted that Niebuhr is finally a defender of the regime. The American Constitution recognizes both the faults and the virtues of man; it looks to the heights of his aspirations without forgetting the stubbornness of his pride. A realistic political system must reflect human nature, and the American Constitution acknowledges the imperfectability of human existence. It is a compromise between the noble and the base in man. Miebuhr attempts to recapture the spirit of the Constitution by showing that man's highest hopes can be as foolish and dangerous as his most hard-hearted cynicism. He teaches us again that a tolerable and even decent life is possible if only we appraise our situation with neither unrealistic jubilation nor undue despair.

NOTES

[1] Reinhold Niebuhr, The Irony of American History (New York: Scribner, 1952), pp. 22, 99.

[2] Ibid., pp. 43-46.

[3] Ibid., p. 11.

[4] Reinhold Niebuhr, The Nature and Destiny of Man (New York: Scribner, 1947), p. 63.

[5] Ibid., p. 14.

[6] Ibid., pp. 17, 54, 55, 72.

[7] Ibid., p. 137.

[8] Ibid., p. 129.

[9] Irony, p. 98.

[10] Ibid., pp. 28, 36, 37.

[11] Ibid., pp. 54, 57.

[12] Ibid., pp. 73-75.

[13] Ibid., pp. 9, 11.

[14] Ibid., p. 10.

[15] Ibid., pp. 8, 83.

[16] Ibid., p. 32.

[17] Ibid., p. 13.

[18] Madison, Hamilton, Jay, The Federalist Papers, No. 10.

[19] Irony, pp. 98, 106, 109.

[20] Reinhold Niebuhr, The Children of Light and the Children of Darkness (New York: Scribner), p. xiii.

[21] Federalist Papers, No. 9 and 10.

[22] Ibid., No. 10 and 51.

[23] George Washington, "Farewell Address," Writings of George Washington, Vol. 35, United States Government Printing Office, 1940.

[24] Irony, p. 37.

[25] Children, p. 131.

[26] Irony, p. 142.

[27] Children, pp. 136, 137; Federalist Papers, No. 10 and 51.

[28] Ibid., pp. 137, 150, 151.

[29] Alexander Hamilton, "Report on Manufactures," in Reports of the Secretary of the Treasury of the United States, Vol. I (Washington, 1837).

[30] Federalist Papers, No. 9.

[31] The same can be said for Madison. See James Caeser, Presidential Selection (Princeton, Princeton University Press), Chapters 1 and 2.

[32] See "Catholic Reflections on the American Proposition" in this edition.

CHAPTER 15
"John Courtney Murray: Catholic Reflections on the
American Proposition"
Rev. Edward Krause, C.S.C.

In his book We Hold These Truths John Courtney
Murray is credited with having written "the most significant Roman Catholic statement on the American
democracy ever published."[1] Originally, he wrote to
belie the assertions of some that Catholic Christianity
was incompatible with democracy or that her theology
contradicted the fundamental principles of a democratic
social order. He also sought to interpret, strengthen,
and reaffirm the underlying spiritual and philosophical
foundations of the "American experiment," having come
with reluctance to the conclusion that these foundations were dangerously eroded. His interpretation of
papal political thought--particularly from Leo XIII to
John XXIII--confirmed the intuition of most second
generation Catholic immigrants that American political
process was fully compatible with Catholic Christian
faith.[2] Murray's work, then, facilitated the assimi-
lation of Catholic ethnics into American pluralism,
making more available to the nation the wisdom and
strength of ancient Catholic tradition. This was
strikingly symbolized in the 1960 election of America's
first Catholic President, John F. Kennedy. A more
lasting and far reaching impact of his thought, however, will undoubtedly be due to its incorporation
into the teachings of the Second Vatican Council (1962-
66) principally the Declaration on Religious Liberty.
This document incorporating as it does the proven
political wisdom of America's First Amendment articles
can be expected to significantly influence worldwide
Catholic polity for many years to come.

Murray was part of an overall attempt endorsed by
the popes to revitalize the thought of St. Thomas
Aquinas and the ancient tradition of natural law. His
earlier writing was influenced by such Neo-Thomists
as Jacques Maritain, Mortimer Adler, and the German
Henrich Rommen. His later writing incorporated many
of the themes and trends of the more existentialist
oriented school of "Transcendental Thomism." With
roots in Hiedeggar and Marechal, this latter school
tended to be more dynamic and historical, as well as
more personalistic, than the earlier neo-Thomist school.
Thus, to characterize the philosophical foundations of
Murray's political thought, one might say that Murray
enlarged upon Enlightenment natural law theory, in

continuity with early Jeffersonian tradition, reconciling it with medieval Thomistic Aristotlelianism.[3]
By contrast, Reinhold Niebuhr, a contemporary and
frequent protagonist of Murray's, drew upon Augustinian
and Lutheran sources to restate and reaffirm the predominantly realist assumptions of James Madison, The
Federalist and the Constitutional Convention of 1787.
Both men were acutely concerned with recovering and
rebuilding "the spiritual foundations" of American
democratic process.

For Murray and contemporary Thomists man is defined as a "rational animal." His reason or intelligence, though limited and easily corrupted by sin, is
taken to be the unique and distinguishing human
characteristic. Further, man's reason is understood
to be essentially related to his spiritual freedom as
both ground and end. It is by virtue of human intelligence that man is capable of surveying a wide range of
truth and goodness, of deliberating about the values
contained in alternative courses of action, and of
judging that here and now such and such a value is
desirable:

> Apart from this previous deliberation
> and judgment, there is no free act.
> And every act is an obedience to a
> judgment of reason. Precisely in the
> privilege of being obedient to reason
> consists the freedom of will.[4]

It should be stressed that Murray, while underscoring
the capacities of human reason, is quite clearly aware
of its fallibility. Moreover, for Murray the failures
of reason are not simple errors. They are partly
deliberate and freely chosen by a disordered or sinful
will. Man is "free" to violate the "dictates of right
reason," though this freedom is only speciously a
freedom, according to Murray, for it cloaks what is in
fact slavery. Sin diminishes and corrupts man's true
freedom and rational nature. Error and the abuse of
liberty in sin are "permanent aspects of the human
condition." There is not and never can be an "Ideal
Republic of Virtue and Truth." Such an ideal is
disallowed on principle "on premises furnished by an
inspection of the nature of man."[5] All of this is by
way of remotely justifying the institutions of democracy in a theory or idea of man. Democracy, for
Murray, is based on the capacities of human reason--

corrupted indeed, but not destroyed.

Murray's understanding of man as intelligent and free undergirds his espousal of natural law theory. Throughout the 1950's and 1960's he was widely looked upon as the "major spokesman in America for the Catholic natural law tradition."[6] He opposed, of course, the many and frequent caricatures of natural law--abstractionist, intuitionist, legalist, static, biologistic, and rationalist versions of the theory:

> Those who dislike the doctrine for one reason or another seem forever to be at work, as it were burying the wrong corpse. For my part, I would not at all mind standing with them, tearless, at the grave of any of the shallow and distorted theories that they mistake for the doctrine of natural law.[7]

He admitted as well that aside from legal theorists there were few non-Thomist political philosophers currently using the vocabulary of natural law. This, however, would be tolerable if the fundamental truths at stake were understood and respected, such as the idea that there are given in nature essential and normative structures of human existence that always and everywhere exert pressure on human thought and conduct. In other words, "reason doesn't create its own laws." Man has the structural laws of his nature given, as nature itself is given. This opposed the asserted "autonomy of human reason" of the secularists and relativists, the idea that every individual is a law unto himself and the sole judge of truth. For Murray, the "American experiment" begins with the assumption that "there are truths accessible to human reason and that they must be held." Truth and its possession by men in a limited political moral con-census is the foundation of American civil unity and political process.

The Founding Fathers accepted in one form or other the concept of natural law. Their main source in the early days of the republic was, of course, John Locke. Although Murray believed Locke's "law of nature" was better than no natural law at all, he goes to con-siderable lengths to rescue Lockean versions of the theory from typically Enlightenment perversions. He was especially critical of Enlightenment individualism

with its concomitant rationalism and nominalism. In
this mode of thought every citizen is a "sort of little
god almighty" and society is not a product of nature
but of artifice and the "Social Contract." The ancient
tradition, by contrast, insisted that sociality was
inherent in the very nature of man, a necessary condition of man's natural perfectability and not simply
a utilitarian convenience for the sake of survival or
the protection of one's property. Murray assumed that
Enlightenment/Lockean individualism was responsible
for the worst flaws of the classical capitalist
economy against which Marxist collectivism was a
reaction. Ominously, this error fostered a false
"individual/state antithesis" and the development of
"Totalitarian Democracy" on Continental Europe which
earlier popes opposed. Locke's theory, Murray argued,
had more felicitous impact in England and America for
a variety of historical reasons as well as the fact
that underneath it all Locke had "restated, and did
not quite succeed in denaturing the great political
truths that were the medieval heritage." In other
words, Murray considered the classical and medieval
concept of natural law considerably superior to En-
lightenment/Lockean versions of the idea, and it was
the strength of this "old idea" which undergirded both
American democracy and the English common law.

The difference between 19th century "totalitarian
democracies" of the European continent, and the
English/American development was crucial for Murray.
Most importantly, the American democracy was clearly
a limited government: limited principally by the
natural law, the constitutional consensus, and the
will of the people. Such limitations imply a crucial
distinction between the larger society and the state.
This distinction is pivotal in Murray's perspective.
With R. M. MacIver, he takes it to be "a primary distinction that lies at the very root of the understanding of government."8 It denies that society can be
completely encompassed by the state. Society is the
more comprehensive term including all the social
aspects of man's nature, the total complex of organized
human relationships, familial, ethnic, economic,
cultural, and religious. The state is only "one form
of the ordering of society" and is limited to specific
ends. It cannot effectively usurp the functions or
rights of other "autogeneous forms" of the organization
of society possessed as they are of their own inherent
dynamisms. By contrast, Continental/totalitarian

democratic ideas, in Murray's view, assumed the juridical omnipotence and omnicompetence of the state.[9] There were no limits on the power of the state or on the will of democratic majorities. If it wished the state would have total control over family structure, economic enterprise, education, scientific research-- everything not strictly private. The state would even presume to control and define the role and nature of the church or establish a "civil religion" at its pleasure. With such an "idolotrization of democratic process" and its concomitant thoroughgoing secularization of society the Church would have no peace, and it was precisely this, the totalitarian pretension of European democracies which earlier popes condemned. The American concept of limited government was distinctly different in Murray's view and it would have to be judged on its own merits.[10]

In American society the limits on government are partly set by the public consensus. The American public philosophy and constitutional consensus is understood to be an essential condition for unified political action in a radically pluralist society. It is the necessary core of agreement and accord in a situation where widely divergent philosophies and theologies of man prevail. In America it began with what the Historian Clinton Rossiter called the "noble aggregate of self-evident truths" as expressed in the Declaration of Independence and later in the Bill of Rights. Among other things the American consensus asserts that government is limited by the sovereignty of God; that government is limited by law, not only its own laws and legal orderings, but most importantly by the universal moral law given in the very nature of man; that government is limited by the will and consent of the people, and lastly, that government is limited by a whole constellation of basic "inalienable rights."[11] The consensus not only limits the power of the government, but also articulates its positive goals, "establishes its identity," sets its purposes, and furnishes a "common universe of discourse in which public issues can be intelligibly stated and intelligently argued." It embraces a whole constellation of principles bearing upon the origin and nature of society, the function of the state as the legal order of society, the dignity of the human person, popular sovereignty, consent, the rule of law and law as a work of reason, the separation of powers, and the "fivefold structure of obligatory political ends:"

justice, freedom, peace, security, and the general
welfare (so the preamble to the American Constitution
states these ends). In sum, Murray states:

> America has proved by experience that
> political unity and stability are
> possible without uniformity of religious
> belief and practice. . . it does not
> follow that this necessary civic unity
> can endure in the absence of a consensus
> more narrow in its scope, operative on
> the level of political life, with re-
> gard to the rational truths and moral
> precepts that govern the structure of
> the constitutional state, specify the
> substance of the commonweal, and de-
> termine the ends of public policy.11a

For Murray the American democracy and its dream,
though based primarily on reason and natural law, was
rooted deeply in religious faith. America was a
"nation under God." It was a creation of Judeo-
Christian tradition and history. The sovereignty of
God over society as well as over the individual citizen
was its "first principle:"

> The first truth to which the American
> Proposition makes appeal is stated in
> that landmark of Western political theory,
> the Declaration of Independence. It is
> a truth that lies beyond politics; . . .
> that the political community, as a form
> of free and ordered human life, looks
> to the sovereignty of God as to the
> first principle of its organization.11b

In broader terms, American constitutionalism recognized
the "primacy of the spiritual" over the political, that
certain basic human things, the "res sacra homo," were
sacredly immune from profanation by the power of the
state:

> The man whose rights are guaranteed in
> the face of law and government is,
> whether he knows it or not, the Chris-
> tian man, who learned to know his own
> personal dignity in the school of
> Christian faith.11c

An exclusively secularist political posture not open to
Divine mystery and God's self-revelation, could not
trace the worth of man to its properly transcendent
foundation in God's gift and grace, where one's identity
as a "child of God" takes precedence over the job one
holds or the wealth one possesses. Murray's deep fears
for the future of the "American experiment" had most to
do with its spiritual substance. The greatest peril to
America's survival was not an external menace or one of
military proportions, but an internal and spiritual
peril. American morale, purpose, identity was nour-
ished historically in Christian faith, and Murray
seriously questioned whether secularist philosophical
assumptions could sustain it.11d

Besides being a product of Christian history and
culture, Murray believed that the American democracy
was a unique human and moral achievement, an instance
of the "adult state," essentially related to its potential for protecting and fostering basic human rights.
These included freedom of religion, freedom of speech,
assembly, association, and petition for redress of
grievance, security of person, home, and property, as
well as rights to trial by jury and due process of law.
He asserted not only the historical, but also the meta-
physical basis of these rights and their corresponding
duties:

> I take it that the political substance
> of democracy consists in the admission
> of an order of rights antecedent to
> the state, the political form of
> society. . . inviolable as well by
> democratic majorities as by absolute
> monarchs.12

In another place he states:

> The American constitutional system is
> based squarely on two fundamental
> principles: first, man is endowed by
> his Creator with certain inalienable
> rights; second, government and the
> order of law exist primarily for the
> protection and promotion of these
> rights.13

Such rights, in other words, inhere in man antecedent
to any act of government; i.e. they are not granted by

government, and cannot be taken away by government. Their proximate source is in nature, and in history insofar as history bears witness to the nature of man; their ultimate source, as the Declaration of Independence states, is in God, the Creator of nature and the Master of history. In this matter, Murray insists that the American Bill of Rights is not to be confused with the French Declaration of the Rights of Man of '89, which assumes that human rights are "man made and look only to man for their creation, realization and guarantee." The asserted "autonomy of human reason" of the French philosophers denied the subjection of reason to a higher law not of its own making. Such doctrines, Murray insists lead logically as they have historically to political tyranny, and claims of juridical omnipotence and omnicompetance by the state.[13a]

The American democracy is taken to be unique and not only because of its success in fostering human basic rights, but also because of its "prejudice in favor of freedom," the "first and most fundamental of our prejudices." America is "an experiment in freedom." She has "passionately pursued the ideal of freedom to new lengths." The freedom sought, however, is not to be confused with sheer libertarianism, as created by "the nineteenth century theory of the outlaw conscience," i.e. the conscience that knows no law higher than its own subjective imperative. Part of the inner architecture of the American ideal of freedom has been the profound conviction that only a virtuous people can be free:

> The freedom toward which the American people are fundamentally oriented is a freedom under God, a freedom that knows itself to be bound by the imperative of the moral law. Antecedently, it is presumed that a man will make morally and socially responsible use of his freedom.[13b]

Murray, then traces critical links between freedom, reason, and the law that are often neglected. He asks, "Has the idea of the free society, perhaps, been strangled?" "Is the free society really free?" In responding, he changes the form of the question to ask, "Is American society properly civil?" In other words, the quality and character of our freedom can be judged by the quality and character of our argument, and public debate. The freedom we have will necessarily be founded on the truths we hold, and the clarity and precision with which we hold them. Freedom is not erratic, but a derivate of intelligence. Far from being hostile to liberty, or even antithetic to it, law as a creation of reason is the intrinsic complement of liberty: Law is "for the sake of liberty":

> The notion of law is to be discovered
> at the very interior of the notion of
> liberty, in such wise that liberty
> itself is unintelligible apart from
> law as its root, support, light,
> guide, and ally.[14]

For Murray the first and foremost of our freedoms is religious freedom. His interpretation of the First Amendment clauses are pivotal. He resolutely resists both secularist and Protestant efforts to give the First Amendment a theological interpretation. He will not make a "Religion out of the freedom of religion." Thus, the First Amendment is not a "piece of protestant ecclesiology" or the "establishment of a rationalist materialist dogma." The articles of the First Amendment are not "articles of faith" but articles of peace. They are not true dogma, but only good law. The First Amendment is not an attempt of government to define the nature of the true Church, but a limitation on government and circumscription of its power. It both forbids the intervention of government and guarantees the "freedom of the Church." It is based on the "non-competence of the state" in matters religious.[15] His then was primarily a "Constitutional--juridical argument" with roots in the sacred inviolability of personal conscience and the notion of the juridically limited Constitutional state. It won the approval of the Bishops at the II Vatican Council. One summary of the case Murray offers puts it in the following terms:

> Inherent in the dignity of man as a
> moral subject is the exigence to act
> on his own initiative and on his own
> personal responsibility, especially
> in that vital area in which the sense
> of his own existence and his necessary
> pursuit of it, are at stake--that is
> to say, especially in matters reli-
> gious. . . . In the name of this
> objective exigence man asserts, in

the juridical order and over all
"the others," his right to immunity
from coercion, especially in matters
religious. . . . If there be an
authority that might possibly enter
a counterclaim to the claim of the
human person to immunity from coercion in matters religious, this
authority could only be government,
which is responsible for the establishment and maintenance of the
juridical order in society. . . .
This, however, it cannot do, except
when its own fundamental responsibility becomes controlling--in the
case of a violation of public order;
a contravention of the necessary
conditions o f social coexistence; a
public offense that imperils the
pillars of society, which are an order
of equal justice for all citizens; the
public peace which is the work of justice; and that minimum of realizable
public morality whose maintenance is
the just requirement of the citizenry.[16]

The American democracy is also unique for its constitutionalism, its respect for law and due process. As
mentioned above, respect for law as a work of reason
and an armature of justice, was the essential correlate
of our "passion for freedom." As "civilization's most
indispensable instrument," it was to redeem man "from
the arbitrary despotism of uncontrolled power," and
from the disruption of life by the irrational forces
of passion, caprice, and chance. "In America Law is
King," was Tom Paine's manner of putting it. The law
makes the king. Constitutionalism, the rule of law,
the concept of government as an empire of laws and not
of men--these were ancient ideas, deeply implanted in
the British tradition at its origin in medieval times.
The major American contribution to the tradition was
the written constitution, and its dynamic "living
quality." The legal structure must both remain true
to the inner spirit that animates its provisions and
reckon with the changing realities of American life.
Though possessed of a moral foundation and quality,
law was surely not the equivalent of morality. In
fact, law as a work of reason and relying ultimately
on coercion, has limited effectiveness in pursuit of

moral goals. It can seek to maintain but a minimum of
actualized morality, only what is socially necessary
for the sake of civil order and basic justice. In a
pluralistic society it should be the expression of the
community's convictions or conscience, without ceasing
to reflect the basic dictates of natural law. Some
measure of general consensus, Murray agreed, must
support the order of law to which the whole community
and all its groups are commonly subject.[17]

     Finally, to early Americans government was not
primarily a phenomenon of force. Though the power to
coerce was taken as integral to government, government
properly speaking was the right to command; it was
authority. And once again its authority derived from
law as a "work of reason." In his debate with American
realists Murray had occasion to reflect on the relationship between law and power. He insisted that the use
of power can and must be invested with moral quality.
The essential distinction was that between force and
violence. Force was the measure of power necessary and
sufficient to uphold the valid purposes of law. What
exceeded that measure was violence. The necessary
standard was "aptitude or ineptitude for the achievement of the obligatory public purpose"--freedom, justice, peace, security, and the general welfare. Murray
believed that what rescued man from the brink of chaotic
power struggles was the resources of reason made opera-
tive chiefly through the processes of reasonable law
and a "discriminatingly apt or legitimated use of
force." Thus, he sees political order primarily as a
matter of rational compromise, consensus, and integra-
tion, rather than of domination. In the explanation
of democratic or civilized unity, according to Murray,
it is not possible to assert the power factor to the
exclusion of its legitimation in moral consensus--be
this implicit or explicit. Law should control the use
of power and it cannot be defined merely by the will of
the one who wields the sword. The use of force must
rest on fundamental principles of justice. The principles are clear, though their pragmatic application in
the "arts" of politics and jurisprudence are always
frought with ambiguities. Still there is no cause to
call in doubt the fundamental principles.

     Since World War II realism has been the predomi-
nant language of American politics. At numerous
symposia organized by the Fund for the Republic and its
Center for the Study of Democratic Institutions, Murray

engaged in intermittent exchange with the "father" and
philosopher of the movement, Reinhold Niebuhr. Murray
understood that there would always be religio-moral
conflict, tension, and competition in a pluralist society. He agreed with Niebuhr that the roots of such
tension and conflict are ultimately human finiteness,
human sin or greed, and human ingenuity or creativity.
Murray does not deny these "obvious facts." But neither
does he focus on them as Niebuhr does. Murray's passionate concern was to know how man could get beyond the
warfare to what he called "civic amity'. His theory was
not as some Niebuhrians read it--a denial of the facts
of conflict and tension among the peoples--but a care
for the kind or quality of conflict which might be
expected to ensue.[18] He would insist that a civilizing
of the conflict was possible and perceived a substantial
difference between civilized and uncivilized modes of
conflict, between humane and inhumane modes of conflict.
He asks what are the necessary conditions for a human-
izing of the inevitable conflicts of a pluralist
society. Thus, in focusing on the political implications of man's moral capacities and his unique powers
of intelligence, Murray clarifies the conditions and
assumptions necessary for effective public argument and
debate. Reason played a necessary and crucial role in
the pursuit of justice for the sake of peace. The
American government for Murray was a government of
reason and law. Because of this it was also a government of justice and freedom.

Murray was a man of reason, but a realistic one.
His expectations were minimal. He sought to "limit the
warfare" of conflicting ideologies, and to "enlarge the
dialogue." He understood that in a pluralist society
civil law could have only "minimal moral aspirations."
It was basic that what was to be commonly imposed by law
had to be sustained by a reasonable consensus of the
whole people. The underlying public consensus, never
finished, in need always of further argument "under pain
of instant decline," related both to more immediate
policy decisions as well as to the wider and broader
issues of governmental structure. It was open civil
dialogue that would foster, recreate, and sustain the
limited, sometimes implicit, but always essential
political moral consensus. Dialogue as Murray saw it
was the very essence of civil society: what makes the
multitude civilized is rational deliberate argument.
The greatest threat to the survival of democracy, Murray
believed, would be the breakdown of civil and orderly

340

dialogue:

> I believe that nothing is more damag-
> ing to democracy than lack of ration-
> ality in public argument. The foun-
> dations of our society are indeed laid
> in an identifiable consensus. But
> they are more importantly laid in a
> reasonable disposition to argue our
> many disagreements in intelligent and
> temperate fashion, using restrained
> language, avoiding misstatements,
> overstatements, or simplifications,
> and endeavoring to define issues with
> precision in the light of all the
> relevant principles and facts. I
> believe that whatever corrupts rational
> public argument corrupts democracy.[19]

In another place he states the rational basis of <u>civil</u>
unity in even stronger terms:

> Civil unity is based on reason. I
> don't want to exaggerate, but I do
> maintain with all my strength and
> conviction that the forces of reason
> are basic in the creation of the
> civil community and its civil unity.
> If, and where, the forces or reason
> fail, civil unity becomes impossible.[20]

In brief, one might characterize Murray's understanding
in these terms: The American democracy represents an
"institutionalization of open civil dialogue in the
pursuit of truth for the sake of justice."[21]

One would have to say that Murray served the
Church first. He brought Catholics into the mainstream
of American politics and pluralism. His thought continues to have vast implications for the internal life
of the Church, its organization, and the "democratization" of its structures. But he also served handsomely
the larger American society and commonweal. He wanted
to recover and help restore American spiritual foundations, her confidence, and her sense of direction.
He believed that the United States was in desperate
need of "a new moral act of Purpose" beyond the "small
souled purpose of mere survival." Without in the least
diminishing either the force of the First Amendment or

341

the integrity of Faith, he showed how the Church and her rich traditions could contribute to such a new act of purpose, up to date but congruent with the one which gave birth to the "New Commonwealth" and its "experiment in freedom." Murray's work, then, is considerably more than "a chapter in recent Catholic history." The American experiment has not ended. The American proposition is still being elaborated. And more than ever we need to know what makes order, and justice, and unity, and civil peace possible in a society increasingly, one might say stridently pluralistic. As Murray states in the Forward of his book:

> Neither as a doctrine nor as a project
> is the American Proposition a finished
> thing. Its demonstration is never done
> once for all; and the Proposition itself
> requires development on penalty of
> decadence. . . Today therefore thought-
> ful men among us are saying that America
> must be more clearly conscious of what
> it proposes, more articulate in pro-
> posing, more purposeful in the realiza-
> tion of the project proposed.[22]

Murray's "reflections" are uniquely provocative with respect to America's place within western political thought, and more importantly with respect to the future of the "American experiment."

NOTES

¹John Cogley, review of We Hold These Truths, The New York Times Book Review Magazine, October 29, 1960, p. 42. The full reference for Murray's work is We Hold These Truths (Garden City, N.Y.: Doubleday & Co., Inc. 1964). Hereinafter referred to as WHTT.

²Murray's was not the first attempt to argue formally the compatibility of Catholic faith and American politics. For an excellent account of his place in the "Americanist tradition" see Donald E. Pelotte, John Courtney Murray, Theologian in Conflict (New York: The Paulist Press, 1975). pp. 141-177.

³See Jacques Maritain, Scholasticisms and Politics (New York: The Macmillan Co., 1941); The Rights of Man and Natural Law (New York: Charles Scribner's Sons, 1943): Christianity and Democracy (New York: Charles Scribner's Sons, 1958); and Man and the State (Chicago: The University of Chicago Press, 1951) which reflects Murray's influence. Also, Heinrich Rommen, The State in Catholic Thought (St. Louis: The Harder Book Co., 1945); and The Natural Law (St. Louis: The Harder Book Co., 1947). Other principal sources for Murray include Jacques Leclecq, Lecons de Droit Naturel (Namur: Maison Wesmael-Charlier, 1934); A.P. D'Entraves, The Medieval Contribution to Political Thought (Oxford: The University Press, 1939); and P.W. Carlyle and A.J. Carlyle, A History of Medieval Political Theory in the West (London: W. Blackwood and Sons, 1936).

⁴Murray, "Freedom of Religion: The Ethical Problem," Theological Studies, VI (June 1945), p. 245. Also, pp. 242, 247, 249, 256 and 258. Theological Studies will hereafter be referred to as TS.

⁵Murray, "Government and the Order of Culture," TS, XV (March 1954), pp. 4 and 12. Also, WHTT, pp. 183-86, 191, 164-65, 24, reflect the seriousness of Murray's understanding of the Christian doctrine of sin and its impact on politics.

⁶See "The Natural Law" in Great Expressions of Human Rights, ed. by R.M. MacIver (New York: Harper and Bros., 1950, pp. 69-104). Also, "Natural Law and the Public Consensus," in Natural Law and Modern Society, ed. by John Cogley (Cleveland: The World

Publishing Co., 1963), pp. 48-81.

[7]WHTT, p. 283.

[8]WHTT, pp. 46, 72-77, and 196-210. See Robert M. MacIver, The Web of Government (New York: The Macmillan Co., 1956), pp. 144-156. Murray calls this distinction the "secular substitute" for the ancient Gelasian dyarchy and all that Christian tradition has meant by the "freedom of the Church." He assumed that Western civilization began when the view of society as a single homogeneous structure was replaced by the radically new idea of a twofold organization of society in church and state. This concept of social dualism along with the development of law and legal process did more than anything else to foster and protect the growth of freedom in the West. He believed that preserving such a dualism on the basis of purely secular institutions was the central problem of modern politics. In this Murray seems in substantial agreement with Dr. Frederick Watkins, The Political Tradition of the West (Cambridge: Harvard University Press, 1948).

[9]Murray, "The Church and Totalitarian Democracy," TS, XIII (December, 1952), pp. 525-63. Murray's concept of Continental Totalitarian democracy relies on J.L. Talmon, The Rise of Totalitarian Democracy (Boston: The Beacon Press, 1951).

[10]According to Murray's interpretation Leo XIII in numerous writings intended to reject precisely these elements in Continental democratic movements: the concept of the social and juridical omnicompetence of the state, the lack of the recognition of an ordo juris antecedent to the state, and the lack of recognition for the rights of social bodies intermediate to the individual and state. Murray published four lengthy articles interpreting the teachings of Leo XIII: "Leo XIII: The General Structure of the Controversy," TS, XIV (March, 1953), pp. 1-30; "Leo XIII: Separation of Church and State," TX, XIV (June, 1953), pp. 145-214; "Leo XIII: Two Concepts of Government," TX, XIV (December, 1953), pp. 551-67; and "Leo XIII: Government and the Order of Culture," TS, XV (March, 1954), pp. 1-33. Later, Pius XI elaborates the "principle of subsidiarity" as a criterior for locating proper limits on governmental power. See WHTT, pp. 314-316.

[11]WHTT, pp. 27-43, and 39-49. For a recent descrip-

tion of the public consensus Murray relies on Adolf
Berle, Power Without Property (New York: Harcourt,
Brace and Co., 1959); and on Walter Lippman, Public
Opinion (New York: Harcourt Brace and Co., 1948).
See WHTT, pp. 105-111.

[11a]WHTT, p. 80.

[11b]WHTT, p. 40.

[11c]WHTT, p. 50.

[11d]WHTT, pp. 204-210, and 227-237.

[12]WHTT, p. 308.

[13]Murray, "On Religious Liberty," America, CXI
(November 30, 1963), p. 706.

[13a]WHTT, pp. 49-50, and 307-309.

[13b]WHTT, p. 162. Also, pp. 47, 48, 152, and 194.

[14]Murray, "Freedom of Religion: The Ethical Problem," TS, VI (June, 1945), p. 249.

[15]WHTT, pp. 55-86. Murray argued mightily against
the injustices of recent Supreme Court rulings in
respect of education which paradoxically violated the
very principles of religious freedom they were supposedly upholding. See "Law or Prepossessions?" in
Essays in Constitutional Law, ed. by Robert G. McClos-
key (New York: Alfred K. Knopf, 1957), pp. 310-343.
Also, "Dr. Morrison and the First Amendment," America,
LXXVIII (February 7, 1948), pp. 627-29; (March 20,
1948), pp. 683-86. For a concise account of the historical development of Murray's thought on Church and
State see Thomas T. Love, John Courtney Murray: Contemporary Church-State Theory (Garden City, N.Y.:
Doubleday and Co., Inc., 1965).

[16]Murray, Religious Liberty: An End and a Beginning
(New York: The Macmillan Co., 1966), pp. 40-41. Other
significant commentary by Murray on the Conciliar doc-
trine and its roots in American experience include the
Problem of Religious Freedom (Westminster: The Newman
Press, 1965); "The Issues of Church and State at
Vatican Council II" TS, XXVII (December, 1966), pp.
580-606; and "Freedom, Authority, Community," America,

345

CXV (December 3, 1966), pp. 734-41.

[17]WHTT, pp. 43-44, 149, 163, and 165-169.

[18]The author agrees with those associates of Niebuhr who believe that the basic positions taken by the
two men are not incompatible, but mutually reinforcing,
even exigent of one another. See Kenneth W. Thompson,
"The Problem of Means," Worldview, Vol. 3 (June, 1960),
pp. 5-6; Will Herberg, "Ambiguist Statesmanship"
Worldview, Vol. 3 (September, 1960), p. 8; and in the
same issue Hans J. Morganthau, "The Demands of Prudence," pp. 67. Also, George Lindback, "Revelation,
Natural Law and the Thought of Reinhold Niebuhr,"
Natural Law Forum, Vol. 4 (December, 1959), pp. 146-
151.

[19]Murray, "The Bad Arguments Intelligent Men Make,"
America Vol. 96 (November 3, 1956), p. 120.

[20]Murray, "The Return to Tribalism," Catholic
Mind, Vol. 12 (January, 1962), p. 10.

[21]By contrast, Niebuhr's Christian realism views
the American democracy as an "institutionalization of
a balance of power for the sake of justice." Although
democracy presupposes some confidence in man's rational
capacities for justice, its primary justification,
according to Niebuhr, is that by arming each citizen
with a measure of political power it acts as a "bulwark
against injustice." As his oft-quoted aphorism has it,
"Man's capacity for justice makes democracy possible,
but man's inclination to injustice makes democracy
necessary." He states:

> The most important thing about democracy
> is that it provides a way of holding
> every public power under public scrutiny,
> challenging every pretension of wisom
> and balancing every force with a counter-
> vailing force.

See Reinhold Niebuhr, The Nature and Destiny of Man,
(New York: Charles Scribner's Sons, 1960), Vol. II,
p. 257.

[22]WHTT, p. 7.